AB 51/23 SOC SCI £6.50

Non fiction Gift Aid
£

0 031140 000780

Paul Baker is Professor of English Language at Lancaster University. His books include *American and British English* (2018) and, with Jo Stanley, *Hello Sailor!* (2003). He regularly gives talks and workshops about Polari and is a Fellow of the Royal Society of Arts.

'By turns deeply edifying and hugely entertaining and unusual for succeeding at being both – a future classic!'
– Damian Barr

'A fascinating and complex story, beautifully told with clarity, passion, and humour.'
– David Crystal

'Glorious! This fascinating and elegiac account of Polari, the Lost Language of Queens, is utterly absorbing. It's history at its best: alive, vivid, fluid, warm, human and humane, and it gets as close as any book I've read to penetrating the mystery-wrapped-in-an-enigma that is camp.'
– Neil McKenna

'Shot through with his nicely dry wit, this is a fascinating and important study.'
– Patrick Gale

'A compelling history of the linguistic lengths to which gay people had to go to hide in plain sight.'
– *Observer*

'A riveting, funny and joyous insight into the story of Polari.'
– Gay's the Word Bookseller Picks 2019

'This is a lovely story, told with charm
and a perfect eye for the anecdote.'
– *Gscene*

'Though a language smacking of Carry On films and saucy
seaside postcards, it's the tragic torment and harassment that
gave rise to Polari in the first place that must not be forgotten
and which is why this book is important.'
– *Daily Mail*

'For anyone interested in finding out more about Polari
– Britain's "secret gay language" – *Fabulosa!* provides
a thought-provoking look at how the language came about
and fell in and out of favour with the gay community
from the days when homosexuality was illegal.'
– *i newspaper*

'The story of Polari – or at least of the world of Polari
and the people who spoke it – is gripping in its own right.'
– *The Oldie*

'[Baker] is especially strong on the changing attitude towards Polari
within the gay community in the '70s and '80s, and on the important
reclamation performed by the Sisters of Perpetual Indulgence.'
– *minor literature[s]*

'A fascinating exploration.'
– *Cent Magazine*

FABULOSA!

The Story of Polari,
Britain's Secret Gay Language

Paul Baker

REAKTION BOOKS

This book is dedicated to Tony McEnery,
my 'friend', boyfriend, lover, long-time companion,
partner, civil partner and finally husband.
For our first date you cooked three main courses,
as you weren't sure which one I'd like, and right
there I knew you were the one.
Thanks for making me laugh so much
– you're top of the pops.

Published by
REAKTION BOOKS LTD
Unit 32, Waterside
44–48 Wharf Road
London N1 7UX, UK

www.reaktionbooks.co.uk

First published 2019, reprinted 2019
First published in paperback 2020, reprinted 2020
Copyright © Paul Baker 2019

All rights reserved

No part of this publication may be reproduced, stored in a retrieval
system, or transmitted, in any form or by any means, electronic,
mechanical, photocopying, recording or otherwise, without the prior
permission of the publishers

Printed and bound in Great Britain
by CPI Group (UK) Ltd, Croydon CR0 4YY

A catalogue record for this book is available from the British Library

ISBN 978 1 78914 294 5

Contents

I

What Is Polari?

Picture it. London, 1953, the A&B Club in Rupert Court, Soho. It is Saturday night, just gone half ten, and there's a sudden surge as the chorus boys make their entrance and everyone looks to the door. Many of them are still in stage slap while a few others, like Bobby (Gloria to her friends), have added a bold bit of blue eyeshadow and rouge to their ekes. They have climbed the stairs to the third floor and knocked to be let in, arriving in twos, threes and fours, parting the fug of vogue smoke, camp little things in tight colourful clobber, gossiping in Polari most bona, luppers flapping around like windmills, oblivious to the effect that they're having on the scattering of respectable and slightly awkward-looking middle-aged omees who have been waiting for just this moment. A couple of off-duty Guardsmen have pitched up in a corner. One, Teddy, is an old hand at this – he's been coming here for a few months now – introduced into the game by an older friend. It's a marvellous way to fill out your packet – catch the eye of anyone who's not completely cod, make a suggestion to take things elsewhere, then he just has to stand in an unlit alley (or sit or even lie back, if the chap's brave enough to take him back home), get plated and earn a few measures in the process. Willing for a shilling – nothing wrong with that. Except the last time, the omee wanted to have it up the dish and offered a lot more, so he thought well why not and gave it a go. And after the first minute, when it stopped hurting, he decided he quite liked it. Have you got any friends, the man asked? There's multi dinarly if there's two of you. So Teddy's brought Arthur along this time – only nineteen, blushes if anyone vadas him – he's been bright red all night. Trouble is, this might have been a mistake. Arthur's getting a lot more attention than anyone else in here.

There's a sudden dip in the din but then it doubles in volume as a bona fide Queen of the Screen comes in. So the rumours are true! She's with a couple of feely omee-palones who must be half her age. Someone tells Gloria that the Screen Queen's been caught with her lally-drags around her ankles at that cottage in the Dilly, aka the meat rack, but her savvy manager's kept it out of the papers somehow. She's playing it like she's the Snow Queen but her orbs are darting round at all the bona omee-palones when she thinks no one's vadering. And yes, she's just clocked Arthur. There's some discreet palarying to one of her consorts and he's been dispatched to where Teddy and Arthur are standing – a request for an audience with her gracious Majesty! Arthur practically spills his bevvy in excitement. 'Say hello to your mother!' says the Queen, holding out her hand graciously. 'And oh, won't someone parker her a Vera!'

～

This is a book about the story of Polari and the people who spoke it – mostly camp gay men. They were a class of people who lived on the margins of society. Many of them broke the law – a law which is now seen in civilized societies as being unfair and cruel – and so they were at risk of arrest, shaming, blackmail and attack. They were not seen as important or interesting. Their stories were not told. If they were ever represented in books, films, plays or songs, they were usually given tiny supporting roles, and the audience was not supposed to identify with or root for them. In the rare cases when they did appear, they were often implied to be silly or sinister, victims or villains. So because of their criminal status, they learnt to speak in an unfamiliar tongue – their voices changed out of recognition so that they could not be understood by others. This is a book which gives them a voice. But first, I ought to tell you about how I got involved in all of this.

A shy boy

It is 1994, I am 22, and I can't get a job. I've just finished a master's in psychology at Lancaster University (a 1960s northern university with a good reputation) but Britain is emerging from one of its periodical recessions, so the prospect for graduates at the time is rather grim, especially if you are a shy boy from a council estate with phobias of public speaking and strangers, and no social skills, only manners.

At the end of my master's I'd plucked up the courage to knock on the doors of the lecturers and asked them, one by one, if they had any research projects I could get involved in. They all said no. So I signed on and applied for a job at a Young Offenders Institution. I didn't get it so I applied for a job as a data analyst at an advertising agency and at the interview was asked to make four triangles out of not enough matchsticks (things like that happened a lot at interviews in the 1990s). I managed it but ●he interviewer looked at me askew and said that that wasn't the solution he had on the answer sheet. I didn't get it. I applied for a job as a trainee accountant and was offered a sum of money so small that I would have had to take out a loan to pay for the travel to work. Then I heard of another job back at Lancaster University, not in psychology but in linguistics. It involved correcting the output of a computer program that was supposed to identify whether words were nouns or verbs but sometimes got it wrong. It was mind-numbingly tedious but I didn't mind. I sat a grammar test and got in. Best of all, because I was an employee of Lancaster University any fees for study were automatically waived. Sign up for a PhD, people advised. You might as well. So I did.

Getting onto a PhD programme isn't easy. You have to have an Idea and a Proposal and then find a Supervisor who thinks you are clever enough to give it a go and not cause them too much trouble. I knocked on the door of the person I liked best in the linguistics department and, stammering, asked her to read my proposal on how academics use politeness – a development of my master's thesis. She agreed, but after several weeks of not hearing from her, I took the hint and decided to have a rethink. I narrowed it down to two options. One was to create and test a computer program that would help people to learn French. The other was Polari.

Polari won.

I'd first heard Polari a few months earlier, on a cassette tape, produced by the BBC, of a radio comedy sketch programme called *Round the Horne*. Two of the characters were named Julian and Sandy, and they were a pair of heavily coded gay friends, living in London and speaking occasionally in a kind of camp jargon. Their sketch began each time with Sandy saying something like 'Oh hello Mr Horne, how bona to vada your dolly old eek!'

I overdosed on Julian and Sandy, listening to lots of sketches in a single afternoon, until it stopped being funny. But afterwards I wondered about it. I'd found that one of the potential advantages of being gay was that I got to socialize with a much wider range of people from different backgrounds and age groups than my straight counterparts, and I'd had plenty of conversations with men in their fifties and sixties at local gay pubs and clubs. But none of them had ever used Polari or even acknowledged its existence. *Round the Horne* had been broadcast in the late 1960s. Less than thirty years had passed but this language had seemingly vanished. It was a mystery, and I liked mysteries. This language was also rude and funny, so I decided it would make a nice counterpoint to my day job with its endless computer print-outs of nouns and verbs. I wrote a second PhD application and this time I was accepted.

My assigned supervisor was called Sally. She was tall and wore lipstick and she had been a punk in the 1980s in Berlin. I thought she was fabulous and quite possibly the coolest person I had ever met. In my head she was an updated Sally Bowles, and that made me a kind of cut-price version of Christopher Isherwood, the writer who claimed, 'I am a camera'. As I was working full-time, I did the PhD part-time from 1996 to 2001. When it was over, the external examiner said that he'd enjoyed reading my thesis but he'd felt I hadn't really put myself in it, and that he didn't know what I actually thought about Polari. At the time, I hadn't felt that doing so was all that important.

I'd been more concerned about giving a voice to the speakers of Polari themselves. But maybe it's disingenuous to think that you can give a voice to someone without acknowledging how it is filtered through your own. I'm the one who was lucky enough to tell their story, but I chose which questions to ask them, and which bits of their interviews to quote from and how to frame those quotes. Despite being gay and from a working-class background like many of the Polari speakers, there are also major differences between myself and them – I was born in 1972, so didn't have first-hand experience of the social climate that they grew up in. And I took a route through education that meant I ended up sounding and acting much more middle class than most Polari speakers – I'd be a posh queen in their eyes. And while I have a sound appreciation of classic camp (I've seen a lot of Bette Davis movies), it's much more an internal aspect of my identity rather than a productive, externalized one. A common word used by Polari speakers was *bold* – it implies a kind of mixture of camp flamboyance and bravery when it came to your sexuality. This kind of boldness does not come naturally to me.

Another reason for not wanting to put myself in my thesis was lack of confidence – young academics are often taught to write in an impersonal, objective style and can be afraid to put their own views into their work. Years later, I'm a little less constrained by those concerns and part of the reason for writing this book is to reappraise Polari from a different, less 'academic-sounding' position. So this book tells the story of Polari, but while I've relied on many voices to tell it, I should stress that the story is told through my worldview and experiences, and also I want to be able to acknowledge the effect that researching Polari has had on me.

Very nice dear, but what is Polari?

One of the earliest issues I faced in my research was what to call Polari and the people who spoke it. Was it a language or just a slang, and is it appropriate to say that gay men spoke it when the term *gay* wasn't used as commonly as it is now and didn't have exactly the same associations? Let's deal with the issue of language versus slang first.

A language usually functions as a system of communication, and human languages normally can be written or spoken and are likely to be distinct from other languages in terms of having a unique set of lexical items (words, phrases, idioms, grammatical rules, pronunciations and spellings). For me, a key test to determine whether something is a full language is the extent to which it can be used to communicate in a very wide range of situations – can you use it to order food, have an argument about politics, tell someone the plot of a film you saw last night or give a maths lecture (not necessarily all in the same conversation)?

Despite the fact that Polari has been used in some unusual contexts, including a full translation of the Bible, I am not sure it is sufficiently versatile to warrant 'language' status, and in some situations its speakers would have to rely quite a lot on English. Another test of whether something is a language or a slang is the extent to which it has its own grammatical rules governing the ordering of words, for example, or how past, present and future tense are expressed. Most languages have a relatively small but very frequently invoked set of 'grammatical items': prepositions, conjunctions, pronouns, articles and determiners, along with various morphemes, like *-ed, -ing* and -*s* (in English), which help to identity features like plural forms or past tense. As Chapter Three indicates, Polari tends to contain words that are lexical items – the nouns, verbs and adjectives – as opposed to grammatical items, and many of its grammatical rules tend to be the same as those of English. Occasionally Polari speakers dropped some of the grammatical items from their speech, giving Polari a kind of telegraphic texture that feels grammatically different to English. In other cases, English grammatical items *were* used but in a distinct way (such as switching pronouns like *he* and *she*). So there have been times when Polari has approached full language status, but not for everyone and not always.

From my interactions with different speakers I get the impression that the ability to speak Polari occurred on a cline. At one end there were those who knew a limited vocabulary of anywhere between ten and forty words and simply used them as slang in place of English ones. At the other end there were those with a wider vocabulary whose conversation included more Polari than English and who would have also been likely to have creatively used a range of different linguistic phenomena, often in real time, to invent new words and phrases that helped to make up for any linguistic deficiencies in Polari itself. I describe this type of ab-libbing in Chapter Three when I discuss how terms like *dowry* and *nanti* could be combined with other words to make new Polari items.

The issue is made more complex by the fact that gay men adopted Polari and ornamented it with words for concepts and various linguistic practices that were most relevant to their situation, but earlier and adjacent versions of Polari were distinctly less gay in nature, being more associated with the theatre or other forms of entertainment. A book chapter written by Ian Hancock in 1984 on Polari barely mentions the connection to gay men but instead focuses more on Polari's link to Romance languages like Italian.[1] As I'll show in Chapter Two, there were links and overlaps between the various social groups who contributed the words that eventually became associated with gay men's use of Polari, and we ought not to view gay men as a separate group, communicating in isolation from other people. Gay men would have held multiple social identities as well as interacting with people from a wide range of other backgrounds.

Two terms I found helpful in terms of conceptualizing Polari during my research were *language variety* and *anti-language*. Language variety is a kind of general term to refer to any set of linguistic items that have a similar social distribution,[2] and the term can refer just as easily to a language as to a dialect or a slang, without forcing us to be more specific. Considering that Polari was sometimes a slang but sometimes felt like it was approaching a language, the term *language variety* allows for definitions to be a little vague and non-committal, although it perhaps also leaves us open to accusations of fence-sitting. An *anti-language* on the other hand is less concerned with the issue of defining the extent to which something actually is a full language, but is more involved with considering its functions. The term *anti-language* refers to forms of language that are used by people who are somehow apart from mainstream society, either residing on the edges of it, perhaps frowned on in some way, or hidden away or even criminalized, with attempts from the mainstream to expel or contain them.[3] These anti-societies are counter-cultures, then: conscious alternatives to the mainstream, existing by resisting either passively or by more hostile, destructive means. Anti-languages are generated by anti-societies and in their simplest forms they are partially re-lexicalized languages, consisting of the same grammar but a different vocabulary, although they can go beyond that to approach fuller approximations of languages. However, the key point about anti-languages is that they aren't just alternative words for existing concepts, but encode something additional, a kind of 'us-against-them' worldview within the meanings of words. In other words, they use language to represent reality in a different way, so that the values of the anti-society are produced, as opposed to the values of the mainstream society. Indeed, the mainstream society may be mocked or criticized in some way by the anti-language. Some of these aspects of anti-language certainly feel like they can be applied to Polari, which had numerous mocking words for the police or heterosexual people as well as representing gender in a very different way to non-Polari speakers. When you learned Polari, you weren't just learning the words but the attitude that went with them.

Early on in my research I got into a bit of a knot over terminology and labels, particularly around how to refer to the people who spoke Polari. The speakers themselves used a range of terms, including *omee-palones* (literally men-women) and *queens*, while the most common term in mainstream society for people who fancied and loved people of the same sex was *homosexual* (usually pronounced *homma-sex-yul* in a posh 1950s newsreader accent). It was a sneery kind of a word, associated with medical and legal pronouncements and used in contexts where such people were often categorized as criminals or mentally ill, at best objects of pity. Another word, *queer*, occurred in more informal contexts – it could appear in a derogatory way, but even in the 1940s it had already begun to be reclaimed. For example, in 1949 Kenneth Williams, who played Sandy in the *Round the Horne* sketches, wrote in his diary that a bar was 'Full of queers and prosts'.[4] However, around the same time, he used the letter *q* as a short-hand for 'queer' – 'I think he's q.!!'[5] – and sometimes spelled *q* as *queue*, perhaps as a way of coding his diary entries so they would not arouse suspicion if they fell into the wrong hands. We thus find other diary entries like 'Richard is queue!!!' and 'Is the whole of London going queue-ing'.[6] By the 1990s, *queer* had been rebadged by activists and academics and no longer meant gay but referred to any form of sexual identity or practice that was seen as against the norm in a particular society (to this end it could be argued that an older woman and her much younger male partner could both be seen as queer). However, in practice, *queer* largely remains synonymous for *gay*, with the additional suggestion of a cool and edgy political awareness. What about *gay* itself, then? This was a word that had been used to refer to people who experienced same-sex desire across the twentieth century, and it was used in this way decades before the Gay Liberation movement of the late 1960s and '70s, although in the UK it had a bit of an elite association. Despite this, I've decided to refer to Polari speakers as *gay* (as opposed to *homosexual* or *queer*) because it's the word that has the most resonance at the time of writing. We should not assume though that Polari speakers or the people who had sex with them would neces- sarily have used that word on themselves or that they would have understood *gay* (as an identity associated with pride and liberation) in the way that it is currently used. Even *gay* has multiple meanings today, being used as a catch-all insult in schoolyard bullying, although that practice seems to be more frowned upon than it was years ago.

While *gay* does not seem to refer explicitly to the gender of the speaker (it can be used to refer to men or women), it is often implied to mostly relate to men – explaining the existence of terms like LGBT or *gay men and lesbians*, where *gay* is positioned separately from a word which refers to women. I also use the term LGBT in this book, particularly in the later chapters, which deal with matters more concerned with the present day, and as a way of referring to the fact that some Polari speakers would have been more likely to identify as bisexual or trans from today's perspective. However, we should also note that the abbreviation LGBT didn't really come into use until the 1990s, so would have not been in the older Polari speakers' vocabulary.[7] While some of the most well-known Polari speakers were drag queens, they did not tend to view themselves as trans, nor did most of them engage in any of the forms of sexual reassignment surgery that had been available since the 1930s, however rudimentary. A Polari word, *remould*, does acknowledge the existence of trans people, although in typical Polari fashion it is unlikely to be seen as particularly sensitive. Compared to the drag queens of today, the Polari-speaking drag queens placed less focus upon contouring make-up and padding or cinching the body or 'tucking' the penis to appear more feminine than they did to comedy routines and parody. Some Polari speakers identified as queens rather than drag queens, though they may have worn feminine clothing, dyed their hair or used the odd touch of blusher, lipstick or eyeshadow. From today's perspective they might be viewed as gender-fluid or non-binary, although these were not terms that were around at the time.

The concept of bisexuality is also acknowledged within Polari with words like *acdc*, *bibi* and *versatile*, although this was an identity that was not always acknowledged or even accepted both within and outside the gay subculture of the twentieth century. Some men who presented as nominally heterosexual but were willing to sleep with other men, either for money or for the purposes of sexual release, were viewed as *trade* rather than bisexual, while there was often the view that bisexual people were gay people who couldn't fully admit it. Considering that we are dealing with an era when being gay was hugely stigmatized as well as being a crime, it is hardly surprising that many people were cautious, ambiguous and non-committal about the sexual labels they used on themselves and others. The larger point I want to make here is that the terms I use in this book would not have been understood in exactly the same way by the people who spoke Polari decades earlier (and perhaps will be seen just as differently in the decades to come).

A couple of questions I am regularly asked about Polari are how many people spoke it, and did women speak it? Taking the first question, there are no official records involving speakers, and it's also difficult to distinguish between people who knew the language but wouldn't have used it themselves for various reasons, those who knew and used a few words, and those who were more proficient users. The UK population stood at around 41 million people in 1961 – a point when Polari was still in use but would start to become less popular in the ensuing years. If we exclude 20 per cent of that number as likely to have been children, that gives around 32.8 million adults. We could then take a conservative estimate about the percentage of people who identified as gay at being 1 per cent of the population, leaving us with 328,000. Within that I will be very pessimistic and estimate that because of the oppressive nature of society at the time, only one in five of those people found their way into some kind of established gay subculture – giving 65,600. Then we could perhaps guess that around half of these people knew Polari (32,800) and of those, only half again would have used it (16,400). However, to this number I would add non-gay users of Polari who may have been friends of existing speakers or would have encountered aspects of the language due to its use in contexts such as the theatre or on ships. I would there-fore estimate the number of speakers as peaking at around tens of thousands but would add that awareness of Polari's existence and some of the basic words is likely to have run into hundreds of thousands or even the millions, especially owing to the publicity given by the Julian and Sandy radio sketches in the late 1960s.

There is not a great deal of evidence regarding the extent to which women spoke Polari. In 1993 female DJ Jo Purvis spoke about using Polari with her friends in the *Summer's Out* Channel 4 documentary on gay history, and one of three sketches featuring conversations in Polari on the same pro-gramme took place between two gay women and appears to have been set in the 1960s. These two female characters use terms like *femmie* and *butch* as well as engaging in gender-switching language (for example, referring to a woman as *George* and using the pronoun *he*). There is little evidence, however, from other oral histories of gay women that Polari was extensively used by them, and I suspect that its incorporation

22

as part of camp parody has tended to be more of an aspect of gay male culture. However, I have been contacted over the years by a small number of women who knew Polari, usually women who did not identify as gay but had several gay friends who used it and had introduced the language to them. And from a present-day perspective, I would say that women seem just as interested in Polari as men – with at least half of attendees at my talks and workshops being female, with good representations from both gay and straight women. It is less usual for straight men to express much interest in Polari, though.

He's got all the Polari, where do you think he picks it up?

I started my research on Polari in the final years of the twentieth century and by this point many of its speakers had passed away. Due to the fact that Polari had started to go out of fashion by the late 1960s, even those people who were still living and had used it were now less likely to be regular users, and some of their knowledge was hazy. I began my quest to find speakers in the Kemptown area of Brighton, checking into a gay-run hotel and asking the owners if they knew any speakers. They put me in touch with a few locals, who then suggested other people I could contact. I used other methods, including placing adverts in newspapers and gay magazines and searching gay websites to find potential speakers. I created a website about my project and this also resulted in people contacting me. I recorded in-depth interviews with around twenty people, although alongside that I have relied on the testimonies of around forty others who have spoken about Polari while being interviewed for books, news articles, radio or television documentaries, such as the drag entertainer Lorri (sometimes spelled Laurie, Lauri or Lori) Lee, as well as people who have published their own reminiscences about Polari, like the journalist and author Peter Burton. Where I've taken quotes from such sources, I've referenced them accordingly. And beyond that are notes I made from many others with whom I conducted shorter conversations or email exchanges about Polari. These often involved people who were not speakers themselves but were able to offer an insight – a small jigsaw piece into the bigger picture – such as the woman who told me that she used to hang out with a group of older gay men when she went to National Union of Teachers meetings and they all used Polari and taught her various words, or the American woman who emailed me and demonstrated considerable knowledge of Polari, indicating that there had been a slight degree of penetration into the u.s. (no pun intended). While being interested in what words and phrases were in Polari and the ways that they were used, I also wanted to know what people thought about Polari, even if they didn't use it themselves, so my net extended to include online discussions, published articles or conversations I had about Polari which helped to reveal attitudes towards it.

It's important to note that interviews tell us what people knew and thought about Polari but it can be difficult to verify the accuracy of such accounts – we are relying on memories of things that happened a long time ago, and even with the best intentions, people may possess different memories of the same situation. Unintentional contradictions, exaggerations or simplifications may also occur during interviews, and many statements can appear more like perceptions than truths. One person I interviewed told me confidently that 'nobody speaks Polari anymore'. A week later, I received a telephone call from somebody who told me that he used Polari every day and, what's more, had taught all of his heterosexual friends at work how to use it. So we should bear in mind that the various interview accounts I quote from are based on memories and perceptions. And while I'm confident that the interviewees were giving what they believed to be honest accounts of their own experiences, they were speaking for themselves, not for every single person who spoke Polari.

As researchers we are trained to follow ethical guidelines and, particularly when working with a group who are seen as vulnerable in some way (such as being at risk from homophobic attacks or who have an identity which has been stigmatized), it is important to handle interviews sensitively and to protect the identities of those being interviewed. Some of my interviewees were concerned about being identified, although others were not concerned at all about having their identities hidden. I have generally erred on the side of caution and changed names, as well as avoiding using surnames for the men I interviewed. I have not changed the names of any people I did not interview directly – in some cases they were already changed but in others the speakers gave their consent to be filmed or interviewed and their identities can be clearly ascertained.

Along with the testimonies of individuals, I've made use of a number of different scripted versions of Polari, of which probably the most well known are the Julian and Sandy sketches that occurred in *Round the Horne*, to which I devote a whole chapter of this book. As well as that, though, there are numerous other sources of scripted Polari – sometimes snatches of a few words spoken in a film, television series or song, some of which are longer recreations of the language, such as the three sketches filmed on a London bus for the documentary *Summer's Out* or the six-minute film created by Brian and Karl in 2015.

Recordings of drag acts also proved to be useful sources of Polari, and I have quoted from the likes of Marc Fleming, Phil Starr and Lee Sutton. The Polari Bible and the Polari Evensong also constitute a form of scripted Polari and are discussed towards the end of the book. Older gay magazines were perhaps a less useful source of information than you'd expect, but I uncovered a few brief uses of Polari in copies of *Gay News*, while another short-lived magazine from the 1970s, *Lunch*, provided a couple of illuminating articles that helped to explain attitudes around camp and older gay identities at the time. Published research on linguistic etymology and history, including the many dictionaries written by Eric Partridge and Captain Francis Grose's *Classical Dictionary of the Vulgar Tongue*, helped me to trace the origins of some of the Polari words.

The one source of information that I didn't have access to involved naturally occurring spoken conversations featuring Polari, such as the snippet at the start of this chapter that I've imagined as taking place at the A&B Club in the 1950s, and is based on various bits of narratives from different interview sources. As a secret language that was already pretty much moribund by the time I started looking for conversations in Polari, the lack of 'authentic' recordings isn't hugely surprising. Kenneth Williams did use the occasional word of Polari in his diaries, especially in entries from the 1940s, and these represent one of the few private, natural uses of the language I've been able to find. However, while access to the men who spoke Polari in the 1940s and '50s is now even more difficult than it was when I began my PhD, the situation regarding access to other forms of information has actually become slightly easier, owing to the fact that the Internet has made the world much more interconnected than it was twenty years ago. YouTube turned up gems like the 1981 BBC documentary on Lorri Lee, as well as old footage of drag acts, helping me to find additional information about Polari that was not available to me when I carried out my original research. There is a good chance that there are other sources of Polari out there, perhaps in letters and birthday cards, home videos or as part of messages recorded on old telephone answering machines. I hope that this book inspires people to come forward so that they can be documented and saved for posterity.

In the chapters that follow I've tried to loosely use a kind of historic structure so that we can see the progression of Polari's story over time. The following chapter delves into the linguistic predecessors of Polari as well as examining some of the sibling language varieties that occurred alongside it, providing new words and ways of forming them. To this end we need to go briefly back to Elizabethan times to consider the Cant of criminals, and then whizz through the seventeenth, eighteenth and nineteenth centuries fairly quickly – covering Molly slang, Parlyaree and its connections to Italian – before looking at earlier twentieth-century influences when Polari became strongly associated with the theatre, as well as borrowing terms from the different local communities in which it was most highly concentrated. Chapter Three takes a scenic diversion from our history lesson by instead considering Polari as a language system, fleshing out the different types of words that were used and providing some information on intonation, accent, grammar and word creation. The story picks up again in Chapter Four, where we look at how Polari was used in the period just after the Second World War, covering a twenty-year period which encompasses the late 1940s, the 1950s and the early 1960s. During this time, Polari had its heyday, with the increasing presence of subcultural (and illegal) establishments and networks of gay people, which regularly came under threat from police scrutiny. As a means of recognizing others, providing secrecy and offering a pressure release in the form of camp humour, Polari played an important part in getting gay people through this difficult time.

Chapter Five focuses on the impact of the Julian and Sandy radio sketches that were broadcast in the mid- to late 1960s, a period when Polari was already starting to go on the wane but was to experience a swansong in the form of a few brief years of mainstream attention. Julian and Sandy represent the most high-profile and long-standing use of Polari in a public context to date, and their impact on people's attitudes towards Polari and the way that it was to be used was considerable. It is no coincidence that their popularity peaked at the same time that homosexuality was decriminalized, and Chapter Six looks at the post-Julian-and-Sandy period, the 1970s and '80s, a time that sees the emergence of new freedoms coupled with continued oppression, a move towards a hyper-masculine gay identity, American influences and a homophobic backlash as a result of conservative and religious responses to the HIV-AIDS crisis. It is during these years that Polari was largely abandoned by the gay community, ridiculed as naff and criticized as a toxic relic of a time that everyone wanted to forget.

Chapter Seven considers the period after the backlash, from the 1990s to the present day, examining how Polari was rediscovered and repurposed, first as part of a positive political message aimed at celebrating gay people, then as an object of academic curiosity, followed by a way of marketing gay identity and, more latterly, as an aspect of highbrow culture. Finally, in the concluding chapter I reflect on my aims in studying Polari's evolution and the effect that my engagement with Polari has had on my own life and identity. I also look at the extent to which the story of Polari is over and what might be in store for it in the future.

Polari is playful, quick and clever – it's a constantly evolving language of fast put-downs, ironic self-parody and theatrical exaggeration. The lexicographer Eric Partridge once referred to Polari as a 'Cinderella among languages', but I prefer to think of it as the Ugly Sisters: brash, funny and with all the best lines in the show. This book is the culmination of a project that I began almost a quarter of a century ago. I learnt a lot, not just about Polari but about myself and about people generally. I also laughed a lot along the way. I hope you'll stick with me until the end of the story. And that you'll laugh a few times too.

FRANCIS GROSE. Esq. F.A.S.

Seeking Vulgar Tongue: Captain Francis Grose

2

Something Borrowed, Something Blue

I t is 1997 and I am 24 years old. I am sitting in the upstairs parlour of a drag queen in a blustery British seaside town, out of season. She is talking away at me very quickly and I am terrified. A hairdresser has arrived in the middle of the interview and has begun the process of attaching an enormous candyfloss-coloured wig to the top of her head. He has teased the wig onwards and upwards until it has become a gravity-defying, Escher-esque illusion. I can't take my eyes off it. Can it really be occupying that space? How can it? How can this *be*?

It doesn't matter that I have no social skills, only manners, because I am not really required to speak. All I have to do is turn on my tape recorder and not bolt out of the door. The drag queen has very kindly consented to talk to me about Polari. It is one of the first of these kinds of interviews that I've done and I feel dangerously out of my depth. Upon arriving, the drag queen seems to go into shock, staggering ever so slightly. She points at a framed photograph on display in the parlour and tells me I look just like her partner from a long time ago, who is now dead. I squint at the picture but can't see the resemblance apart from the fact that we are both young and have old-fashioned haircuts. I don't know how to respond. There was nothing about this in any of the books I'd read on doing interview research.

The drag queen lives above the restaurant/cafe she runs as a sideline and everything is very chaotic – I feel as though I'm in that scene at the start of *All About Eve* when Eve first meets Margo Channing (Bette Davis), backstage. There are three or four other gay men, employees, running around, popping in and out, interrupting, shouting. Someone steps halfway into the room and yells, 'Go away and fuck off!' to someone else outside, and the drag queen hisses majestically, 'I'm taping this!'

Another man bursts in later on, looks me up and down and then turns to the drag queen pointedly. 'Who *is* he?' he asks, gesturing at me. 'Is he an actor?' The drag queen manages to dispense with him, but we can still hear him shrieking at someone in the corridor: 'I'm sorry! I'm not prepared to sit in all day waiting for you!'

'Her voice unfortunately,' the drag queen says. I am not sure if this is an apology or an explanation or merely an observation. Without missing a beat, she continues talking. 'Hugh Paddick. He's still around. Also, Su Pollard – Su uses it a lot. Mark Fleming actually put Su onto the scene. Because she was sitting in the Union Tavern when we used to be down there . . .'.

When the interview is over, she turns to me. 'You've got them all excited, they'll have the porn out this afternoon.' I smile and thank her, then run all the way back to my hotel, feeling giddy and exhausted, like I'm a real researcher. What the drag queen has told me, she has probably told to dozens of people before, but for me it is gold dust. I will conduct lots of these interviews and they will always leave me feeling both drained and excited at the end. Every time.

Another question I often get asked about Polari is: where did it come from? Apart from saying 'It's complicated', it's not a question that can be answered briefly. And it can also be difficult to be confident that the answer is fully accurate. Polari was a secret, mainly spoken form of language which occurred in private conversations among people who were not part of a social elite, and has roots in forms of language that were around long before the invention of recording devices, so we often have to rely on secondary sources, hearsay, theories and educated guesses. Apart from by a couple of notable exceptions, such as Eric Partridge, it was not viewed as especially interesting or worth researching. The few attempts to provide written accounts of the language or transcriptions of it illustrate the lack of standardization. This was very much a language variety that was subject to change and developed on the fly by groups of people who belonged to multiple communities, as opposed to it existing within a single community where everyone knew everyone else. Even by the time we get to the early twentieth century, the notion of a single gay community who all knew the same Polari words and used them in the same way is mythical. So, a health warning – a lot of this chapter is speculative. Without a time machine we simply cannot know the truth. But with that said, let's start somewhere near the beginning, with Cant.

Cant

It's likely that what later became known as Polari was influenced by a much earlier secret form of language known as Cant, also known as St Giles Greek or Pedlar's French. The most famous compiler of Cant was the fabulously named Captain Francis Grose (1731–1791), whose *Classical Dictionary of the Vulgar Tongue* had over 4,000 entries by the publication of its third edition in 1785. Captain Grose was an unusual man for his time – coming from an upper-class background and receiving a classical education, he served in the army and captained the Surrey regiment, although he seemed to prefer working as a draughtsman and lexicographer. He was a true ethnographer, working through the night to find new words and phrases by mixing with the 'rough squads' of London who worked around the slums of St Giles, Turnmill Street, St Kitt's and Saltpetre Bank.

Cant was used by criminals in the sixteenth to the eighteenth centuries, although its roots have been traced back as far as the eleventh century, when under conquest by the Normans some Saxons became outlaws and robbers, with their language reflecting that of a conquered class and continuing for centuries afterwards with little change.[1] Cant is also linked to an earlier form of slang called Elizabethan pelting (paltry) slang, which had a large number of terms relating to criminal activities.[2] For example, there were over twenty terms for different classes of vagabond in pelting slang, including *prigger of prancers* (horse stealers), *jarkman* (forger), *bawdy basket* (seller of pins, tapes, ballads and obscene books) and *dell* (a young girl of the vagrant class), as well as words describing criminal strategies, which were collectively known as *laws*. A *lifting law*, for example, related to stealing packages. There were also names for tools (*wresters*: for picking locks), the spoils (*snappings*) and various penalties that would be incurred if caught (*trining on the chats*: being hanged). Cant was a technical language, concerned with a trade (albeit an illegal one), and there were additional words for objects, body parts, animals, institutions and places.

One of the most characteristic aspects of Cant was its use of the word *cheat*, which had a general meaning of 'thing which'. A *hearing cheat* was an ear – literally a thing which hears. Other body part words that were derived using the 'cheat' rule were *smelling cheat* (nose), *prating cheat* (tongue) and *crashing cheat* (teeth), although the rule could be applied to a range of objects: *belly cheat* (apron), *lullaby cheat* (infant), *trundling cheat* or *rattling cheat* (carriage, later car or taxi) and *muffling cheat* (napkin). This aspect of Cant – naming something via an aspect of its essential nature – occurred in other forms: sometimes a single descriptive word was enough on its own, so horses were *prancers* because that's what they did.

Other productive Cant terms were *queer*, *cove* and *cull/cully*, which could all be combined with other words. *Queer* was not associated with homosexuality or even strangeness but referred to something bad, often a threat to criminals. So a *queer rooster* was an informer, a *queer cuffin* was a Justice of the Peace and a *queer ken* was a prison house. *Cove*, *cull* and *cully* referred to a man and could be combined with other Cant words (often adjectives or verbs) to specify different types of men, such as *flash cove* (master of the house), *milling cove* (boxer) and *smacking cove* (coachman), and we also have *bob cull* (good man), *chaunter cull* (writer) and *bleeding cully* (one who parts easily with his money). *Cully* could refer to a thief's mate but could also mean testicles, and it has been wryly observed that speakers of Cant had a particular interest in finding words for sexual body parts and the bodily evacuation of waste.[3]

The distinctive way in which many Cant terms are formed – by combining two words to make a compound term, with the first word often being an adjective or verb that describes a stereotypical activity associated with the object in question – is something which links Cant to Polari, particularly in the way that numerous words are derived from the term *queen* (*drag queen*, *bold queen*), *fake* (*fake riah*) or *omee* (*bevvy omee*, *kosher omee*). This kind of compounding can result in combinations of three words, such as *gentry cove ken*, meaning a gentleman's house.

I would not count most Cant words as 'core' Polari words, however, and none of the older speakers I interviewed for my PhD research knew any of them. But one group of newer speakers has incorporated them into the version of Polari that they use. The Sisters of Perpetual Indulgence is a charity, protest and street performance organization of gay men that began in San Francisco in 1979. They wear nuns' habits and use camp as a form of political statement, raising money to help people with HIV-AIDS and LGBT-related causes. The organization has numerous 'Orders' around the world, including several in the UK where the British Sisters have adopted Polari in their rituals (described in more detail later). It is likely that this adoption of Polari occurred in earnest in the 1980s and '90s, and probable that some of its members would have known Polari before they joined the Sisterhood.

During my PhD research I was given a small handmade paper booklet produced by and for the British Sisters, which was used as a Polari dictionary. I recognized many of the words from Cant, and the dictionary's version of Polari relies much more on Cant than other sources like the drag acts or the Julian and Sandy sketches described later. The Polari Bible (also described later) was created by one of the Manchester Sisters and also contains a high ratio of Cant words. However, I do not have much evidence that Cant was a large part of Polari as it was used in the 1950s and earlier. Does Cant count as Polari, then? I suspect it formed part of the earlier, pre-Polari influences on the language, and its much later adoption by the Sisters is a fascinating example of reclaiming Polari. It also indicates how nobody 'owns' Polari, and it offers a unique illustration of how the language variety changes over time. It is ironic, then, that Cant occurs at the start of our story, when in fact it should also appear at the end.

Cant also contributed to some of the later language varieties or slangs which eventually found their way into Polari, so *ken* retained its meaning in Polari as a house,[4] while we could make a link between Cant's *mish* (shirt) and later words like *camisa* and *comission*, which had the same meaning and occurred in the later Parlyaree. Additionally, a *poll* (wig) in Cant could be connected to the later Polari word *palone* (woman), as a wig could have been used if a man wanted to dress as a woman. Other Cant words, like *dudds* (linen) and *booze* (alcoholic drinks), have found their way into mainstream slang, although *dudds* (or *duds*) now refers to clothing generally.

Mollies

While speakers of Cant would have identified largely as criminals rather than men who were interested in sex with other men, there was such a group in existence alongside Cant speakers who were known as Mollies. These men had emerged as a social group by around 1710. Prior to that, there had been 'rakes', who were viewed as religious libertines and politically republican. They were also supposed to be sexually interested in men, taking the penetrative role with younger, sometimes adolescent males (rather like the ancient Greek or Roman acceptable configuration of male–male desire). Around the same time as the rakes there were another group of men known as 'fops', who were feminine in dress and manner but not really associated with having sex with other men. Mollies were a new group, both feminine and interested in sex with men. They existed as a subculture based around semi-public meeting spaces known as Molly Houses, which were clubs and taverns where men of different social classes could socialize and pick each other up for sex. Randolph Trumbach refers to them as 'adult passive transvestite effeminate male[s]', although Rictor Norton suggests that Mollies were more 'vulgar than aesthetic, and evinced more vitality than effeteness' – that is, their dressing up was more a means of 'letting off steam'.[5]

It's not the case that we can draw a straight line between Mollies and the future Polari speakers of the twentieth century, although both groups had a number of similarities that are worth noting. As well as enjoying sex with other men, both groups used performance, parody and camp humour and built a social identity around this shared sexual preference, resulting in

'Confirmation; or, the Bishop and the Soldier', 1822. Satirical print showing the discovery of the Bishop of Clogher soliciting soldier John Moverley in the back parlour of the White Lion pub, Haymarket. Subsequently, both men were dragged through the streets, severely beaten and jailed

a community or subculture. Both groups were criminalized by mainstream society, too, and so were driven underground, and both groups had specific words that were not known by others.

Mollies had plenty of words for sex between men (*riding a rump, the pleasant deed, do the story, swive, indorse, caudle making*) as well as cruising for partners (*strolling and cater-wauling, bit a blow, put the bite, make a bargain*). Other Molly words are also found in Cant – *flash ken*: house of thieves, *nubbing cheat*: the gallows, *mish*: shirt, *shap*: hat, *stampers*: shoes, *poll*: wig, *queer ken*: prison, *queer booze*: bad drink, *queer cull*: fop/fool. As with Cant speakers, Mollies did not use *queer* to refer to homosexuality, although it is possible that its use as an (initially) pejorative term for such men might have become associated with them. A couple of Molly words can be traced through to Polari slang more generally – *trade* (a masculine sexual partner) and to be *picked up* (to find a partner). Mollies also called each other by female names and used the term *queen* to refer to each other. The phrase 'Where have you been you saucy queen?' is attributed to a Molly.[6]

Mollies had a range of customs and rituals that subverted traditional heterosexuality, which bring to mind latter-day drag acts. In Molly Houses 'marryings' would occur, a euphemistic term for when two men would slip off to a private room (referred to as the Chapel) to have sex. Mollies also engaged in 'lying in', where one man would pretend to be female and 'give birth' to a wooden baby, which would then be christened. A similar tradition is reported in the context of *femminielli* in Naples, Italy, a name given to people who are born as men and go on to live as women. *Femminielli* would also hold weddings and enact *figliata*, a ritual involving the phases of pregnancy, culminating in the *femminiello* giving birth to a child (usually a wooden puppet the size of a newborn male baby with a huge phallus).[7]

In Britain, there was a somewhat censorious moral climate in the late seventeenth and early eighteenth century, partly as a result of the newly forming middle class, who wished to set themselves apart from the other classes and turned to religious edicts as a way of judging and punishing others. A number of societies for the reformation of manners were formed throughout the country, which effectively policed a range of behaviours like swearing and public drunkenness.[8] Within this context, the fact that 'sodomy' was a crime, punishable by a prison sentence, meant that Mollies were a despised and vulnerable group. Rictor Norton reports on the famous raid of Mother Clap's Molly House in 1725 or 1726 in Field Lane, Holborn. By an early hour of the morning, forty 'sodomites' had been rounded up and taken to Newgate prison. None of the men were caught having sex, although some had unbuttoned breeches. Several of them were subsequently fined, imprisoned and put in the pillory, while three were hanged at Tyburn. This was just one of a series of raids, probably the result of a smaller number of informers who were either embittered at being accused themselves, or prostitutes who had subsequently been used as agents provocateurs by the police.[9] It is perhaps unsurprising then that Mollies, viewed as criminals, would have mixed with actual criminals, either due to being driven underground or through imprisonment, which helps to explain the overlap between Molly slang and Cant.

Parlyaree and its variations

As the eighteenth and nineteenth centuries progress, we find a successor to Cant,[10] referred to as Parlyaree. This was a language that was influenced by Italian and spoken by a range of overlapping groups who tended to exist on the margins of society and often led itinerant lives. Some of the speakers of Parlyaree were influenced by Romany, a dialect of Roma spoken by Gypsies who had migrated to England via India, Ukraine, Poland, Germany and the Low Countries. However, Parlyaree is a distinct form of language from Romany. A second lexicographer, Eric Partridge, enters our story at this point – and it is his work that I have drawn on most in trying to understand the role that Parlyaree played in what was eventually to become Polari. Born in New Zealand, Partridge became a school teacher briefly before serving in the First World War, where his travels inspired his interest in the 'underside' of language. He wrote over forty books on the English language, with many works on slang and the origins of words. His dictionaries of slang reveal a great deal about the origins of Polari words, although they sometimes present more information than is helpful. Consider the following entries, taken from the 1964, 1970 and 1974 editions:

> **parlaree** or **-ry; parlyaree;** or with capitals. The language of circusmen, showmen and itinerant and/or low actors; based on Italian and to some extent on 'Lingua Franca' . . . It often merges with the language of tramps.[11]

> **Parlyaree**
> In 1. 3, read 'C. 18–20 actors', for a few terms (e.g. *letty*) survive among troopers and traditionalists.
> In 1.10 *pargliare* is a misprint for *parlare*, which accounts for the *parlaree* (*-ry*) form; the *parlyaree* form has been influenced either by **palarie** (p. 601) or by e.g., *parliamo*, 'let us speak' . . .
> *Parlyaree* is both less general and less serviceable than *Parlary* or *parlary*. In late C. 19– early 20, *palarey* or *palary* was very common esp. among music-hall artists; after ca. 1945, *palary* is demotic, *parlary* hieractic.[12]

> **parlary.** Slang: prostitutes': since ca. 1930.[13]

This isn't easy (or necessarily useful) to pick apart. There are references to *parlaree*, *parlary* and *parlyaree*, all with or without capitalization. Then there's something called *pargliare*, which at least can be discounted as a misprint in an earlier book. Then we have *parlare, palarie* and *Parlary* (in upper case). And in addition are *palary* and *parlary* (now in lower case). A number of groups are mentioned: circus men, showmen, itinerant and/or low actors, tramps, costermongers, music-hall artists and prostitutes. Earlier, in 1950, in an essay entitled 'Parlyaree', Partridge uses his first sentence to say that Parlyaree is also occasionally known as Parlaree, Parlarey, Parlary or Palarie.[14] He probably should have just left it at that.

From examination of some of the different sets of slang associated with these different groups, it is clear that there are a range of overlapping and unique terms, and that Partridge was attempting to tease them all apart, but it is difficult to know the extent to which any of his accounts in different editions of his books are accurate. Instead, it is easier to note that there was something called Parlyaree (with numerous pronunciation and spelling variants) that was used in the eighteenth and nineteenth centuries and which was spoken by different groups who coincided. Some of these speakers belonged to various travelling groups, often involving entertainment or performance, and some were criminals or on the fringes of society. Two of the groups mentioned by Partridge who are associated with Parlyaree are unlikely to be familiar to present-day readers: costermongers and cheapjacks. The former were people who sold goods (often fruits, vegetables and meats) from a handcart in British towns and cities. The latter were also known as pedlars – they were tradespeople who moved from place to

London street traders, Clapham Common, late nineteenth century

place and would have mingled with showmen in fairgrounds or performers in travelling shows or circuses. Similarly, beggars and prostitutes might have also been likely to travel around more than most people, while actors would have also toured with shows. Actors were a despised social group until the end of the eighteenth century, so their use of Parlyaree would have functioned as form of protection, secrecy and bonding in a similar way to Polari.

Like Cant, Parlyaree was a technical language, with words relating to the occupational aspects of speaker's lives. Partridge cites an out-of-print essay by Sydney Lester written in 1937 called 'Vardi the Parlary', where terms for numbers and money are given. The words to count up to twelve are *una, dewey, tray, quattro, chinqua, say, setter, otter, nobber, daiture, lepta, kenza,* while monetary terms include *saltee*: penny, *bianc*: shilling and *funt*: pound. Lester has a nice example of a Parlary conversation between two people (possibly entertainers, beggars, thieves or sellers of goods) who are counting up the day's takings:

'What's the bottle, cull?'
    'Dewey funt, tray bionk, daiture soldi medza, so the divvi is otta bionk nobba peroon and tray medzas back in the aris.'

Translated, this reads:

'How much have we taken, pal?'
    'Two pounds, three shillings and ten-pence half-penny, so we get eight shillings and nine-pence each and put three halfpence back in the bottle.'[15]

Aris (most likely Cockney Rhyming Slang from the word *Aristotle*) translates as *bottle* and refers to the day's tak-ings (possibly not a literal bottle). Notably, *aris* occurs in the Julian and Sandy sketches as a Polari word (most likely meaning arse).[16]

We also see the word *cull* in Parlyaree, which links us back to Cant and Mollies, who used it too. *Divvi* perhaps comes from 'division' and means to share – a similar slang word is used in some regional forms of English today (as in 'to divvy something up'), while *peroon* could mean 'per person', 'per man' or 'per one'.

Partridge also describes a busker's song, sent to him in a letter by Herbert Seaman,[17] which contains a number of words that are likely to have been understood by Polari speakers:

Nantee dinarlee: The omee of the carsey
Says due bionc peroney, manjaree on the cross
We'll all have to scarper the jetty in the morning,
Before the bonee omee of the carsey shakes his doss.

Translated, the song means:

We've got no money: The landlord
Says two shillings per person, we've got our food by
    cheating
We'll have to leave in the morning
Before the good landlord wakes up.

Again, there is *peroney*, and words for money and numbers, but also *nantee* (no, none), *omee* (man), *carsey* (house), *scarper* (leave/flee), *bonee* (good) and *doss* (sleep). While some of these words (*carsey*, *scarper*, *doss*) are also found in Cockney, others are more clearly linked to Polari words (*bonee* is very

Champagne Charlie
(George Leybourne),
darling of the music halls

close to Polari's *bona*, while *omee* and *nantee* are definitely core Polari words).

Related to the various versions of Parlyaree which Partridge tried to delineate is Thomas Frost's 'circus slang',[18] which contains numerous terms relating to circus acts (*jeff*: rope, *ponging*: tumbling) but also more general words that are suspiciously similar to Parlyaree ones. For example, Frost's *John Scarpery* (to abscond without paying) looks connected to the *scarper* meaning in the song above. Additionally, *dona* in circus language is not a stretch from *donna* and has the same meaning (woman), while *letty* (lodgings) is the same in both forms of slang. Frost's circus slang also has links back to Cant, with terms like *cully* (mate) being congruent in both lexicons. One of the verses of the circus song 'The Man on the Flying Trapeze' written by George Leybourne (also known as Champagne Charlie) in 1868 contains the line 'This young man by name was Signor Bona Slang'. While *slang* referred to a gymnast's performance rather than language, note the similarity between *bona* and Frost's *bono* – both meaning good.

Another of Partridge's sources was Philip Allingham, who wrote the book *Cheapjack* in 1934, a largely autobiographical novel which told of his 'adventures as a fortune-teller, grafter, knocker-worker and mounted pitcher on the market-places and fairgrounds of a modern but still romantic England'. Allingham refers to Grafter's Slang in his book, which also shares more than a passing resemblance to Parlyaree, with the following overlaps: *bevvy*: drink, *charver*: despoil, *chavvy*: child, *denar*: shilling, *donah*: women, *homey*: man, *letty*: lodgings, *munjary*: food, *nanty*: beware, *scarper*: run, *tober*: fairground, *tober'omey*: toll collector, *tosheroon*: half a crown. As with many of the other 'occupational' slangs referred to in this chapter, there are also a set of trade-specific words such as *dookering*: to tell fortunes, *flash*: grafter's display, *gear*: stock, *lark*: line of business, *tober*: fairground, *vardo*: caravan, along with terms for money and crime. Allingham has *phunt* to refer to a pound, while Lester has *funt*, and *nanti* means beware for Allingham but Partridge gives the meaning as 'be quiet', 'no', 'none', 'nothing' or 'don't'. *Charver* is another shared word; here's an example of it from *Cheapjack* – note also the use of Cockney Rhyming Slang (*apples and pears* for stairs):

'E'll keep you gassing all the blinking night if you let
'im,' he said to me. 'What about slippin' up the apple
and pears and getting in feather? I'm just about charvered.' . . . 'Charvered' is not a very nice expression,
and no doubt Charlie would not have used it had he
realised that Madam Eve was present.[19]

Around the same time that Allingham was writing
Cheapjack, another writer, George Orwell, had worked on
a similar semi-autobiographical novel, focusing on the lives
of tramps and low-paid kitchen workers in *Down and Out
in Paris and London* (1933). In the second half of this book,
Orwell returns to London and finds out that the job that had
been promised to him is not available so he becomes a tramp,
living on the margins of society and sleeping in spikes (Salvation
Army shelters). Although the book does not refer to Parlyaree,
there is a chapter on the slang of beggars and tramps that contains a number of words also used in Allingham's *Cheapjack*,
including *deaner/dener*: shilling, *clod*: money, *kip*: lodgings,
tosheroon: half a crown, *sprowsie/sprasy*: sixpence, *gee*: accom-
plice, *Smoke*: London, *mug-faker*: photographer. Orwell also
(unintentionally) implies a potential way that some of these
slang words could have crossed over into the language use of
the gay men of the period. In one part of the book he describes
how a tramp makes a sexual advance towards him when they
are locked up together, explaining that owing to their status,
sex with women would be out of the question, so most tramps
of the time had sex with one another. In another part of the
book Orwell describes a doss-house that contained 'ambiguous-
looking youths in smartish blue suits', as well as wealthier

men who were prepared to slum it, perhaps because they were seeking sexual contacts.

The Italian connection

Readers familiar with Italian are likely to have recognized some of the words mentioned so far, and it's certainly the case that Parlyaree and some of its close relatives had Italian origins. This link has been best explored by Ian Hancock in an essay published in 1984 that considers Shelta (a form of language spoken by Irish Travellers) and Polari.[20] Hancock does not go into much detail regarding Polari's use by gay men but instead focuses on its relationship to Italian, providing some interesting lines of reasoning that suggest some of the ways this may have come about. He notes, for example, that Britain saw the arrival of a relatively large number of Italian Punch and Judy men, organ grinders and pedlars during the 1840s, who would have been incorporated into existing networks of travelling enter-tainers, adding to the slang lexicons already in use. A second source of Italian into British itinerant communities is due to the importation of a large number of children from Italy in the nineteenth century, who were sent out to busk, and were controlled by 'padroni' (a person who secures employment for immigrants). These children are unlikely to have known much English and most of their communication would have been with other street performers, offering another glimpse into how Italian entered the slang of travelling entertainers.

About two-thirds of Hancock's 109-word Polari lexicon appears to contain Italian-derived slang words. Some relate to sex – a *kerterver cartzo* is a venereal disease (literally a 'bad penis') – while he also includes *charver*, *punk* and *carsey* (which has the meaning of a brothel). Other words relate to performance (*wallop*: dance, *mazarine*: platform below stage, *fake the fatcha*: shave the face, and *muck*: stage make-up), while *barkey* (sailor) suggests a link to Lingua Franca (a form of language used by sailors around the Mediterranean) or the docklands. Interestingly, as well as including some of Partridge's Parylaree words for numbers, there are several variant forms – so seven translates to *say oney* (literally six and one), while eight is *say dooey* (six and two) and *long dedger* is eleven, as opposed to Lester's *lepta*. As Partridge gives the word *daiture* as ten, perhaps *dedger* is a variant term, with *long dedger* being considered a 'long ten', similar to how a baker's dozen is thirteen.

Henry Mayhew documented the speech of the Punch and Judy men in the third volume of his *London Labour and the London Poor* series, with the following account:

That's the way to do it! An eighteenth-century Italian puppet show

Bona parlare means language; name of patter. 'Yeute munjare' – no food. 'Yeute lente' – no bed. 'Yeute bivare' – no drink. I've 'yeute munjare', and 'yeute bivare', and what's worst, 'yeute lente'. This is better than coster's talk because that ain't no slang at all, and this is broken Italian, and much higher than the coster's lingo. We know what o'clock it is, besides.[21]

The excerpt contains words that would later be found in Polari, notably *bona* and *parlare*, although note how the pronunciation of *lente* is close to the more commonly known *letty* for bed, and the similarity between *bivare* and *bevvy* (to drink) found in Allingham's Grafter's Slang described earlier. Similarly, *munjare* (food, to eat) is likely to be linked to *jarry*, which was sometimes used metaphorically by Polari speakers to refer to oral sex (*jarry the cartes*). However, *yeute* does not appear to have survived into Polari, as *nanti* became more commonly used as a negator. It is interesting how Mayhew's speaker casts the *parlare* that he speaks as more comprehensive and complex, being 'higher' (most likely approximating a full language) than the slang of the costermongers.

Mayhew outlines another piece of conversation from a Punch and Judy man:

'How are you getting on?' I might say to another punch-man. 'Ultra cativa,' he'd say. If I was doing a little, I'd say 'Bonar.' Let us have a 'shant a bivare' – pot o' beer . . . 'Ultray cativa slum' – not a good call. 'Tambora' – drum; that's Italian. 'Pipares' – pipes. 'Questra homa a vardering the slum scarpar it, Orderly' – there's someone

a looking at the slum. Be off quickly. 'Fielia' is a child;
'Homa' is a man; 'Dona,' a female, 'Charfering-homa'
– talking man, policeman.[22]

Again, we see links through to later Polari words, albeit
with slightly different spellings or pronunciations. *Fielia* is close
to *feely* (child), *homa* was later *homie* or *omi*, and *charfering-
homa* becomes *charpering-omi* (policeman). The authors doing
this kind of lexicography work at the time were making their
best guesses at spellings of words, though, and did not have
access to recording equipment, so we need to allow for discrepancies. And as with *yeute*, not all of these words appear
to have survived into Polari – I haven't found cases of *ultra/
ultray* (very) and *shant* (pot) being used later on.

However, what become known as Polari in the twentieth
century retained such a strong Italian flavour that care needed
to be taken when considering potential audiences. One of my
interviewees, Keith, offered to tell me 'the shoe shop story',
which describes how two of his friends were on holiday in Italy
and decided to buy a pair of fancy shoes. It was a crowded
shop and the man who attended to them was very attractive, so
this inspired some commentary between the friends, who used
Polari to communicate what they thought of him. However, the
Polari words that they used were so similar to Italian that the
object of their desire looked up and said, 'Thank you.' It transpired that everyone in the shop had understood the Polari and
they all started laughing. The friend who'd spoken Polari was
so embarrassed that he ran out of the shop. The moral of the
story is that if you wish to use a secret language to talk about
how good-looking someone is, it is a good idea to investigate

where the words come from. Let's hope that the shoes at least impressed people back home.

Romany

One of the Polari speakers I interviewed claimed that Polari came from Romany, a member of the Indo-European family of languages which was spoken by an ethnic group who are sometimes referred to as Gypsies (possibly a variant form of 'Egyptians' and likely to be a misnomer). The Romany people originated in Northern India and the Romany language is rooted in Sankrit grammar structures. Romany speakers moved westwards at some period, no later than the ninth century AD, across western Asia, Europe and eventually America. By the early sixteenth century they had reached Britain, the first recorded account being 1505.

The claim of Polari originating from Romany has been made by others, including Paul O'Grady, who performed a drag act as Lily Savage from the 1970s to the 2000s. In a book published under Savage's name called *Lily Savage: A Sort of A to Z Thing*, O'Grady gives a 58-item Polari lexicon, describing it as a 'slang that originates way back with the Romany gypsies'.[23]

Peter Burton, a journalist and gay rights activist who spoke Polari and wrote about it in the 1970s and '80s, also notes the link to Romany: 'It owed allegiance to and was curiously linked with the curious argots developed by the "underworld groups" – the Gypsies, the blacks, the drug sub-culture, the criminal, the racing fraternity.'[24] The idea of Romany feeding into Polari makes sense, especially if we look at the other kinds of groups whose language influenced its development. Gypsies

are likely to have some shared characteristics, at least superfi-
cially, with travelling entertainers, cheapjacks, costermongers
and beggars. Hancock, however, disagrees:

> Burton's labelling of Gypsies and Blacks as 'under-
> world' peoples speaking 'curious argots' is scarcely
> justifiable . . . there is nothing clearly Gypsy or Black
> in Polari, and Sephardic immigrants would more likely
> have contributed Romance words to the dialect than
> would have Ashkenazim from Russia and Poland.[25]

Donald Kenrick suggests that the form of Romany spoken in
Britain originated as a pidgin – in this case a simplified form of
communication that merged aspects of English and the Gypsies'
native language.[26] This later developed into a creole (a fuller
version of the pidgin) although by the twentieth century it had
lost its distinctive syntax, phonology and morphology (in that
order) and was simply a lexicon consisting mainly of verbs,
adjectives and nouns. Looking at a lexicon of Romany English
first published by George Henry Borrow in 1874, there are a
handful of words that appear to be related to Parlyaree or Polari.
These include *boona*: good, *chavi/chavali*: girl/daughter, *chavo/
chauvo*: boy/son, *dui*: two, *gajo*: outsider, *moey/mooey*: mouth
or face (from *mooi*), *warda*: guard or take care, *pani/pawnee*:
water.[27] The Romany English word *fake* (work illegally or steal)
is also found in Thomas Frost's list of circus words, with a
similar meaning. Additionally, there are words from Romany
that can be linked to Cockney slang, such as *wonga* (money in
Cockney and close to the Romany *wanga* where it meant coal)
and *cushty* (good), which is close to the Romany *kushtipen*.

So there are potential links between Polari and Romany, although they are slim and therefore should not be overstated at the expense of closer language varieties like Parlyaree or Italian. It could be the case that any lexical similarities between Polari and Romany English are the result of overlap with a third variety. However, Polari and Romany were both used as 'insider' languages to exclude outsiders, unlike, say, Lingua Franca, which was used in order to allow different groups of people to communicate, and perhaps this is why the link between the two has been emphasized in some quarters.

The Dancer's Language

As the nineteenth century progressed, Eric Partridge notes that Parlyaree became 'moribund'.[28] The strolling players and performers were gradually succeeded by entertainers who may still have travelled but were more likely to be associated with music halls and theatres, particularly in London but also in other British cities. London's West End was home to dozens of these venues and it was no coincidence that these entertaining classes overlapped with other social groups, including gay men, trans people and prostitutes. With its larger population, thriving nightlife, liberal attitudes, opportunities for work and affordance for anonymity, cities like London were popular destinations for people whose gender or sexuality went against the mainstream in some way. Homosexuality had been illegal since 1533 when Henry VIII had made all male–male sexual activity punishable by death (the Buggery Act), and after a succession of various repeals and reinstatements by Edward VI, Mary Tudor and Elizabeth I, the Act had been in force since 1558.

Despite this, James I and possibly William III had male lovers. The Buggery Act was repealed and replaced with the Offences against the Person Act in 1828, and while the death penalty for 'buggery' was not abolished until 1861, it still remained a crime, with 8,921 men being prosecuted between 1806 and 1861, and 56 executed.[29] Section 11 of the Criminal Law Amendment Act in 1885 prohibited 'gross indecency' between men and covered a wider range of sexual activities than buggery. It was this act that would bring homosexuality to public attention with the celebrity case of Oscar Wilde. The playwright was accused of inciting twelve boys to 'commit sodomy' between 1892 and 1894, resulting in his imprisonment in 1895. The case may have scandalized the upper classes but it did not destroy the strengthening networks of gay people over the early decades of the twentieth century. Although Wilde used coded language in his plays, he does not seem to have used Polari. However, it was within theatrical circles that Polari began to properly establish itself, to the extent that for some it was a theatrical language first and a form of language used by gay men second.

In a letter to *The Guardian*, the actors Glyn Jones and Christopher Beeching give a couple of interesting examples of nineteenth-century music-hall slang. They reference a theatrical newspaper called *The Magnet*, which in 1874 referred to Harris and Crossling, a music hall act:

They were in Edinburgh, standing outside what they believed to be the Waverley music hall, but which was in fact a first-class hotel called the Waverley. I quote: 'This is a bona crib,' said Harris to Crossling. 'Proper, my boy,' replied his companion. 'Who's that homo standing on the

steps?' cried Harris. 'Nanty,' says Crossling. 'He's piped
your nibsgigging!' – and thus the exchange went on.[30]

The passage contains a couple of well-known words that were
used by twentieth-century Polari speakers: *bona* (good) and
nanty (don't – most likely used in this context to mean don't
speak). There are other terms which I have not come across
elsewhere, though: *crib* probably refers to the building under
discussion while *he's piped your nibsgigging* could mean he's
heard you talking. The online OED gives a nineteenth-century
use of to *pipe* as meaning to 'watch, notice, look at; to follow
or observe, especially stealthily or with criminal intent'. *Nibs*
was also used in the nineteenth century as a way of referring to
someone, later being used somewhat mockingly to imply that
a person was self-important. If this is the case, then *gigging*
could be seen as a separate word from *your nibs*, although its
meaning becomes difficult to ascertain.

The use of *homo* also raises a question – are the speakers
using the word as a shortened version of *homosexual*, or (more
likely) as a variant of Parlyaree *omee* (man)? There doesn't
appear to be enough context for us to be sure.

Jones and Beeching give a second example in their *Guardian*
letter, which involves George Leybourne, mentioned earlier in
this chapter.

In January 1866, the music hall star George Leybourne
(Champagne Charlie) wrote and sang a song in which
he impersonated Chang the Fychow Giant, who was
then causing a sensation in London. The chorus is,
for the most part, nonsense 'Chinese'. However,

Canterbury Hall, a music hall in Lambeth, 1856

Leybourne throws in this line of polari: 'Varder me nibs parladering'.

A couple of the words are most likely variants of twentieth-century Polari: *varder* (later spelt *vada*, meaning look at) and *parladering*, which is possibly the same as *palarying*, meaning talking. The term *me nibs* suggests further evidence that *your nibs* is being used in the earlier instance to refer to a person, and a possible translation of this phrase would be 'look at him talking'.

Within the music halls and theatres, dancers were known as *wallopers* and singers were *voches* (voices). Other words were taken from the older Parlyaree, with the updated version variously called Parlare or Palari. Chorus boys, many of whom were gay, were especially taken with the language, as it enabled them to communicate about matters of a sexual nature in public spaces, protecting them from persecution, and they adopted the language as their own, adding in new words and phrases that enabled the discussion of more risqué topics.

The composer and lyricist Sandy Wilson, who is thought to be the inspiration for Sandy from the *Round the Horne* sketches, was interviewed for a BBC Radio 4 programme about Polari in 1998. He described the link between Polari and the theatre. 'I was living with a dancer . . . and they all talked it, regardless of sex, it was nothing to do with sex – it was just a kind of professional slang.'[31] In 1969, Peter Gordeno, a dancer, cabaret singer, choreographer and occasional actor, published a short article in *TV Times* magazine (a popular television listings magazine aimed at a family audience) referring to something called the Dancer's Language.[32] He included a nineteen-item list of words, including *camp*: outrageous, eccentric or twee, *omme-polone*: homosexual and *frock*: female attire. Gordeno stated that the language came from the circus and was known by thousands of dancers all over the world. This was clearly Polari, just not labelled as such.

And of course, Polari's links with the theatre were also acknowledged in the characters of Julian and Sandy, two out-of-work actors who took on various temporary jobs between roles.

Love for sale

A further influence on Polari's development was through people who worked as prostitutes. Partridge had referred to *parlary* as being a prostitute's slang since the 1930s. Quentin Crisp, one of the grand 'effeminate homosexuals' of London in the interwar years, describes how he hung out in Soho with other queens and male prostitutes, the line between the two sometimes being blurred. For six months he worked as a prostitute himself, describing how, during the repressive atmosphere of the period, accepting money for sex absolved him 'from the charge of enjoying sex for its own sake'.[33]

There were plenty of words in Polari or related forms like Parlyaree that referred to prostitution: *charvering donna*, *bitaine*, *brass*, *aspro*, *pont*, *ponce*, *punk* and *rent* all referred to prostitutes, while to *go on the batter* was to walk the streets as a prostitute, and a prostitute's client was known as a *steamer*.

The painter Francis Bacon described Soho as a place of excitement: 'The prostitutes were all over the streets. The streets were more fun, more amusing. The prostitutes gave a living sense to the streets.'[34] In past decades, before the establishment of legal bars or clubs or online cruising apps, the streets of cities were places where sexual pick-ups were much more likely to take place. The author W. Somerset Maugham has one of the characters in his novel *The Narrow Corner* reminisce about the area around Piccadilly Circus:

There was a part that in his day they called the Front, the street on the north side that led from Shaftesbury Avenue to the Charing Cross Road, where from eleven to twelve people walked up and down in a serried throng. That was before the war. There was a sense of adventure in the air. Eyes met and then . . . The doctor smiled. He did not regret his past; he regretted nothing.[35]

Quentin Crisp : 'Treat all disasters as if they were trivialities but never treat a triviality as if it were a disaster'

There was often a fine line between cruising and prostitution. The Dilly boys – young, feminine men who powdered their faces – operated as street prostitutes around Piccadilly Circus and constituted a distinct set of Polari users. They were likely to have contributed to Polari's status as a highly sexualized language with numerous words for sexual acts and body parts. Quentin Crisp describes their 'mannequin walk' and their conversation: 'As I wandered along Piccadilly or Shaftesbury Avenue, I passed young men standing at the street corners who said, "Isn't it terrible tonight dear? No men about. The Dilly's not what it used to be.'[36] The Dilly boys' use of language was acknowledged decades later in a song by Morrissey called 'Piccadilly Palare', released in 1990. The song is voiced by a Dilly boy who refers to Palare as 'silly slang' and contains the words *bona, vada, eek* and *riah*.

The Street Offences Act of 1959 was designed to clamp down on people who loitered or solicited for sex in public places and it also included special provision to prosecute owners of night cafes which sex workers sometimes used. The Act had the effect of driving prostitution further underground (and indoors), and the kinds of cruising activity described by Crisp, Bacon and Maugham could now be used more easily as grounds for arrest. Legal terms like *importuning* and *soliciting* were incorporated, most likely ironically with scare quotes round them, within Polari, to refer to cruising. A link between gay men and female prostitutes is given by Jim, one of the men interviewed for a BBC television documentary on gay history called *It's Not Unusual* in 1997.[37] He describes how they each gave one another protection:

> If girls were caught with condoms they would be charged with prostitution. If a gay guy was caught with a tin of Vaseline he would also be charged with prostitution. So the girls would carry the Vaseline and the boys would carry the condoms. It made for a rather strange relationship.

Sailors and sea queens

We now move on to consider the role that the sea and the people who travelled on it played in Polari's development. As already noted, despite being a form of language spoken in Britain, there were strong links with Italian, and during the nineteenth century the only way to reach the UK from abroad was to travel across the sea. During these voyages the Italians who came to Britain to work as street performers would have had contact with seafaring people and may have exchanged slang words with them, even during brief voyages. A lingua franca can refer to any situation where people possess different native languages (say English and Spanish), so they communicate in a (usually simplified version of a) third language that they both know. However, the term *Lingua Franca* also refers to a form of language that was spoken by sailors in ports along the Mediterranean coast, originating from the time of the Crusades.[38] The Mediterranean Lingua Franca contained a few words that were also reasonably familiar to Polari speakers, such as *barca*: boat, *mangia*: food, *bona vardia*: all's well, *capello*: hood and *parlamento*: conversation.[39]

Many English seafarers in the eighteenth and nineteenth centuries would most certainly have known Lingua Franca and are likely to have brought elements of it back to Britain. Wounded seamen in particular would often be put to shore miles from their home or the place where they were to be paid and would be obliged to take to the roads against their will, becoming cheapjacks, beggars or petty thieves to survive.[40] Additionally, some retired sailors would have joined travelling fairs or circuses in order to make a living.[41] An Act of 1713 made wandering illegal, except for sailors, and as a result of this distinctions between sailors and other travelling people were often confused as some travellers pretended to be sailors until 1792 when the Act was repealed. There are numerous ways that the language used by seafarers would have cross-pollinated the language of travelling entertainers, beggars and pedlars in this period.

Bona drag? Sailors pose as couples on the deck of a ship, 1920s

As Polari gradually became more firmly associated with gay men in the first decades of the twentieth century, we can point to the sexual fascination that many Polari speakers had with various types of men in uniform. Jonathon Green writes that 'The automatic union of . . . sailors ("rum, sodomy and the lash") and the gay world is clichéd, politically no doubt far from correct, but unavoidable,'[42] while Stephen Donaldson describes the 'erotic mystique' of sailors, who in their figure-hugging uniforms could be seen as sexually casual, easily plied with alcohol and willing to do almost anything for money.[43] Kenneth Williams described an encounter with sailors hanging around outside an establishment that was popular with gay men in Hong Kong in a diary entry of Thursday, 11 September 1947: 'Sent up silly by seaweed outside the building – gay place this.'[44]

Despite the fact that homosexuality was illegal in the Navy, the all-male environment is likely to have resulted in men having sex with one another, possibly without viewing themselves as gay. Such men may also have been more willing than others to accept the attention of other men in shoreside pubs and bars, especially if they were offered money. Kellow Chesney suggests that 'it was probably in the great ports that the most genuinely professionally male prostitutes were found'.[45] Additionally, during the first two-thirds of the twentieth century, a sizeable number of British gay men joined the Merchant Navy or worked on passenger cruise ships as stewards or waiters as a way of seeing the world and escaping the drab atmosphere back home.

Men interviewed for Channel 4's *Summer's Out* documentary series described the existence of different varieties of Polari, particularly making a distinction between the version used in the West End of London and another used in the East End. Activist and member of the Gay Liberation Front Michael James noted that there was a geographical difference, with the East End queens being more rooted in their community whereas the West End queens were like gypsies, moving from place to place. James sees West End Polari as being fundamentally influenced by Theatre-Speak (the Dancer's Language described earlier), while the East End version was based on the boat queens (the gay men who worked in the Merchant Navy) as well as Yiddish and other communities, so this form of Polari became embellished with a wider range of linguistic influences.

David McKenna, an East Ender also interviewed in *Summer's Out*, describes how the West End queens were more restricted by societal norms because they worked in offices during the day and had to wear suits and ties. They would be called George by day but Fishy Frances by night. He goes on to outline the ways that the different communities would use Polari.

The sea queen would accentuate or elaborate a lot more on the Polari. If you were going to say, 'Look at that guy standing next to me,' the shore-side Polari part would be 'Vada the omee standing next to me.' A sea queen would say, 'Vada the schwawarly on me jaxys way out.' They just elaborated on it, because it was meant to sway people, so they didn't understand what you were talking about. Even with the sea queens not wanting a shore-side West End queen to understand what she's saying. You'd be standing there and you'd say, 'Oh vada that naff queen. What a coddy kaffall dear. Oh vada the schnozzle on it dear.' And you'd be doing all this Polari, they'd understand the basics. They understood bona and camp and cod and riah and things like that, but the sea queens would really go to town.

East End Polari is represented as more complex than the West End version – the latter is probably best seen as closer to the form used in the Julian and Sandy sketches (although it's likely that Julian and Sandy used an even simpler version still). David McKenna's Polari is among the most complex that I've heard as he appears to embellish a number of words – *ajax* becomes *jaxys way out*, for example. Let us consider, then, some of the other influences on the form of Polari spoken in the East End of London.

Cockney Rhyming Slang and Back Slang

Capital cities, with their large, densely packed, continuously changing populations which tend to be socially and ethnically diverse, are often places where new forms of language thrive and distinct languages are combined, resulting in hybrid forms. At the start of the twentieth century, London was the largest city in the world, being home to 6.5 million people,[46] and arguably the United Kingdom was the world's most powerful country, spanning an Empire upon which the 'sun never sets'. The influence of London on Polari should not be underestimated, and if anywhere was Polari's home, it was 'the Smoke', or *Eine* as it was known.

Working-class people in London spoke (and to an extent still speak) a dialect called Cockney, which is sometimes seen as limited to people living in London's East End. Cockney involves distinct pronunciations of certain sounds, including use of the glottal stop (so *butter* can sound like *bu'er*), *h*-dropping, replacement of the *r* sound with something approximating *w* (*three* can be pronounced more like *fwee*) and the vocalization of the *l* sound so *mill* can sound like a bit like *me-ul*. Cockney uses *ain't* for *isn't*, and double negatives are also fairly common (for example, *I didn't see no one*).

The first Cockney Rhyming Slang lexicon was published in 1821 as *The Flash Dictionary*, and was reprinted as appendices to *Poverty, Mendacity and Crime* (1839) and *Sinks of London Laid Open* (1848), both without acknowledged authors. Although it has been suggested that the rhyming and Back Slang used by costermongers derives from a secret language of the criminal underworld, Julian Franklyn notes that there were differences between Thieves' Cant, which was 'complex and grim', and rhyming slang, which was amusing and intelligible even to the uninitiated.[47]

Many Polari speakers would have come from or lived in London at some point and are likely to have had at least traces of the Cockney accent. In addition to this, though, are a number of Cockney slang terms that were used by Polari speakers so often that they became incorporated into Polari's vocabulary itself. Cockney used a form of rhyming slang whereby terms are derived from their rhyming qualities with other words or phrases. For example, the word *street* rhymes with the phrase *field of wheat*, so a street would be known as a 'field of wheat' or, more commonly, just a *field* – the first part of the phrase. The fact that the rhyme typically involved a two- or three-word phrase but usually only the first, non-rhyming part of the phrase was used meant that it was not easy to decipher Cockney Rhyming Slang without a little effort, so the slang acted as a form of code that could be difficult to crack, even if you knew the general rule behind it. Commonly used Cockney Rhyming Slang words that found their way into Polari included *Barnet* (meaning *hair*, derived from the phrase *Barnet Fair*), *Irish* (meaning wig, from *Irish jig*), *minces* (eyes, from *mince pies*), *plates* (feet, from *plates of meat*), *scotches* (legs, from *scotch peg*) and *steamer* (mug, from *steam tug*). The last one is a little more complex to decipher in that *mug* is slang itself for someone who was the client of a prostitute. It is notable that apart from *steamer*, these other terms all reference body parts, and this perhaps helps to explain why they became popular with Polari speakers whereas other Rhyming Slang words, like *Rosie* (tea, from *Rosie Lee*) and *apples* (stairs, from *apples and pears*), did not.

A less frequently encountered form of slang used in Polari also involves linguistic word play, and is slightly less complex although it works in a similar way – that is, having an initial rule that can be used to derive new words. Back Slang simply

Vada her titfer:
Cockney Pearly King
and Queen, 1961

involved pronouncing a word as if it was spelt backwards, and
this trick was used in the creation of a number of Polari terms:
knife was *efink*, face was *ecaf* (sometimes shortened to *eke* or
eek), while hair was *riah*. The two last terms, along with the
Cockney Rhyming Slang words mentioned above, were used in
the *Round the Horne* radio sketches. A less common Back Slang
word, not used in *Round the Horne* but mentioned by Polari
speakers I interviewed, was *esong* (nose). As with Cockney
Rhyming Slang, most of the Back Slang terms used by Polari

speakers refer to parts of the body. Jonathon Green in *The Big Book of Filth* gives a few additional Back Slang terms: *doog gels* (good legs), *foop* (poof) and *larro* (oral sex),[48] but while these three all look like reasonably good candidates for Polari, I have not found verification that any Polari speakers used them.

Yiddish

Another influence on Polari's development in London involved the sizeable Jewish community who were particularly concentrated in London's East End and contributed towards the mix of slangs that were spoken there. There were 100,000 Jewish people living in London between 1870 and 1914, and many times that number stayed in the East End before going on to New York.[49] Yiddish was a form of language used by Jewish people, containing words from Rabbinic Hebrew, Loez or Laaz (Jewish dialects of Old French and Old Italian), dialects of medieval German and forms of Slavic. It dates back to at least the fifteenth century when it was introduced to Poland from Germanic lands. Like Polari, it has borrowed and adapted words from many different sources. At the start of the Second World War there were 11 million speakers of Yiddish, comprising between 65 and 70 per cent of the world's Jewish population.[50]

Links between Polari and Yiddish are found in a number of words used by Polari speakers including *kosher homie*: Jewish man, *schinwhars*: Chinese man,[51] *schonk*: to hit, *schvartz homie* or *schvartzer homie*: black man, *vonka*: nose, *meese*: unattractive, *meshigener*: crazy, *sheitel/shyckle*: wig, *schlumph*: to drink, *schnozzle*: nose and *nosh*: oral sex. With Yiddish being extremely popular in the East End of London around the start of the twentieth century, then, it is not surprising to see some of these words merging with the other slangs which gay men of the time absorbed into Polari. And in addition to the East End/docks connection, another source of contact is likely to have been through Parlyaree-based theatrical slang via the Yiddish spoken by Jewish performers.

National Service and American Air Force slang

The Second World War had the effect of uprooting established social and familial networks and temporarily replacing them with new ones, as those who were called up for national service were stationed across the UK or transported to a wide range of different countries. Dudley Cave, who served in the Royal Army Ordnance Corps as a driver, described how gay and straight people worked together as a team because their lives might have depended on it:

> People were put in the army regardless of whether they were gay or not . . . It didn't seem to bother the military authorities. There was none of the later homophobic uproar about gays undermining military discipline and effectiveness. With Britain seriously threatened by the Nazis, the forces weren't fussy about who they accepted.[52]

The campest gay men were drafted as morale-boosting drag performers to perform in travelling concert teams. Lee Sutton, for example, who later performed as a drag queen and incorporated

Dudley Cave

Polari into his songs, joined the RAF in the Second World War as a flight mechanic and soon got involved in putting on performances for the forces, being posted to India where he wrote shows for the troops and staged military entertainment for hospitals and convalescent homes.

These men were regarded with affection and helped to lift spirits. In some cases, gay soldiers provided sexual relief to colleagues, a service which was overlooked by all but the most zealous of officers.[53] One of my interviewees, Robin, describes the popularity of Polari as linked to national service, which ran from 1939 until 1963 and would have helped to propagate the spread of different linguistic forms far beyond the more traditional pockets of speakers. Kenneth Williams, for example, was stationed in Singapore when the war ended, and he stayed on in the Combined Services Entertainment Unit, which put on revue shows. As mentioned earlier, his diary entries from the

1940s offer a few Polari phrases, and while the Second World War probably didn't in itself result in many new terms being added (although *black market queen* is a good candidate), it is likely to have helped to provide a great deal of social mixing, which helped to introduce Polari to larger numbers of speakers.

At the start of the Second World War, Quentin Crisp describes how he was rejected from the army on the grounds of 'suffering from sexual perversion', but 'as soon as the bombs began to fall, the city became like a paved double bed . . .'.[54] With the Blackout and a greater sense of the precariousness of existence brought about by the threat of attack, especially during the Blitz years of 1940–41 when people were thrown together to sleep in shelters, anonymous, semi-public sex was more available than it had been before. Doorways, parks and underground stations were viable locations for a chance encounter.

The first American servicemen arrived in the UK in 1942, and by the late spring of 1944 the UK had become home to 1,421,000 Allied troops.[55] American GIs (named after the term Government Issue, which appeared on their equipment) formed the majority of these, and for Crisp and his friends these handsome young men, in their tight uniforms and speaking in voices straight out of Hollywood movies, were a breath of fresh air.

As they sat in the cafés or stood in the pubs, their bodies bulged through every straining khaki fibre towards our feverish hands . . . Above all it was the liberality of their natures that was so marvellous . . . Never in the history of sex was so much offered by so many to so few.[56]

Fiction of the time offers a glimpse into the effect that GIS had on the lives of Londoners. Rodney Ackland's play *Absolute Hell* was first performed in 1951, although it was subsequently revised to make some of its themes more explicit. It is set in a dilapidated Soho drinking club at the end of the Second World War. Several of the main characters are gay, using slang terms associated with Polari like *drag* and *camp*. A wealthy female character is referred to as the Treacle Queen, and one of the handsome GIS who visits the club is called Butch, probably named after the short haircut style favoured by the American military. In one scene Butch asks the play's protagonist, Hugh, where he can find 'a piece of ass' and says he'll do anything involving sex except pay for it. Hugh asks, 'Does it have to be a woman?', resulting in Butch instructing Hugh to meet him at his hotel, room number 37, which Hugh repeats as 'Dirty Heaven' so he can remember it.

The comedian Tommy Trinder described the GIS as 'overpaid, oversexed and over here', and most accounts in popular culture have focused on the heterosexual relations between American GIS and the British women who were attracted to them, possibly hoping to be presented with nylon stockings, soap and chewing gum. The GIS had average salaries around five times that of British soldiers so they could afford to be big with the gifts. As a result of falling for their charms, around 70,000 British women married GIS. Unsurprisingly, numbers relating to how many gay relationships occurred between British and American men during this time were not collated, but the fact that American slang terms start to appear in Polari around the time of the Second World War suggests that they were not insubstantial. When the war ended, the Americans returned home,

Got any gum, chum? American GIs

but gradually Polari speakers began to adopt Americanisms including *butch*: masculine, *cruise*: look for sex, *blowjob*: oral sex, *naff*: bad, *fruit*: gay, *fag*: gay, *fag-hag*: female friend of a gay man, *glossies*: magazines, *Mary*: gay man and *rim*: anilingus. Some of these types of words would have been used by American GIS, especially those who identified as gay. Others, like *fag-hag*, are more likely to have been picked up by Polari speakers in the decades following the Second World War, as a result of increased travel and communication between Britain and the u.s. We return to American influences on gay culture later, but for now let us move on to a final, post-Second World War influence on Polari's development.

1960s drug culture

The 1960s saw a change in many societal attitudes, especially among young people living in urban areas, and along with this there was an increase in drug use for recreation or experimentation. Drugs were popularized by accounts in America from writers and poets such as Allen Ginsberg, Jack Kerouac, Neal Cassady and William Burroughs. In 1966 Timothy Leary advocated to 30,000 hippies at Golden Gate Park in San Francisco that they 'turn on, tune in [and] drop out'. Cultural influences from the u.s. on the uk had by this point an almost instantaneous effect. And while people who used drugs were criminalized and the popular press was quick to sensationalize and stigmatize those who were caught, unlike earlier generations of drug users, this subculture did not consider itself in terms of being criminal or hopelessly addicted. Peter Burton's 1979 article on Polari in *Gay News* asserts that during this time a few words and phrases referring to drug use entered some Polari lexicons:

> Many of the words used in Polari also belong to the slang of . . . other groups . . . dubes, meaning pills, had – and may well still have – exactly the same meaning in drug-users' slang. And of course, at that point in time, a lot of us seemed to live on 'uppers' and 'downers'.[57]

Uppers referred to stimulating drugs like cocaine and speed whereas *downers* like heroin, alcohol, sleeping medication and tranquillizers create a calming 'high'. Mods had popularized the use of drugs such as Drynamil, which were prescribed for anxiety but also had an amphetamine effect, especially when two or more were taken together. Drynamil tablets were colloquially known as *purple hearts* because they were shaped like a rounded triangle and had a reddish-blue colour. In the 1960s they would have been taken by gay men in order to give them enough energy to dance the night away. Burton describes other terms in his list of Polari words – to get high on pills was to be *blocked*, while a desire to have sex as the effects of a drug were wearing off was known as a *randy comedown*. As well as referring to pills, *doobs* (also *dubes* or *doobies*) was slang for marijuana cigarettes. These were not words which appeared in the 'safer' version of Polari that was popularized by Julian and Sandy around the same time, however, and by this point Polari itself was already starting to wane to the extent that it becomes difficult to trace the social groups that were to influence it further.

In 1970 Eric Partridge acknowledged, a little late in the day, that 'gay slang has come to be known, in raffish, homosexual circles, as *polari*', as the historian David Halperin claims that by the late 1960s, Polari had become 'almost extinct'.[58] We'll discuss Polari's demise in more detail later so instead here I want to consider how we start to untangle what is ultimately pretty much an incomplete etymological mess of knotted historical threads, with more than a few conjectures and contradictions to complicate things further.

One problem is that even some of the Polari speakers I interviewed made a distinction between Polari words and what they referred to as nelly or nonce words or just gay slang. The gay slang words would include terms like *camp*, *rimming* and *bitch*, which have survived to the present day, whereas the Polari terms would be those which appear to have fallen into disuse like TBH (*to be had*), *dish* and *eke*. However, there are other words that could be seen as gay slang rather than Polari which are also less popular today (such as *cottage*, *chicken* and *fish*[59]). Do we view Polari as only those words that appear to have been invented and used by gay men and disregard the others as 'borrowings' from other forms of slang?

An article in the *Spectator* magazine in 2016 dismisses the claim that Polari is a language at all, with the author (who uses the pseudonym Dot Wordsworth) describing how she did an online search of Jonathon Green's *Dictionary of Slang* for Polari, and came up with 25 terms. Ms Wordsworth notes that many Polari words 'properly belong under European Lingua Franca, Yiddish and Romany' and goes on to write that 'it's all nonsense that Polari was a secret language. If used in a pub the police were among the most likely to understand it. Its few dozen words didn't even begin to be a language.'[60] In some cases, Dot is quite right – we could probably conceive of a kind of curve of speakers, with many people knowing a few words of Polari, and a few people knowing many and being more fluent and creative with the way they used them – a topic which is discussed in more detail in the following chapter. However, in giving workshops on Polari, I've noted how people quickly get confused when the ratio of English to Polari words tips in favour of Polari – and phrases like *order lau your luppers on the strillers bona* tend not to be understood by newbies every time they first hear them, even if they've had a fresher course in the basics.

English itself has borrowed words from numerous languages over time, as words like *thug* (Hindi), *cherub* (Hebrew), *cotton* (Arabic), *yoghurt* (Turkish), *tsar* (Russian), *wanderlust* (German), *gusto* (Italian), *embargo* (Spanish), *rendezvous* (French) and *kimono* (Japanese) attest to. Three difficult questions to answer are: at what stage do we accept that a word has become part of a language as opposed to being from another language or in some intermediate stage? What percentage of words need to be spoken in Polari, rather than English or something else, to earn Polari language status? And who decides? Unlike, say, nuclear physics, where only a small number of people can claim to be experts, everyone uses language, everyone has an opinion and those with the strongest opinions have a tendency to pronounce them rather loudly.

In the case of Polari, matters are made more complicated by the fact that we are considering a mostly 'dead' form of language where records were not kept, and if there were, they tended to be written somewhat after the fact, like Peter Burton's account, or else they were degrees away from authentic usage, documented by interested observers but non-speakers like Eric Partridge. None of the men I interviewed completely agreed on what was and what wasn't Polari, and there was quite a bit of disagreement around what certain Polari words meant or how they were pronounced.

So if we want to come up with a definitive account of what Polari was, is or should be, then we are asking the wrong question. It is too late for that. The best we can hope for is a partial account of some of its influences, propped up by some educated guesses, although we have no way of fully confirming who came up with certain words and the extent to which they were popularly used. Instead we have a form of language, spoken by people who identified as gay and who took words from here and there and combined them in new ways, changing some of the original words, and adding their own where they saw fit. Some were competent and fluent in doing this, others less so.

An important point to make is that the identity of 'gay man' is not a definitive identity – it's one of the reasons that I inwardly cringe when people use *gay* reductively as a noun in phrases like 'there were a group of gays over there'. Nobody is ever just a gay. They can also be defined by their age, their gender, their profession, their health, their religion, their social status, their hair colour, their sex life, their politics, the music, books and films they like and hundreds of other features. And this is something to consider of all the people who spoke Polari. They were not just gay – they were lots of other things too. They may have worked on a market stall, or in the theatre or in a dockland pub. They may have had a Jewish father or an Italian mother. And the people they met would have had equally complex, multifaceted identities. This helps to explain to an extent how Polari evolved from so many other forms of language, although a key part of the puzzle is that many of its influences were on the edge of society in some way. Like gay men, the contributors to what became Polari were frowned upon to an extent. They were largely outside of what was considered normal – they were foreign or had jobs that people looked down on, or were viewed as not having enough money or eyed with suspicion as likely criminals or sexual deviants, or were moving around the country so never really able to integrate into the community of a single place. For these reasons, the people in these groups developed ways of communicating with one another, of recognizing one another, of strengthening their bonds and, where necessary, of protecting themselves from everyone else. This helps to explain the overlap in linguistic terms between the different sets of speakers and the fact that some of Polari's words can be traced back across the centuries.

But if we cannot give a fully confident answer to 'Where did Polari come from?' then what questions can we ask instead? How about we move to the next chapter, where we consider how Polari worked as a language variety, and where there is firmer evidence to support our claims.

3

How to Polari Bona

It is the last year of the twentieth century and I'm in Washington, DC, to talk about the different words in Polari at the world's only conference dedicated to language and sexuality – Lavender Linguistics. As an impoverished student I've been put on the cheapest route to get there from the UK – three interconnecting flights taking a total of twenty hours. When I arrive at my hotel I sleep for a day then get up and have a bit of an incident on a subway escalator when my legs won't move. But I don't want to think about why that's happened, as I have worse things to worry about. It is my first ever conference talk and in the parlance of Polari, I am not feeling very bold. I don't know anyone at the conference, and I've been dreading giving the talk for months. During the coffee breaks I hide in a toilet cubicle and look at my watch until the talks start again. By the day of my talk I am a nervous wreck and my shirt is soaked with sweat before I've even left the hotel. Thirty minutes before I am due to go on, I am checking the handouts I've prepared and notice an error. It's a tiny spelling mistake. But despite this I freak out. I'll look shoddy, like I haven't prepared. In typical drama queen fashion, I think, 'IT'S ALL RUINED!' But then I remember seeing a print shop downstairs. There is still time. I can redo my handouts and get them all printed again. So I dash downstairs, queue behind students who are having their essays printed, correct the mistake, redo the handouts, pay for them, bin the old ones and race back up the stairs, just in time for my talk.

I am introduced and open my mouth. Then everything goes black and when I come round it is twenty minutes later and there is a smattering of polite applause. It's finished but I have no recollection of what has just happened. Back in my seat, I don't hear any of the next talk. I look down at the few remaining handouts and spot the spelling mistake. Somehow, in my panicked state, I must have thrown away the wrong set. I think, somewhere, in heaven, the long-gone Polari queens are looking down at me and thinking, 'This! This dizzy queen is meant to be our representative on Earth! Scharda dear! Scharda!'

That's the background to how this chapter came about. I'll be revisiting that talk here (in less panicked circumstances), giving an overview of some of the most commonly used Polari words along with a discussion of the worldview that these words evoked and how new words were derived. The chapter acts as a Polari primer, so if you want to learn how to Polari bona, then this chapter is for you.

Finding the voice

Perhaps we should start with how Polari should sound. Many speakers had regional accents, of which a good proportion were London, especially East End or Cockney, ones, as London was Polari's spiritual home. You don't need a Cockney accent to speak Polari, though – I interviewed speakers with strong Scouse and Glaswegian accents. And Liverpudlian Paul O'Grady, who performed as Lily Savage, knows plenty of Polari.

Speaking in a 'posh' upper-class or a middle-class 'received pronunciation' accent, sometimes thought of as standard English or what people say when they claim (incorrectly) to have 'no accent', isn't great for Polari, unless you can also sound very camp. Ideally you should have a regional accent, Cockney if you can get away with it, but then overlay that with the occasional affected attempt to sound as if you're descended from your actual royalty. Just as the word *queen* was used to describe men who often came from modest backgrounds, the accents of these men also had majestic pretensions. Kenneth Williams is a good role model. He grew up above his dad's hairdresser's shop, but in his many Carry On film roles he acted with an upper-middle-class provenance, playing a variety of haughty doctors and professors, presenting a slightly stern posh accent when trying to impress, although slipping into Cockney when highly excited. Kenneth's Sandy exploits the Cockney accent in the *Round the Horne* sketches to insert more Polari into the dialogue. In a sketch called 'Bona Homes', where he and Julian play landscape gardeners, he opens with, 'Oh hello Mr Horne, we're bona 'omes you see.' By dropping the *h* in *homes*, he is able to make the word sound more like *omee*, the Polari word for man.

Or listen to the recordings of Lee Sutton's drag acts.[1] Compared to Williams, who always sounds animated, Sutton has a deadpan comedic delivery – and although he's in drag there's scant attempt to contrive to the audience that he's female: his voice is unapologetically gravelly. However, he sounds like he is having a good time, and that's key to Polari. Even if your heart is breaking on the inside, you keep up the act, whether you're in drag or out of it. A Polari queen never cried, until she got home and drew the curtains.

The 'pseudo-posh' bits of Polari can come across in a variety of ways. Some Polari speakers could sound quite cosmopolitan as they threw bits of classroom French (or, less frequently, German) into their conversation. While, as we've seen in the previous chapter, Polari has a complicated history, picking up all sorts of linguistic influences over the decades, my guess is that use of French was more about showing off than there being a more substantial French connection. For the average working-class Brit in the 1950s and '60s, holidays 'abroad', as the world beyond the English Channel was known, were much less common than they are now. A bit of French could imply that the speaker was a glamorous jet-setter or at least had a foreign boyfriend. However, I don't think that most speakers were convincing anyone of this, other than the most naive chicken. Instead, use of classroom French was more parodic, based on the understanding that it is funny to pretend to be someone who thinks that speaking French is glamorous. Attempts to speak those little bits of French in an actual French accent are therefore to be frowned upon – that would be trying too hard and indicate that the speaker really knew French as opposed to be pretending to know it (although using an exaggerated French pronunciation is acceptable). Julian and Sandy regularly made use of a set of stock French phrases, including *artiste, tres passé, intimé, pas de deux, entrepreneur* and *nouvelle vague*. And one of Kenneth Williams's party pieces was to sing a song called 'Ma Crêpe Suzette', which consisted of a string of unrelated French phrases that have been absorbed into English, put to the tune of 'Auld Lang Syne'. The phrase *gardy loo* (meaning beware) is derived from the French *garder l'eau* (beware the water), originally used when the contents of a chamber pot were thrown out of a window onto the street below. Lily Savage has noted that some Polari words also have -*ois* added to them – such as in *nanteois*, none, and *bevois*, drink.[2] This has the effect of making them appear as if they are French, introducing a further level of complexity (and also acting as a marker of snobbishness).

Polari, when spoken naturally, can have an exaggerated intonation style. Vowel sounds can be dragged out and within longer words there can be multiple rises and falls across the different syllables. Take for example *fantabulosa*, which contains five syllables: *fan-tab-u-los-a*. If used as an exclamation, as Sandy would sometimes do, the 'a' sound in the syllable 'tab' would be extended while the following 'u' would have a falling intonation. Then the 'los' part would have an almost hysterically rising or a rise-fall intonation, along with another lengthened vowel sound, with a final, slight falling intonation on the last syllable, making the speaker appear exhausted but triumphant. But there are numerous other combinations of rises, falls or accented syllables that can be applied to *fantabulosa* – try enunciating it in at least three different ways, aiming for the campest intonation you can find!

Exclamations were an essential part of speaking Polari, being associated with 'stereotypically feminine' language, as they are reactive. If we say, 'oh!' or 'really!' or 'fabulosa!', we're usually reacting to some sort of external event such as someone's wig falling off or a claim about how many men someone danced with at last night's ball. There have been claims by some feminist linguists that women carry out what has been memorably described as 'shitwork' in conversations, especially with men.[3] This shitwork involves all the little things that people do to keep a conversation running smoothly – asking questions, showing that you're listening with little 'ohs' and 'ahas', choosing topics that you know the other person will want to talk about. It's very tiring. Men, on the other hand, aren't meant to even acknowledge that someone else has spoken – they just stand a little away from everyone, facing the wall in a murderous sulk, or they simply bludgeon their way into an ongoing conversation, interrupting whoever is speaking to tell them they're wrong (usually on a subject they know nothing about), or to change the subject to sport or cars or politics. If they can get a little boast in about their sexual prowess or how much money they make, then all the better. That's the stereotype at least, and while it holds for a small number of men and women, some of the time, actually most of us are pretty versatile communicators and there are more similarities than differences between the sexes.[4] Polari, then, with its exaggerated exclamations and its *dears* and *duckies* and empty adjectives (*bona!*), feels like a hyper-realized version of stereotypical women's speech – a parody of how women talk taken to a hilarious extreme – a linguistic form of drag.

There are different ways to speak Polari, then, linking through to personas – the piss-elegant posh queen, the world-weary seen-it-all tired old queen, the excited, breathless young queen, the witty, caustic queen, the gossipy queen who knows everyone's business. Each would use a different set of intonational patterns for different effects.

The social whirl

Polari is about drama and Polari speakers were drama queens par excellence. Another feminine stereotype – gossip – is meat and drink to Polari. Polari was essentially a social language, and many speakers lived in densely packed urban areas and had numerous friends, acquaintances, lovers, one-night-stands, exes, crushes, stalkers, rivals, enemies and frenemies. They also had a perfect recollection not only of all of their current relationships but of the status of the relationships of all of the other people that they knew, and social occasions would be spent updating one another on these relationships *in great detail*. As a young and introverted man on the gay scene, I often found this volume of gossip to be dizzying and overwhelming. I'd sit in the living rooms of some new friend who'd invited me round and then three or four of his other, more long-standing friends would arrive and there they'd sit all afternoon, drinking cups of tea and talking about all the people they knew, with me a sullen presence in the corner, to the point where I was sure they were simply making up names – nobody could know that many people! There couldn't be that many people in existence! Gossip is one of a queen's weapons – you never know when it'll come in handy, and much of it is, of course, geared towards the possibility of having sex with someone at some later date. Keeping track of who has split up with who, who is rumoured to have been seen down the cottage, who made a clumsy pass at who, whose wig fell off on the dance floor – these are all matters of state importance to Polari speakers.

The large number of words that relate to people indicates the importance of gossip in the Polari speaker's world. As we've seen, the generic term for man, usually a heterosexual man, was *omee* (also *omi* or *homi*), while a woman was a *palone* (sometimes pronounced to rhyme with *omee* as *paloney*, sometimes not). A gay man was named by combining the Polari words for man and woman together into *omee-palone*, whereas a lesbian was the reverse order – *palone-omee*. There's a conflation of gender and sexuality here which from some later perspectives might be seen as problematic – to say that a gay man is literally a man-woman keys into negative stereotypes about gay men as effeminate or women trapped in men's bodies. This was the general thinking of the time, so it is hardly surprising that these ideas found their way into the Polari mindset. However, many Polari speakers *were* very camp and a good number were what people might nowadays call gender-creative. They dressed in women's clothes – either by dragging up as female impersonators, or in a relatively more low-key way, by dyeing hair, wearing a touch of make-up or accessorizing with a colourful scarf. These speakers enjoyed the aspects of their identity that were feminine and felt that they were being true to themselves when they expressed them – they may have looked and sounded like camp stereotypes but most of them didn't view themselves or people like them negatively. Accordingly, *queen* keyed in to the imaginary world of Polari speakers as (female) royalty. If you are going to emulate a woman, why not be the most powerful woman in the country?

In 1981, a documentary called *Lol: A Bona Queen of Fabularity* was broadcast on BBC2. Starring London drag queen Lorri Lee, the documentary cuts between Lorri's drag act at a hen night, hoovering her flat and reconstructions of her younger days coming out of national service and joining the Merchant

Navy (with Lorri playing her younger self in flashbacks). Lorri waxed lyrical on the word *queen*, providing a lesson in the different sub-classifications:

Well what is a queen? Well you've met one, that's the drag queen, that's me . . . There's also the camp queen, that everyone sees in the street . . . you know, 'alright duck', that type of queen . . . There's what you call a black market queen. Now that's the type of queen that an ordinary everyday person, and even me, could look at it, and you'd never suss that it was a queen in a million years, but they're the types, I don't really admire terribly . . . that usually sort of creep up on people and then strike, you know, sort of lull them into a false sense of security and then strike, and I think they're the ones that usually get smacked in the face because of it. But then . . . you've got your blob type queen, this a queen of no account, you know, she's a little dumpy queen, walks around, usually follows a drag queen and sort of hangs on to every word it says, hoping a bit of the glitter's going to fall off on her and one day she's going to wake up like Prince Charming, suddenly turn into something different . . . After that you've got . . . your cottage queens. Now a cottage queen is a queen that would get her trade from a cottage naturally . . . it means a man's toilet. And I know queens . . . couldn't pass a cottage dear, would have to go in, some would even take sandwiches and a flask, would spend a pleasant day.[5]

In the Polari speaker's world, gender was linguistically reversed – *he* was *she* and (less commonly) *she* became *he*. This practice of feminizing through language, referred to by artist and Sister of Perpetual Indulgence (Manchester branch) Jez Dolan, is referred to as 'she-ing'. She-ing is one of the aspects of Polari that has survived into more recent decades, and the practice was so pervasive at a particular bar on Canal Street in Manchester's Gay Village that a 'She-box' was installed a few years ago, akin to a 'Swear-box', where patrons would have to put in a few coins if they she'd someone, with the proceeds being donated to charity.

In the Julian and Sandy sketches, *she* is occasionally used to refer to the (male) partner of a (butch) man. In the following exchange, from 'Bona Bijou Tourettes', the pair refer to their friend Gordon, who wears leather and rides a motorbike, bearing some of the identity markers of rough trade (discussed later in this chapter). Julian and Sandy discuss how Gordon had set himself up with a bar in Tangiers, although the venture has recently fallen through:

> Julian: She walked out on him.
> Sandy: Oh, that old American boiler.
> Julian: Yes.
> Sandy: Oh.
> Julian: She moved on.
> Sandy: Mm, Mm. I thought she would.
> Mr Horne: Look, erm.
> Sandy: I could tell you a thing or two there.
> Mr Horne: Yes, er, now look.
> Sandy: Make your hair curl. Don't you talk to me ducky.[6]

As there are enough clues regarding Gordon's sexuality else-where in the sketches, we can interpret *she* as referring to a male partner.

Hypothetically, almost everything can be referred to as *she*, including oneself. Polari speakers would routinely call one another *she* – normally in an affectionate, sisterly way, although if they knew that the person being spoken to didn't identify as a queen, there would be a more confrontational aspect to the pronoun. *She* effectively drags up the most masculine of men, without the need for a trip to the make-up counter at Selfridges, and it also acts as an insinuation that the man being talked about may not be as fully masculine or heterosexual as he presents himself to be. To an extent this may have been wishful thinking – for many Polari speakers the ideal part-ner would be a butch man who did not identify as gay, the Great Dark Man of Quentin Crisp's fantasies. However, there was also a more spiteful side to 'she-ing' – the Polari speakers would have known that such men would have found the use of feminine pronouns on them to have been very insulting, so to use them was a way of taking them down a peg or two. This explains the large number of feminizing terms for the police, who were rightly seen as natural enemies: *Betty Bracelets, Hilda Handcuffs, Jennifer Justice, orderly daughters, Lily Law*. These terms indicated that Polari speakers were able to turn a threat into a joke, with the added advantage that they could act as coded warnings – uttering 'Betty Bracelets!' at the local cot-tage would have the effect of sending queens scattering in all directions.

The gender politics behind the feminizing pronouns are complicated. When gay men use *she* on themselves and their friends, are they parodying women in a way that borders on offensive? Are they simply complicit in their own oppression by adopting language and labels that are used in homophobic ways, and then using that oppressive language on their enemies, knowing it will hurt them even more? Am I over-thinking it? Polari speakers simultaneously reclaimed and weaponized *she*. We could argue that they were a product of their time, but after decades of Gay Liberation, *she* is still used by (some) gay men. I like to think of it as an affectionate word – and if it was used to hurt, then it was more about the drag queen's uncanny ability to find a person's weakness rather than saying anything about the speaker's own politics.

Another pronoun, perhaps even more problematic from later perspectives, was *it* – which Lorri Lee uses three times in her discussion of queens quoted earlier. *It* was sometimes used to refer to a one-off anonymous sexual partner – signifying a form of objectification which can appear dismissive, even callous. Consider the following, from Kenneth Williams's diary:

> I met Harry who said Tom picked up a boy in the Piano and Harry said 'It's got a huge cock so Tom is silly, with that pile and all . . .' so I thought hallo! It certainly gets around in Tangier.[7]

To an extent such partners appear to be reduced to their physical body parts. As mentioned, another term for a sexual partner was *trade*, which had a range of slightly overlapping meanings. It could refer to a potential, past or current sexual partner, and usually indicated a temporary sexual relationship, sometimes a one-off. *Trade* sometimes, but not always, indicated a masculine man who might not have identified as gay and would have been likely to have taken the 'inserter' role in sex. Such men who were classed as trade did not usually speak Polari and probably would not have identified as trade or talked much about their sexuality.

Trade could also literally refer to a male prostitute, or to someone who would occasionally take money for sex but might not typically be viewed as a male prostitute – sailors on shore leave, for example, or Guardsmen who traditionally cruised parks looking for well-off men. Money might exchange hands; it might not. Sometimes the money would have been nominal, a way for the trade to establish his masculine, normally heterosexual credentials. This was in a time when some men felt that they had to engage in elaborate excuses to justify having sex with one another. However, trade could also be a station on the way towards a more established gay identity. Gardiner notes the aphorism 'today's trade is tomorrow's competition', which indicates a downside to the endless hunt for new partners in a finite context.[8] Internalized homophobia or just plain nastiness might make the trade attack their sexual partner or demand money from them, hence the term *rough trade*, although this term could also refer more generally to working-class casual male partners. Quentin Crisp, despite being a camp gay man, did not really use Polari in his autobiographies, although in the televized dramatization of *The Naked Civil Servant* he does refer to *roughs* – aggressively masculine working-class men who disguised their attraction to other men through harassment: 'Some *roughs* are really queer and some queers are really *rough*.'[9] And Lee Sutton cracks, 'I've been feeling a little rough all day,' in his drag act.[10]

Another way of referring to people was to use terms like *ducky*, *dear*, *heartface*, *girl* or *treash* (a shortening of *treasure*), which often acted as a kind of full stop at the end of every utterance. One of my interviewees, Lucas, explained why these terms of endearment were so common:

> I myself use *sweetie* a lot because it is very convenient if you don't remember the other person's name, a very frequent occurrence on the gay scene. Older people use *dear* for that reason, as well as its camp value.

With the large cast of characters passing through the Polari speaker's world, it is perhaps understandable that there would be occasional memory lapses, so simply using a generic and feminizing term of endearment for everyone is safer than getting a name wrong, but also helps to contribute towards the speaker's own feminine performance. With that said, a couple of the men I interviewed noted that these words could also have a sting. To call someone *heartface*, if they are not attractive, would be rather cutting, while *dear* can appear somewhat patronizing or dismissive. And if everyone is called by the same term then the effect is to diminish the importance of individual relationships. You are signifying 'I can't be bothered to learn your name', so there is a slight put-down behind these seemingly affectionate terms, if used in certain contexts. However, there's potentially an additional level of meaning behind all of the implied rudeness in Polari – a sense of playfulness or parody, of not really meaning it. The Polari speaker who calls everyone *dear* may only want to appear a bit dismissive and forgetful – she is doing it because she feels close enough to you to know you'll take the joke in the right spirit. It's a shared joke, rather than a joke at your expense. The worst thing you can do with a Polari speaker is to take her seriously. In other words, we should bear in mind the importance of *not* being earnest.

Perhaps a kinder set of words are those based on family metaphors – an *auntie* or *mother* indicates an older gay male, usually a friend or mentor where there is no sexual relationship. On the other hand, the term *sisters* indicates two gay men of usually similar age, who have probably previously had sexual relations, but the initial physical attraction has given way to a more companionable situation.

Another important aspect of Polari was the assignation of a camp name, or a christening. Such names were given to you by other queens; you were not supposed to pick one for yourself. They thus marked your camp identity and acceptance into the gay subculture. Your camp name could be merely arbitrary, but in many cases it would reflect an aspect of your provenance, personality, physical appearance or sexual behaviour, although as with other aspects of Polari, while given affectionately, there could be an element of sarcasm attached to it – a little sting designed to take an arrogant queen down a peg or two. So a very attractive queen might be given a dowdy name like Mavis. Lorri Lee describes the process:

Being young queens, everybody had camp names, what we called other names, mostly girl's names. So Crystal, who's name isn't Crystal – I said to her, you must be called Crystal Spring and she said 'Yes, I will be.' In those days, I was very partial to sailors, who we referred to as seaweed. So I got the name of Lorelei, a rock in the river Rhine, which is reputed to give out vibrations luring sailors to their doom. At sea the boys couldn't get their tongue round the name so they used to call me Lol or Lola or Lolly, anything.[11]

Martin, a steward I interviewed who worked on cruise liners, describes some of the sea queens that he knew and how they received their names.

You had Prissie – she was a prissy queen; Mother, who was one of the older queens – she was like a mother hen with all her young chicken queens who confided in her; Olga, because her grandmother was Russian; Lana Turner, who always wore sweaters and dyed her hair peroxide to convince us that she was a natural blonde; Mata Hari, who was always snooping around at night looking for trade; Poppy, who used 'Californian Poppy' perfume by the gallon; Molly Brown, who got torpedoed in the war and still survives to tell the tale. Some of them, I didn't know their real names.

There is less evidence that gay women referred to each other by camp names, although in the 1964 play *The Killing of Sister George* (filmed in 1968 with Beryl Reid in the title role), the soap opera actress June Buckridge is widely referred to as George, based on the nickname of the character she plays in the fictional soap opera *Applehurst*.

Sexuality, gender and sexual availability and desirability were all important ways in which individuals were categorized, with numerous Polari words given over to this task and some words referencing multiple categories. *Manly Alice* describes a gay man who is also masculine, whereas *Zelda* is a woman who is also unattractive. The abbreviation TBH (to be had) functions in a similar way to *trade*, in that it has multiple meanings. If someone is TBH then they are sexually available (that is, willing to engage in gay sex), and/or worth having (in other words, physically attractive). As Michael Davidson wrote in 1962:

> The word 'queer' then hadn't been invented; the cryptic designation was 'so', corresponding *comme ça* in Montparnasse. 'Oh, is he *so*?' one would ask, giving a slight italic tone to the syllable. Another verbal cipher in use was the initials *t.b.h.* 'My dear,' someone might say standing outside Wellington Barracks, 'the one third from the right in the front rank – I know he's t.b.h.!' – meaning 'to be had'; as the modern queer will say 'he's trade'.[12]

An extension of the abbreviation, NTBH, means someone who is not to be had – for example, hopelessly heterosexual or simply ugly. Related to NTBH is *naff*, possibly derived from another acronym, although with many differing origin stories, it is difficult to confidently pinpoint where it came from. Perhaps the most satisfying explanation is that it stands for 'not available for fucking', although this could be a backronym – whereby a meaningful phrase is found to spell out the individual letters at a later stage of the word's development.

Naff was used to refer to heterosexual people generally and could be either an adjective or a noun – 'Don't waste your time on her, she's naff!' or 'Awful – the place was full of naffs!'

Naff therefore also has the overlapping meanings attributed to NTBH – someone who is either unavailable (owing to the unfortunate condition of being straight) or not worth pursuing, or a mixture of the two. It is a word with an amusing later development, as it was one of the few core Polari words to cross over into mainstream slang. *Naff* was regularly used by characters in the 1970s prison sitcom *Porridge* to mean something bad, especially in the phrase *naff off*, which stood for a softened version of *fuck off*. The word gained notoriety in 1982 when it was reportedly used by Princess Anne, who fell off her horse during the Badminton Horse Trials and told photographers to 'Naff off.' Once a swear word has been embraced by real royalty, it inevitably loses some of its lustre and *naff* diminished in use from the 1980s onwards. However, we can perhaps take a certain amount of gratification from the fact that it was naffs who adopted the word *naff* themselves, not realizing that they were the original target of it, and that by the time they were using the word themselves, this was simply a marker of how naff they were.

There is a proliferation of classificatory words that relate to camp mannerisms – *outrageous*, *screaming*, *nelly*, *dizzy*, *swishing* and *bitchy*, which are likely to have had subtle distinctions between them, as opposed to being merely synonymous. Related to these words was *bold* – a favourite of Julian and Sandy, who would instantly label any sexually suspicious behaviour of Mr Horne with 'Ooh, in'e bold!' To be bold was to be fairly open and/or obvious about one's sexuality, and considering the taboos and dangers associated with this state, this really was an act of boldness. Despite the fact that Polari enabled secrecy, many Polari speakers were bold queens in reality. A bold queen does not mind that she will be identified as a queen. In fact, this queen *wants* to be identified as a queen and would be rather upset if nobody noticed her. This is a queen who is used to being the centre of attention. She sees herself as Scarlett O'Hara, surrounded by eager suitors hanging on her every word. The bold queen will be dressed as a bold queen, in eye-catching colours and patterns, clothes that are a little too tight in places, a little too fashionable, a little too daring. Her hair will have been worked on in some way – dyed, gelled, teased up or forward to hide any unfortunate balding areas – and she is likely to be wearing make-up. Her goal is to signify that she is gay and available – and to attract the attention of the most masculine, handsome man she can find. Her voice will be a little louder than everyone else's, her walk exaggerated, her mannerisms larger and more affected.

Moving on to a related use of Polari, we find a class of nouns that refer to body parts, which comprise around one in five of all Polari nouns. These enabled Polari speakers to refer to themselves and one another in a more technical way. About a third of the body words relate to the face, with another third referring to sexual organs. There were about equal numbers for male and female organs, although we might want to bear in mind that gender switching could be used to apply to sexual organs in the same way that it was used on pronouns. So a man might be referred to as possessing a *minge* (vagina) or might even be given the nickname *Minge*. The relatively high number of sexual body words indicates an explicit aspect to Polari that did not appear very often in the Julian and Sandy sketches (although see the discussion of *dish* later). *Dish* (bum) implies a food metaphor that was present in other words – *beef curtains* (vagina), *brandy* (backside), *meat and two veg* (penis and testicles), *minces* (eyes), *pots in the cupboard* (teeth), *plates* (feet), *winkle* (small penis). Similarly, a young man was a *chicken* – a term that was sometimes used on me when I went on the gay scene in the 1990s. I was told very markedly that you were a chicken only until you were 25, this age magically representing a kind of cut-off of desirability, with thirty being the next cut-off (and simply meaning 'old'). Sex is likened to a tasty meal in the Polari speaker's worldview, although this is not unique to gay men – similar food metaphors are found in slang used by heterosexual people (for example, referring to a woman as *crumpet*).

Clothing words comprised around 15 per cent of Polari nouns, with again around equal amounts of words to refer to male and female clothing and many of them relating to accessories like jewellery (*groinage*) and spectacles (*ogale fakes*) or hats (*cappella*), wigs (*sheitel*) and shoes (*batts* – pronounced *bates*). Clothing itself was simply *drag* but could also be *clobber*.

A significant number of Polari verbs refer to sexual acts – *charver/charva* and its clipped spelling *arva* refer to penetrative (vaginal or anal) sex, and there are a number of other words which specifically denote oral sex (*gamming, blowjob, plating, reef, tip the velvet, jarry, nosh*), many which are synonymous with the concept of eating. We should note that *plate* could refer to both feet and oral sex. Drag performer Lee Sutton makes the following joke in one of her acts, describing how she was an apprentice for a photographer's assistant:

> The first day he took me into the darkroom, just to get
> the feel of things. The second day he taught me how

to touch up and develop. The third day he showed me
how to make a good enlargement. We started off with
postcard size and ended up with whole plates.

On my recording, the word *plates* produces audience laughter,
indicating that the ruder Polari meaning was recognized.[13]

Verbs could be conjugated in much the same way as English
verbs. So *varda* or *vada*, which meant look, can have the forms
vadaed (looked), *vadas* (looks) and *vadaring* (looking). Applying
a little creativity results in *bona vadering* (good looking). While
vada generally refers to the acting of looking (and can be used
as a directive – *vada the omee ajax*), other verbs referred more
specifically to the practice of looking for sexual partners, *cruise*,
troll, *cold calling*, and two were taken parodically from legal
language, *solicit* and *importune*.

Other categories of verbs relate to performance – as we've
seen, to *wallop* is to dance, for example, and again we can apply
English grammatical rules to derive other forms – a dancer
becomes a *walloper*. Many words that were nouns could also
be verbs without modifying them. So while a *bat(t)* was a shoe
it could also refer to shuffling or dancing on stage. Similarly,
a *bevvy* was a drink but it could also mean to drink or could
be modified as *bevvvied* to refer to being drunk. In the same
way, to be *charvaed* (fucked) meant to be exhausted.

Clothing and dressing-up verbs could also be linked to
the more performative, theatrical aspect of Polari or could be
due to the fact that gay men paid attention to their physical
appearance in order to attract partners, with both actors and
gay men likely to talk of *dragging up*, *putting on the eke* or
zhooshing the riah.

Some words refer more to social interaction, with *polari* itself not only standing for the language itself but functioning as a verb which meant to say or speak. *Bitch* (in the verb sense) referred to complaining or criticizing someone, and there are other words or idioms which indicate interactions: *mogue* (to tell a lie), *do the rights* (seek revenge), *turn my oyster up* (make me laugh). Some verbs indicate conflict, violence or crime: *barney*, *battery*, *battyfang*, *schonk*, *sharper*. These words perhaps remind us how dangerous it could be to be gay in the twentieth century. Finally, a collection of miscellaneous verbs suggest more wide-ranging activities and can be applied to a range of contexts: *order(ly)* (go, come), *screeve* (write), *savvy* (know), *parker* (give), *lau* (put/place) and *dhobie* (wash).

A little Polari goes a long way

The next most important class of Polari words comprised different types of modifiers, many of which were adjectives, which are used to describe nouns, although some adjectives could just as easily function as adverbs. Probably the most well-known adjective is *bona* (occurring very frequently in the Julian and Sandy sketches as part of the opening line *how bona to vada your dolly old eek again*). However, it also works as an adverb in phrases like *order lau your luppers on the strillers bona* where *bona* means 'to do well' (though some Polari speakers used *strillers bona* to refer to a grand piano, as opposed to an upright one, referred to as a *cottage upright*).

Many of the Polari adjectives are evaluative in some way, rather than neutral, conveying the speaker's opinion (positive or negative) towards what they are talking about. Polari is a highly critical language, again often relating to questions regarding the sexual availability or desirability of people. Some Polari terms were superlatives: *too much*, *gutless*, *large*, *mental* – and these could be used to refer to something as extremely good or bad, with context needing to be taken into account for the interpretation. If someone's *riah* is described as *too much* it is being marked as worthy of attention but it may be lovely or awful.

Words relating to quantities or gradations played a particularly important role, as they could be combined with other words in order to create new meanings. Two especially useful words were *nanti*, which functioned as general negator and could be variously used to mean none, no, not, nothing or don't, and *dowry*, which meant many, a lot of or very. *Nanti* could be used to signify that there was nothing of something: for example, *nanti handbag* or *nanti dinarly* meant I've got no money, and *nanti kip* meant I've had no sleep. *Nanti* could also be used with a verb to act as an imperative to the listener. *Nanti Polari, Lily!* means don't say anything, the police are nearby. Other, less immediately obvious uses of *nanti* were *nanti that*, meaning don't worry about it or forget about it, and *nanti worster*, meaning I'm no worse or not bad, when someone asked you how you were doing. When combined with the preposition *ajax* (which meant nearby, from the word *adjacent*), *nanti ajax* stood for far away. Lee Sutton used *nanti* even more creatively in his Union Tavern act, immortalized in his *A Near Miss* LP:

> Are you aware of personal freshness? Or do your mates all call you pongo? If so use nanti poo and show them you're not to be sniffed at.

Here *nanti poo* translates to 'no poo' or 'no smell', with Sutton taking advantage of its similarity to the word *shampoo* – where *nanti* replaces *sham*. Similarly, *dowry* could be combined with various nouns to signify something that was the biggest, best or ultimate of that class. A *dowry lattie* was a palace, a *dowry aqua* was a flood and a king was the *dowriest omee*. The basics of Polari are pretty easy to pick up – there is a limited vocabulary that shouldn't take too long to learn – but these queens made the most of what they had, just like Maria in *The Sound of Music* making new outfits out of curtains. If a word didn't exist, they'd see if an existing one could be altered in some way and if that didn't work, then they'd marry up two words to imply the meaning. Learning new ways to employ old words is one of the pleasures of engaging with Polari – and in the workshops I teach, there is always a nice 'aha!' moment when the class learn that they can combine terms to make new concepts like *dowry lattie* or *nanti ajax*.

The combination of the basic numbers is another way in which people realize that they actually know a lot more Polari than they thought they did. My workshops usually begin with me getting students to say the numbers one to ten (*una, dooey, tray, quattro, chinker, say, setter, otter, nobber* and *daiture*) as well as half (*medza*) and a hundred (*chenter*). Knowing just these few words allows us access to much larger numbers: fifty, for example, is *chinker daiture*, while seven hundred is *setter chenter*. Thus the number 956 becomes *nobber chenter chinker daiture say*.

This versatility on behalf of the speakers potentially means that old words can be adapted to refer to new contexts. The noun *vacaya*, which refers to something that makes a noise, can be used to refer to a mobile phone, indicating that later Polari speakers appear to have invented new terms as other technologies came along – the telephone is known as the *polari pipes* whereas television is *vadavision*. Both words employ a form of alliteration that has been seen elsewhere in terms like *Betty Bracelets* or *Lily Law*.

Other ways of compounding words to make new ones involve terms like *queen, omee, fake, covers* and *cheat*. We have already seen how *queen* could be modified to refer to different types of gay men (*cottage queen, drag queen*) and in a similar way *omee* could be paired with other words to suggest professions – *strillers omee* (musician), *butch omee* (soldier), *charpering omee* (policeman), *joggering omee* (entertainer). *Fake*, while having a noun meaning (as an erection) and a verb meaning (to make something), also had a modifying use where it could be attached to other words, often to signify clothing or accessories. *Fake ogles* were spectacles while a *fake riah* was a wig. *Goolie ogle fakes* (literally black eye fakes) were sunglasses and *aunt nelly fakes* were earrings. In a similar way, *covers* could be used in order to refer to different types of clothing with *lally covers* being trousers and *mart covers* being gloves.

Cheat plays a particularly interesting role in Polari, coming from Cant and acting as a kind of dummy noun for 'thing that . . .'. It can therefore be combined with a variety of verbs to create new nouns, as in the phrase given in the last chapter: *hearing cheat*, to mean an ear (a thing that hears). Animals also featured in Cant using *cheat*, such as *bleating cheat* (sheep), *quacking cheat* (duck), *cackling cheat* (fowl). Polari speakers, particularly some of those linked with the Sisters of Perpetual Indulgence, incorporated aspects of Cant into their Polari, updating some of the old words to have slightly new meanings to reflect twentieth-century objects. For example, a *trundling cheat* initially referred to a cart or carriage, but in Polari it would refer to a taxi or car.

The process of referring to a noun via some aspect of its nature is called synecdoche and is found in a few other Polari words like *smellies* (perfume), *glossies* (magazines), *timepiece* (watch) and *remould* (sex reassignment surgery), with the process potentially enabling the creation of new Polari words as required.

We have already seen how -*ois* can be added onto the end of an existing Polari or English word in order to make it appear as if it were derived from French, making the speaker appear more multilingual than they are. However, another suffix, -*ette*, not only signifies that a word is Polari but creates new meanings. Putting -*ette* at the end of a word both feminizes and reduces the implied size of something: for example, an *usherette* is a female usher, whereas a *kitchenette* is a small kitchen. Julian and Sandy used the -*ette* suffix to camp effect, with some of the titles of their businesses incorporating this form: Guided Trippettes, Bona Song Publisherettes and Bona Bijou Tourettes. Their use of -*ette* usually implied something small, as it was paired with words like *bijou*, *tiny* or *mini* (bijou treashette, a tiny drinkette, a mini glassette). However, as with a lot of Polari, there's a seam of irony running through the discourse, and a mini glassette of Chablis could actually refer to an enormous glass of wine, held by someone who likes their drink but wants to humorously downplay the fact.

Does Polari have a grammar?

Grammar is the system of rules in a language which help to determine the order in which words occur in order to make sense and how different tenses like past, present and future are marked. Has something happened, is it currently happening or is it going to happen at some point? It is also grammar that lets us distinguish between who takes on the active role in a sentence (the doer) and who is the person having something done to them (something which is often of great interest to Polari speakers!). Without grammar a language is just a list of words and that won't get us very far.

Up to this point we have considered the types of words in Polari and how new words can be created or old words can be combined to make new ones. However, we have not considered in much detail the way that multiple Polari words can be strung together to create a meaningful spoken utterance or a written sentence. There do exist a number of idiomatic phrases within Polari that tend to work as fixed expressions and express a certain meaning, which sometimes cannot be literally translated word for word. These are often euphemisms that make use of English words, such as *what's the colour of his eyes?* (how big is his penis?), *don't be strange* (don't hold back *or* goodbye), *that's your actual French* (I've just spoken some French, aren't I sophisticated!), *in the life* and *on the team* (both meaning to be gay). Other idiomatic phrases can incorporate a mixture of English and Polari: for example, *nanti pots in the cupboard* means no teeth, while *scharda there's nada to vada in the larder* means it's a shame he has a small penis.

However, these idiomatic uses tend to have a single meaning, so function more like a single word rather than a bona fide combination of words. In order to think about the grammatical aspects of Polari, then, we initially need to consider three important grammatical categories or sets of words that I've mentioned so far in this chapter – these are nouns (words that name things), verbs (words for doing things) and adjectives (words for describing things). I've noted already how we can apply English derivational rules to Polari words in order to create different forms of a base word. So if *lally* is leg we can apply the normal rules of pluralization to form *lallies* – legs. The same applies to verbs – so as well as *vada* (look) we can have *vadas* (looks), *vadared* (looked) and *vadaring* (looking) – and adjectives – *naff* (bad) can be extended to *naffer* (more naff) or *naffest* (the most naff). Additionally, adverbs can be derived from adjectives, so if I say, 'he took his part bona', the word *bona* functions as an adverb to mean 'well', as opposed to its more typical adjectival meaning (which is 'good').

If we simply focus on the nouns, verbs and adjectives but keep everything else in English, we can go a long way. Julian and Sandy made use of this 'basic' form of Polari in phrases like 'scotches may be naff but his plates are bona'.[14] We could swap out the Polari for the English equivalents and very easily glean the meaning 'legs may be unattractive but his feet are nice'. Julian's sentence here is missing the initial 'his', but this is implied. While Polari has a reasonably good coverage of nouns, verbs and adjectives – grammatical categories that are sometimes called 'open-class' because we can go on inventing new words to put in them – it hasn't really developed equivalents for what are called the closed-class grammatical categories, a much smaller set of words incorporating prepositions (such as *by*, *of*, *in*), conjunctions (*and*, *or*), determiners (*that*, *a*, *the*), auxiliary verbs (*be*, *do*, *have*) and modal verbs (*could*, *can*, *would*). These grammatical categories are called closed-class because we generally can't invent new conjunctions or prepositions in the same way that we can create new nouns or verbs. Indeed, *ajax* (next to) and *nanti ajax* (far away) are two rare cases of Polari prepositions.

So some Polari speakers simply use the English closed-class words, as in 'scotches *may be* naff *but his* plates *are* bona'. However, another option is to miss a few of them (but not too many) out. If this can be done without completely obscuring the meaning of the utterance, then it can work. Take the phrase 'palone vadas omee-palone very cod'.[15] A word-for-word translation of this – 'woman looks gay man very bad' – is ambiguous because the closed-class words are missing. If we knew more about the context that the utterance was made in, we could probably start to piece it together, though. In this case, imagine it is being said by one Polari speaker to another and they are in a cafe with a rather frosty-faced woman sitting at a nearby table, close enough to hear their conversation. If we know that there are no other gay men around, then we can deduce that *omee-palone* is being used to refer to the speaker himself – he's describing himself as a gay man rather than using the first person pronoun *me*. This enables us to have another go at translating: 'woman looks me very bad'. And now we can start to guess at what the missing closed-class grammatical words would be: 'That woman looks at me very bad.' This still doesn't sound like a well-formed English sentence though, so we'd need to engage in a little glossing in order to reach the final translation: 'That woman is giving me dirty looks.'

Paul O'Grady is one of the last connections to the drag acts who used Polari, and one of the few queens who broke into the mainstream, becoming a much-loved household name. In *Lily Savage: A Sort of A to Z Thing*, O'Grady gives a few examples of Polari sentences, some of which mirror the simple type of Polari used by Julian and Sandy and can be reasonably easily translated.[16] These include 'varda the naff hommie with nante pots in the cupboard' (look at this unsightly wretch with the appalling dentistry) and 'get that bona jarrie down the screech' (eat this wonderful food). However, a couple of Lily's other Polari phrases require a little more guesswork. Lily writes that 'naff feeley hommie' (which literally means awful young man) translates to 'I'm very jealous of that young man'. Here, as with the *palone* giving the *cod vada* above, context is important. Another example of Lily's is 'palare the antique h. for the bevois'. The literal translation is 'talk the old man for the drink'. Once we make an educated guess at the missing grammatical words we have 'talk to the old man for the drink' and a final gloss gets us to 'If you engage our elderly friend in conversation he might stand a round of drinks'. So while some Polari phrases when written down and presented out of context are difficult to follow, we need to bear in mind that this is not the way that Polari was ordinarily used. The speakers would be taking their immediate surroundings into account and this would have aided translation considerably. In a BBC interview broadcast in 2017, O'Grady reminisced about Polari, describing being in a taxi with a friend who was an adept Polari speaker.[17] The friend elbows him and says, 'Nanti

Lily Savage (Paul O'Grady): 'I know it's a cliché,
but I didn't want to work in an office'

Polari, omee aunt nellying.' Again, a word-for-word gloss would
be 'Don't speak, man listening', but O'Grady translates it as
'Don't speak, the driver is listening'.

Another point of note about Polari's grammar is that there
is evidence that it borrowed from French on occasion. Consider

the following quote from one of the *Summer's Out* Polari sketches: 'Vada well: zhooshed riah, the shyckle mauve, full slap, rouge for days, fake ogle-riahs, fortuni cocktail frock and mother's fabest slingbacks.'[18]

The part of this sketch I'm most interested in is 'the shyckle mauve' which translates word-for-word to 'the wig mauve'. This word order (putting an adjective after a noun) is not typical of English but is more commonly found in French. The speaker in this sketch also uses French phrases like *mais oui* and *la tout ensemble*, employing occasional idiomatic French as a way of projecting a pseudo-sophisticated identity, so the word order of *shyckle mauve* also suggests an adoption of a French grammatical convention, indicating a way that Polari grammar could sometimes differ from the expectations of English grammar.

Polari certainly does have the makings of a grammar, then, although depending on the complexity of its use, it either adopted the rules of English grammar or developed a grammar that was highly dependent on open-class lexical grammatical categories, requiring hearers to rely heavily on context in order to make sense of utterances. The elision of the closed-class grammatical categories has the effect of making Polari utterances rather reminiscent of telegraph messages. As the cost of such messages was often calculated by the number of words, people tended to remove small words like conjunctions and prepositions since they could often be inferred due to the context. For most speakers, Polari did not have a unique grammar, then, which makes it wholly different from English, although its telegraphic nature did start to approach a form of grammar and some speakers combined words in unusual ways, making it difficult to decipher utterances if the contextual aspects were not present.

In covering some of the most commonly used types of words in Polari, we can start to get a better idea of the kinds of topics that typical speakers were interested in – with the high number of words for people, clothing and everyday objects indicating that this is a social language. This, coupled with the words for sexual body parts, sexual identities and sexual acts, also points to another aspect – a form of language for talking about sex and sexuality, especially gay sexuality. However, as we have seen, focusing on the words themselves can only take us so far. Polari is highly dependent on context for meaning, and without knowing more about the context we may make inaccurate interpretations. The following chapter moves away from the nuts and bolts of the language itself to consider social context – asking under what circumstances and with what motivations Polari was spoken.

4

A Bad Time to Be Gay

I get in from a particularly dull trip to Sainsbury's and have a phone message. I've put adverts in several local newspapers around the UK, concentrating mostly on the south coast, where I've judged that older gay men might now be living. For this round of interviews I want to contact men who worked in the Merchant Navy or on cruise ships from the 1950s to the 1980s.

I play the message back. It's a male voice which sounds elderly and articulate and from the south. 'I saw your advert in the newspaper,' the voice booms, 'and I would like to say that what you are doing is *disgusting*!' The voice continues to develop this theme for a while, noting that he was a sailor and claiming that my so-called research is bringing shame on a fine establishment. Then it hangs up. No name has been left. I look at my partner and for a few seconds nobody speaks. Then we both start laughing at the same time.

'What you are doing is *disgusting*!' repeats my partner, in the same voice. His skill as a mimic is rarely surpassed. The phrase instantly gains star billing in our household, being uttered several times a day, sometimes in the most incongruous of situations.

Later, in bed, I put down my book and say, 'But it's 2002! How can anyone still be bothered by any of this?'

'It cuts deep,' says my partner.

'Poor thing,' I say. 'Life can't be much fun for him.' I kiss my partner goodnight.

'What you are doing is *disgusting*!' he says.

This chapter focuses loosely on the period from the end of the Second World War to the early 1960s, just before the broadcast of the Julian and Sandy sketches. This was one of the worst times in recent history to be gay if you were British, and Polari played a role in helping LGBT people of the time get through it – not just in terms of enabling them to hide their identities but as a way of expressing them in a cheerfully and sometimes defiantly camp way. While the previous chapter looked at Polari as a language system in terms of its constituent parts, this chapter is concerned more on the various contexts in which it was used. I'll consider the motivations for speaking Polari – what it was used to achieve, and also some of the places where you would be likely to hear it. Towards the end of the chapter I discuss the types of people who used it most, along with those who didn't, looking at two of the most common contexts in which it was found – the Merchant Navy and drag acts.

Welcome to the '50s

Being gay in Britain in the 1950s was not easy. This was an uptight, grey little decade, with the country victorious from the Second World War and paying the price, with rationing lasting until 1954 and National Service not being fully phased out until 1963. The war had played havoc with personal relationships. Families had been split up, children were sent off to the countryside and those who were called up were posted all over the place, forced into close contact with strangers. Around 450,900 British people were killed as a result of the Second World War, many of them while serving in the military, but there were around 67,000 deaths as a result of airborne attacks on British towns and cities, including two of my great-uncles who were killed as children when a bomb was dropped on the house they had taken cover in during an air raid. Britain was a nation in grief.

My grandmother fell in love with a man she'd met who was posted near her town during the war, marrying and moving to Wales to live with him once the war had ended. It was a mistake – they had nothing in common and it didn't last. Such hasty matches were both frequent and understandable, given the circumstances. Thinking that this might be your last few hours alive, during night after night of air raids, has a way of making you live for the moment. And a lot of clandestine sex happened, in lodging houses, in the Blackout, in army bunks, in the back rows of cinemas, in public loos, in parks, in alleys, and, well, people often turned a blind eye because there was really too much else going on to worry about. Even in the armed forces, homosexuality was mostly tolerated, with Dudley Cave noting that 'With Britain seriously threatened by the Nazis the forces weren't fussy about who they accepted.'[1]

And then the war ended – or, as Quentin Crisp put it, 'that terrible evening' peace 'broke out'[2] – and the survivors came home, to the other survivors. Many people who had lived through the war wanted everything to return to normal quickly. There was a reassertion of family values and a baby boom, as new couples set about making families. Wartime indiscretions needed to be put aside, and homosexuality, which had fallen off the moral agenda during the war, was suddenly back on it. A survey of British values in 1949 found that most people were horrified and disgusted by it.[3]

After the war, the political landscape across the world was somewhat different from how it had been before. From around 1947, there was a state of political tension referred to as the Cold War between the Eastern Bloc (comprising the Soviet Union and various satellite states) and the Western Bloc (chiefly the U.S., NATO countries and other allies). In 1951, British-born Guy Burgess fled to Moscow, realizing that he was about to be unmasked as a Soviet spy. Burgess was Cambridge-educated and had worked for MI6 and the Foreign Office. He was also gay, as was Anthony Blunt, another member of the spy network referred to as the Cambridge Five. With few (if any) positive depictions of gay people in public life at the time, Burgess became a kind of stand-in for homosexuals – not only were they criminals but they were also likely to hold all sorts of sympathies for those who wanted to threaten our way of life, and that included becoming a traitorous communist spy for Russia.

And there was a dolly new queen in town. Her name was Elizabeth and her coronation was about to take place in 1953. The eyes of the world were on London and some of the other queens around at the time noted that the authorities seemed especially keen on imposing a kind of clean-up campaign on the country. Drag queen Ron Storme observed that during this time drag shows were banned and that if you went out in drag, even if you were just sitting in a car minding your business, the police would make you get out, then arrest you for soliciting.[4]

It's certainly the case that the number of reported indictable 'homosexual offences' was going up and up – 178 such convictions were reported in 1921, but by 1963 it was 2,437, more than double the number for heterosexually related offences that year.[5] The police had long known that convicting gay people was easy. Gay people were not real criminals, of course – they were often polite, cooperative, terrified and ashamed of being caught – so there was little threat to those making arrests of getting injured in a struggle. They usually didn't appeal or complain at their treatment for fear of attracting publicity, so for police who wanted to make a slew of easy arrests and convince others that they were cleaning up Britain's morals, staking out the local public park or loo was a doddle. Young attractive policemen were employed as agents provocateurs, enticing men into engaging in sexual contact and then clocking up the arrests.

No gay man was safe during this period, with stories of persecution appearing like a sinister combination of George Orwell and Franz Kafka. In January 1952 Alan Turing, the man who had cracked Germany's Enigma machine codes in the Second World War, making a significant contribution to ending the war and saving countless lives in the process, reported a burglary at his home after one of his partners, nineteen-year-old Arnold Murray, told him that the intruder was an acquaintance of his. Turing acknowledged his relationship with Murray to the police, who then decided to prosecute Turing instead. His security clearance was removed and he was banned from working with GCHQ or entering the U.S. On his conviction he was given a choice between prison or chemical castration with probation. He chose the latter, which meant receiving injections of synthetic oestrogen. Turing grew breasts and became impotent. He was found dead on 8 June 1954, with the post-mortem establishing the cause as cyanide poisoning. There is speculation about whether this was an accident owing to him storing laboratory chemicals at home or suicide. There was a half-eaten apple beside Turing's bed, which many believe he had dosed with the poison – his biographers have suggested he was enacting part of the story of Snow White and the Seven Dwarves.[6] But whatever the cause, there is no changing the facts about his disgraceful treatment by the British authorities. The government did not apologize until 2009 and he was not pardoned for 'gross indecency' until 2013.

Turing's is a high-profile case, as Oscar Wilde's was a half-century earlier. This should not detract from the thousands of gay people who were convicted for their sexuality during those decades, turned into criminals for loving or fancying someone, another adult, consensually. And beyond those thousands are countless others who were not convicted due to either good luck or constant vigilance, those who lived secret gay lives, worrying that today was going to be the day they would be caught. And beyond them are more still who decided that the risk was too much, that they would repress their feelings and be celibate or get married for the sake of appearances. How cruel to feel you had to live a lie and involve others in it too – the disappointing honeymoon, the decades of sexual frustration and fear of having your secret exposed. No wonder that academic research has indicated that some of the more strident homophobes tend to harbour attraction to members of the same sex.[7]

The police were roundly hated and feared by gay people, although there is that characteristic defiance in the Polari words that were employed for them – *Betty Bracelets*, *Lily Law*, *Jennifer Justice*, *Hilda Handcuffs*, *orderly daughters*. *Betty Bracelets* is my favourite – it doubly feminizes the police, both referring to them as Betty and casting their handcuffs as a form of jewellery. We might ask whether this feminization was properly intended as an insult, especially as Polari speakers 'christened' one another with female names and often used them with real affection. I suspect it was an insult – but it's only an insult if the target views it as such, and while Fishy Frances and Diamond Lil wouldn't have minded their own female monikers, they knew that the police would have hated them.

The police weren't the only Establishment figures who targeted gay people. The medical profession viewed homosexuality as a mental illness, sometimes conflating it with transgender identity, while psychiatry was inclined to spout nonsense about having a dominant mother and an absent father, a belief which doubled as a subtle way of policing the behaviour of straight people. Don't be an assertive woman or your son will be gay – best to let your husband be in charge. And if you're a father, don't desert your family, even if you and your wife can't stand one another – your boy needs a good male role model, or else he'll turn into a woman!

As the decade wore on, a new medical procedure joined the chemical castration endured by Alan Turing – aversion therapy.[8] Some who had been arrested for being gay were made to undergo this kind of 'treatment', whereas doctors referred others who had been exposed to so much societal homophobia that they wished they could be straight. The idea was that participants would be shown sexy pictures of people they fancied, while being given electric shocks or being made to vomit through injections of apomorphine. That anyone thought this might work beggars belief – it demonstrates such a basic misunderstanding of the human brain and body that anyone advocating it should have been immediately struck off. But perhaps it was really more about punishing gay people than actually curing them.

The media were equally hateful towards gay people during this period, contributing to the climate of fear and intolerance. The *Sunday Pictorial* published a series of articles called Evil Men in 1952, describing homosexuality as a 'spreading fungus',[9] and in 1963 the *Sunday Mirror* offered a handy article entitled 'How to Spot a Possible Homo', coming out with a plethora of lazy stereotypes which included 'The Over-clean Man', 'The Fussy Dresser' and 'The Middle-aged Man, Unmarried'. It also evoked the 'gay men are paedophiles' myth by referring to 'The man who has a consuming interest in youths'. The article came on the back of another gay spy scandal involving a British government agent, John Vassall, who had been blackmailed into spying for Russia after compromising photos had been taken of him with other men while drunk at a party.

With the government, the law, the medical profession and the media being purveyors of homophobia, not to mention the Church and the education system, the hands of the British Establishment had gay people in a stranglehold. It is perhaps surprising that anybody was brave enough to acknowledge their own sexuality, let alone do anything about it. But people, of course, did. The human drive to 'only connect', as E. M. Forster put it, is stronger than any form of social sanction. And in reality, some people had more to lose than others, while some, through their positions, were able to minimize their chances of being found out. During one of the talks on Polari that I gave in Manchester, an audience member, now well into retirement, took me for a coffee afterwards and told me about when he had been a young man, in his late teens. He and a couple of friends had been regularly escorted to London, their transport, food and lodgings all paid for, where he had been paired up with various rich and important older men. At the time, I'd naively wondered why anyone would go to the trouble of having to import their trade from Manchester to London, especially as there would have been plenty of pickings to be had there already, but on reflection it makes sense – those young men would have been easier to manage and less likely to blab to the wrong people than if they were locals, as they could be dispatched back home after the weekend. His story indicates the presence of informal secret networks, and it's likely that some upper-class, famous or well-connected gay men were able to use their money, position and influence to find and get what they wanted. A well-known comedian I had become friendly with around the same time told me about performing on a Royal Navy ship during the Second World War, and the captain letting him pick which sailor he wanted to spend the night with. Another friend told me about a 'birthday present' arranged for a wealthy closeted gay man which involved a visit by several Guardsmen and their captain, who barked the order for his men to drop their trousers as if it were just another command. So much for the illegality of homosexuality in the armed forces.

The rich were normally able to stay out of trouble, although blackmail of well-to-do gay men was a constant concern, with one team of blackmailers reported as making around £100 a night, amassing £15,000 (the equivalent of around £500,000 at the time of writing) over seven months.[10] And being rich and titled did not mean that you were completely above the risk of arrest and scandal. In 1954, the public were shocked by news reports of the arrest, trial and imprisonment of Lord Montagu of Beaulieu, his cousin Michael Pitt-Rivers and their journalist friend Peter Wildeblood. In 1952, Wildeblood had brought two young RAF servicemen, Edward McNally and John Reynolds, to a beach hut near Montagu's country estate, where the five men apparently 'had some drinks, we danced, we kissed, that's all', according to Montagu.[11] However, the courts charged the three men with 'conspiracy to incite certain male persons to commit serious offences with male persons'. Montagu received a twelve-month sentence while his two friends were sentenced to eighteen months each. Wildeblood's subsequent book, *Against the Law*,[12] described his experiences in prison, encouraging both prison reform and homosexual law reform, and the case is widely seen as helping to instigate the end of the widespread and open persecution of gay people. But that was not to happen for years to come.

The middle classes had an even weaker safety net, with novels by authors like Rodney Garland and Martyn Goff describing the climate of the time. Garland's *The Heart in Exile* gives an account of a psychiatrist's efforts to uncover the truth behind the suicide of a man who had been his lover years previously.[13] Rodney Garland was the pseudonym of Adam Martin de Hegedus, who committed suicide himself five years after the book was published. Goff's *The Youngest Director* follows 32-year-old Leonard Bissel, who has a good job and a nice house in Chelsea, but his boss and family expect him to marry.[14] Leonard defies their expectations, moving his boyfriend John in, and gradually his world goes to hell – he loses his job and his father disowns him. Leonard isn't convicted of a crime but he is socially excommunicated and loses his livelihood.

And for working-class men, many of whom would have had fewer chances to conduct relationships in the privacy of homes that they owned, the alternative – casual sexual encounters in the cruising grounds of parks, public loos and cinemas – would have resulted in more immediate dangers, such as physical attack from 'queer-bashers' and arrests from the constabulary, followed by prison sentences or fines, shaming in their local communities and job losses. And it was not just the shame and scandal that you incurred upon yourself; it was on your wife, your parents and your children. For many gay men, that was the greatest fear and source of regret: not that their own lives were ruined, but that the people they loved would be drawn into the mess.

Speaking in secret

Even attending a private drinking club was putting oneself at risk, as such clubs could be raided, resulting in mass arrests. David, interviewed for *Summer's Out*, describes what would happen:

> The pub was raided. They took your names and addresses. It was a form of harassment in those days.

The pub would go quiet for a week or a month, and then people would start drifting back again . . . If you had a height of powder too much on one cheek, you might have missed it as you got ready to go out. The barman would say, 'Sorry dear, out.' And you'd have to leave.[15]

John Alcock talked about a collective feeling of panic during the 1950s:

I thought that every policeman coming up to me on the street was going to arrest me. I always looked over my shoulder when I was bringing a gentleman home to entertain, usually a labourer . . . The temperature of the time was quite unpleasant. We thought we were all going to be arrested and there was going to be a big swoop.[16]

And so it was in this climate of state oppression that Polari came into its own. One of my interviewees, John, described how Polari was used 'specifically as a hidden language': 'You would say "Vada the cartes on the omee" because nine out of ten times [heterosexuals] wouldn't understand what the hell you were talking about.' And Polari was especially useful for conducting conversations in public spaces, especially on public transport. DJ Jo Purvis described how she 'could sit on a Tube train or a bus and talk about the person opposite using this Polari which no one could understand except theatrical people'. There was no such thing as a 'safe space' in 1950s Britain, but Polari helped to create a kind of symbolic safe space for gay people of the time by allowing them to talk in ways which otherwise would have revealed their sexuality to anyone who was listening. And there was a real danger of this – people in the 1950s could be rather nosy, and Quentin Crisp describes how his neighbours used to look through his windows and then report him to the police.[17]

It is simplistic though to think that at the time people were consciously aware of how speaking Polari was helping them to cope with the oppressive times; this was perhaps more likely to come in hindsight. Drag queen Bette Bourne, interviewed in 2014, recalls:

> You never thought, 'Oh God I'm so oppressed I can't speak about myself,' you just did it. You just slipped into it [Polari] without even thinking really ... It wasn't like this great terrible thing hanging over me, which eventually ... we realized yes it was a fucking drag, the whole thing was terrible and awful and made people very secretive and suspicious and wary, very wary, but once you got that together it was fine. You had the equipment ... Those things are forced upon you. They're not just invented as a camp joke. They're practical.[18]

Polari could also be employed as a kind of 'secret handshake', enabling recognition of a shared sexuality between two strangers – a careful way of coming out of the closet, or at least of opening the closet door a crack. One of my interviewees described it as a 'non-giveaway that you were gay', while Dudley Cave described Polari words as 'secret passwords. You could identify with other gay people if you thought they might be – you could drop a word in like "camping about" or "I'm going camping, but I'm taking my tent".'[19] Such code words would be likely to result in a nonplussed reaction if the hearer wasn't gay so were a reasonably safe way of revealing one's identity without being overly explicit, and could be shrugged off as a simple misunderstanding if someone had the wrong quarry.

Camp names had a secrecy function too. In an interview in *Gay Times*, David, who was 56 in 2002, describes his early experiences on the gay scene in the 1960s, watching Mrs Shufflewick perform at the Black Cap and modifying his language so his parents wouldn't know that he was gay:

> A guy I met at the Black Cap was a nurse, so I could say to my parents, 'Oh I've met a nurse called Susan'. You just got used to it. Madge was a particularly popular name.[20]

The need for secrecy helps to explain the set of Polari words that function as euphemisms, being taken from English words but having altered meanings. For example, one of the men interviewed by Porter and Weeks described how another word, *so*, was used to mean gay, whereas the phrase 'to be had' was put into abbreviated form, again making it difficult for outsiders to understand its meaning:

> We were 'so'. Have you heard that word? We were so. Is he so? Oh yes. Oh he's so so, and TBH (to be had) was a very famous expression. The sentence would go simply like this, well he's not really 'so' but he's TBH. And you would know exactly.[21]

While it's definitely the case that Polari helped to obscure the content of one's conversation, it wouldn't necessarily completely hide the fact that someone was gay. For a man like Quentin Crisp, who dyed his hair red with henna, wore feminine clothes and make-up and walked in a mincing fashion, people passing him by on the street wouldn't need to wait for him to say anything before they had him pegged as 'queer'. Crisp describes being followed and physically assaulted by members of the public while simply walking down the street,[22] so no amount of Polari was going to keep his sexuality a secret. Thus Polari helped you to 'pass' for straight or 'not gay', but only if you visibly conformed to expected standards of heterosexual dress and behaviour in all other ways.

The journalist and author Peter Burton describes a fascinating use of Polari which was more about confrontation than conformity. Burton was born in 1945 so he is likely to have been a Polari user in the 1960s and '70s, when the social climate was starting to thaw a little, and flamboyant attire was seen as fashionable on young men.

Burton writes: 'We flaunted our sexuality. We were pleased to be different. We were proud and secretly longed to broadcast our difference to the world: *when we were in a crowd*.'[23] He acknowledges that in hindsight it must have been obvious to everyone what he and his friends were talking about when they used Polari. In such cases, Polari with its strange words and exotic intonational patterns would have probably helped to identify some speakers as gay – being just one symbol among numerous others of their sexual difference. Burton's use of Polari, then, is suggestive of a bolder queen – one who clocks the dirty looks and laughs from straight strangers and responds

Peter Burton

with a mouthful of insulting Polari – the language could be used to 'confound and confuse', in Burton's words. The target of the verbal abuse would know they were being insulted but unable to respond because they couldn't understand the language – a little like receiving a gypsy's curse. There is something particularly frustrating about being insulted in a language that you don't understand – you are instantly wrong-footed and it can be difficult to respond in kind. In such cases, Polari assumes an occult, almost magical quality, taking on the form of a withering spell.

The 'twilight world'

The private clubs, pubs, bars and cafes of London and other large cities around the UK are the places where Polari was most likely to have been heard. In the late 1920s and early

1930s, Quentin Crisp's hangout was the Black Cat cafe in Old Compton Street (nobody bothered to refer to it as Au Chat Noir, which was the sign over the window), where many of the customers were on the game – Crisp talks about spending night after night there, drinking endless cups of tea so the owner wouldn't throw them out. The Gateways Club from 1931 onwards, in the King's Road, Chelsea, was down a vertiginous flight of stairs and was the most popular place for women – it was made famous in the film *The Killing of Sister George*, which had scenes depicting many of the regulars dancing cheek-to-cheek. Also on the King's Road was Le Gigolo, which had a dance floor in the basement. One of the sailors I interviewed described how he had been taken there in the 1960s by a friend:

It was very crowded and hot, and when I went onto the dance floor, I discovered that it was not so much a dance but more of an orgy, and the further one got sucked into the heaving mass of bodies, the more overt the sexual activity became. In no time at all I found my trousers round my ankles, and my dick in someone's mouth, all the while trying to fend off others who were anxious to stick their dicks up my rear end. I couldn't spend more than half an hour on the dance floor, it was almost difficult to breathe and the crush was frightening. One had to literally fight one's way out. I developed a way of simplifying my exit. I would just say, 'Excuse me, I'm going to throw up!' and the crowd would part like the Red Sea!

Bona palones at the Gateways Club

An equally notorious establishment was The Caravan Club, at 81 Endell Street, which opened in 1934, promising 'All Night Gaiety' and claiming to be 'London's Greatest Bohemian Rendezvous said to be the most unconventional spot in town' – for those in the know, this was a coded indication of the type of clientele that could be found there. The club was popular with men and women, with prostitutes of both sexes being patrons. The owner, Jack Neave (or Neaves), known as Iron Foot Jack for his lengthened metal boot which corrected a short leg, had been an entertainer – a strongman and escapologist – and the club soon earned a name for itself, with the entertainment involving a bare-chested man who passed burning papers over his body. Complaints, in the form of letters to Holborn council, were made about this 'sink of iniquity', and when the police made three visits in July, one constable reported that men were dancing together as well as describing a conversation that he had had with a man who called himself Josephine.

The club was raided in the early hours of 25 August, with 103 people arrested, most of whom were in their early twenties. The subsequent trial attracted a crowd of around five hundred people outside the court, cat-calling the defendants as they arrived. The court had to be locked, and the reading of the names took ten minutes, with many of those accused giggling as they were called out. One constable testified that five of the men present at the club were collectively known as Cochran's young ladies, while another two were called Doreen and Henrietta. Two of the defendants were commissionaires who appeared in their uniforms. While many of the defendants were found not guilty or given short sentences, Neave was sentenced to twenty months hard labour, although he was still a frequent character around Soho in the 1950s, appearing in a Pathé Newsreel in 1955 called 'Soho Goes Gay'.

Along with the A&B (formerly the Arts and Battledress) Club, with its alluring mixture of military men and West End actors, was the Blue Posts at the other end of Rupert Court, and the Rockingham Club, also in Soho, which was popular with closeted politicians and other men who stood to lose a lot if their sexuality were made public.

While those were pretty much exclusively gay, there were other places, like Lyon's Coventry Street Corner House or the Salisbury Pub in St Martin's Lane, Covent Garden, which appeared in the 1961 Dirk Bogarde film *Victim*. The Salisbury had more of a mixed crowd and was a favourite of Kenneth Williams. Further north, at 171 Camden High Street, was the

Dowry Polari at The Black Cap, 171 Camden High Street

Black Cap – a stately building with the bust of Mother Black Cap, a local witch, atop it, looking down imperiously at the passing trade. It was popular from the mid-1960s onwards, and spiritual home to the drag cabaret act Mrs Shufflewick (Rex Jameson), who played on Sunday afternoons to a packed house. Over the river, in Camberwell, Phil Starr played at the Union Tavern, going on to run the Two Brewers pub at Clapham Common where there was nightly cabaret, sprinkled with Polari.

Then there was London's East End, which had pubs like the Royal Oak (Columbia Road, Hackney), and the pubs of the docklands, like Charley Brown's in Limehouse, which ran from the 1920s to the 1990s. Seafarers' pubs like the Ken and the Round House, positioned outside the dock gates, attracted West End queens on the lookout for seaweed (sailors who were trade), as well as being popular haunts for the sea queens themselves, gay guys who sailed with the Merchant Navy, often as waiters, cabin staff or porters. Drag entertainer Lorri Lee recalls how when a ship was coming in, the sea queens would have a reunion, not dressing in full drag, which may have been too much, but perhaps teasing their riahs or plucking their eyebrows a little, and wearing fluffy sweaters.[24]

London may have been the focal point of Polari, but it could also be heard all over the country. In Liverpool, the Royal Court and the Magic Clock were similar pubs popular with sailors and theatrical types. The gay clientele used the snug at the back of the Royal Court, which was next to the theatre, and according to Able Seaman Don Trueman, the sailors would blow kisses to them and make the odd flirtatious comment like 'nice arse', although such comments were often purposefully ambiguous. The queens could usually tell who was seriously interested and would flash their tackle in the loos if they thought they stood a chance. Trueman notes how if girls came into the snug, the gay guys would spit at them and call them 'slut', angry about the potential competition.[25]

In Southampton, the Juniper Berry and the Horse and Groom were used by gay seafarers who were well-versed in Polari, whereas a drag cabaret club in Sydney, Australia, called Les Girls, kept the Polari tradition going, with the female impersonators using it in the dressing room. Stan Monroe came to Australia from Wales in 1963, joining Les Girls as a performer. He describes how the compere, Peter Moselle, was a British man who had worked in travelling Soldiers in Skirts entertainment outfits in the war, where he'd picked up Polari. He subsequently popularized it among the performers at the club.[26] Monroe himself had first heard of Polari aged around fifteen from a friend who'd been to London.

Along with the bars, there were other gay meeting places where there was more emphasis on sex than socializing. Many British cities had Turkish bath complexes, which were same-sex segregated and where to a greater or lesser extent gay activity was sanctioned as long as it didn't attract too much attention. In London, the Savoy Turkish baths on Jermyn Street allowed patrons to let 'bachelor chambers' and after the Second World War, the staff increasingly turned a blind eye to the cruising Guardsmen, happy enough that business was going well. Christopher Isherwood, W. H. Auden, Benjamin Britten, Derek Jarman and even the film star Rock Hudson all reportedly enjoyed the baths there. Kenneth Williams used to visit the Grange Road Turkish baths in Bermondsey, which was perhaps the inspiration for the South Mimms Men's Slipper Baths A-Go-Go, a fictional establishment mentioned in the sketch 'Bona Tax Consultants', where Mr Horne describes meeting Gordon, an acquaintance of Julian and Sandy, who worked as the steam room attendant there. The Bermondsey baths is also described in Rodney Garland's gay novel *The Heart in Exile*.

The public cruising grounds were riskier – parks, public toilets, cinemas and theatres, where darkness, anonymity and an ever-changing clientele afforded easy access to a wide range of potential trade, but also brought with it the greatest dangers. Police entrapment was an occupational hazard, as was homophobic violence. Some men simply enjoyed physically assaulting queers; others saw the chance to make a few pounds through blackmail and intimidation or were conflicted and, once they had experienced sexual release, would externalize their guilt and shame by beating the other party up, in order to prove, somehow, that they were not gay really – until next time.

Owing to its telegraphic nature and vocabulary of sexual words, Polari was useful as a form of quick communication among friends and passing acquaintances in these cruising grounds. Jim C, one of my interviewees, noted that it was 'useful shorthand when you're cruising', while David A described how speakers could alert one another to someone attractive who had just arrived: 'It was used . . . to draw attention to someone. Like as we were saying "Vada the homie" instead of saying "Look at that gorgeous person over there".' There were also words and phrases which alerted one's co-cruisers to the presence of danger in situations that could result in arrest. As noted in the last chapter, a phrase like 'Nanti Polari, Lily!' warned that the police were present, while other Polari phrases could alert people to other dangers such as someone with a sexually transmitted infection (*catever cartzo*) or a sexual partner who is likely to turn violent: 'Gardy loo – she's rough trade!' There's an illustrative 'warning' use of *Lily* in an early issue of *Gay News* from 1972, in 'Julian's Column' (perhaps echoing the Julian of the next chapter), where the writer gives film reviews for the Biograph (a cinema in the Victoria district of London, which was an extremely popular cruising location for gay men):

Remember I was saying in the last issue to watch out for 'Lily Law' and her wandering at the Bio. Well, she seems to have got bored and is keeping herself busy somewhere else. Now you can get on with your relaxation without any interference, apart from that silly usherette man who still can't keep his hands off his flasher. I hope that the batteries of his torch run out soon.[27]

All the nice boys love a sailor

What about other places where Polari would have been heard? The theatre and the Merchant Navy were two professions where people of different sexualities would have mixed together in a more liberal atmosphere than the usual workplace settings, with Polari being spoken by gay men, but also known and sometimes used by their straight compatriots.

Joining the Merchant Navy allowed gay men to escape the atmosphere back home, travel the world and mix with a wide range of people from different social backgrounds. In the BBC documentary *Lol: A Bona Queen of Fabularity*, Lorri Lee re-enacted how she and her friend Crystal got signed up on a ship. They had followed a couple of attractive men into the Shipping Careers building, not realizing what it was:

> 'Where've they gone?' 'They've gone in that door,' I said. 'I bet it's a club.' It was only a shipping pool wasn't it. And they're all round the door these geezers, saying, 'Go on girls,' and pushed us right up the front. And the geezer who's giving out the jobs he says, 'Yes? Do you want a ship?' So I says, 'In for a penny, in for a bleeding pound,' so I says, 'Yes, you got any?' So he said, 'Well, what are you? Are you a waiter?' I said, 'Oh yes, I've been waiting a long long time.'[28]

Forging their references, they embarked on the voyage of a lifetime and never looked back.

The passenger ships of the 1950s and '60s were places of mass festivity with a holiday atmosphere. In this setting, flamboyant behaviour was tolerated, helped along by the fact that the ship could be hundreds of miles away from anywhere – they were liminal spaces, and there was little chance of running into your neighbours. The ships were not just conveyances to holiday destinations – they were holiday destinations in themselves with food and entertainment laid on. Working-class gay men tended to take on domestic roles like stewards, porters, waiters, pantry-boys, cleaners or cooks, and also contributed towards the evening entertainment, putting on shows for passengers and one another. And there were parties, so many parties, where fancy dress was often required and drag was encouraged rather than frowned upon. Dave, who had worked his way up from waiter to wine waiter to head waiter, describes the organization of crew parties:

> Little notices would go up on noticeboards that Janice or the Black Widow or Diamond Lil, they all had names, was throwing a party. And if you're bona, because the old Polari was in use in those days, and any bona lads could come along, as long as they'd bring a bevvy, welcome, so we used to go along with two or three Allsopps, they were the beers. The music would be played – it was a bit tricky when the ship was rolling, we had these wind-up records, then battery, because it was 110 volts so we'd got nothing that could run off that. So we had fun, they'd all come in their party frocks and wigs and things like that.

Ian, who worked on the *Sea Princess*, describes how 'gay reigned'. He says:

Miss Everton 1954 (there wasn't much competition that year)

[It was] a very camp ship to work on. I think they [gay men] created an atmosphere for the passengers that really made cruising so special, because it made an atmosphere, wherever you were on the ship, whether you were working or below decks, there was always a laugh. You could always hear people laughing or joking, or having camp jokes all the time, just laughing. It just sort of rubbed off, I think. I'm sure the passengers must have just felt this as soon as they came on. As soon as you get on, it's really relaxed and everyone was happy, genuinely happy.

Younger gay men, on their first voyage, were to discover a tight-knit gay subculture which welcomed them, and part of the subculture was to learn Polari, as Robin described to me via email (note the alternative spelling of Polari):

Palarie was very common-place on board ships when I was at sea. I joined my first ship at 16 and there were a lot of unfamiliar [Palarie] words to learn . . . There were many, spoken by everyone, Officers and Ratings. I was a Steward, like the airlines today, many were H.P.'s [Homee Palones]. The older Queens looked after me though and I was soon christened my camp name, Rose. A lot of the older Queens spoke only Palarie . . . The 'Merch' was a good way out for the more feminine men at the time, when the Liners were in their hey-day.

Polari was a kind of family tradition, helping gay seafarers form new bonds with each other, with words and phrases handed down from generation to generation. The practice of giving camp names to new sailors was very common, according to Dave:

Voche out! Sailors in drag put on a show

There was always a Diamond Lil somewhere. She always seemed to be the Queen Bee. Tall elegant thing, didn't want a promotion, been doing it for years, slim, very good looking, glasses, knew her stuff. The Black Widow: she used to wear black all the time. And there was Big Freda.

The sea queens had their own version of Polari, with terms like *seafood* as well as *seaweed* referring to sexually available sailors. *Black market queens* (BMQS) or *phantom* (*gobblers*) would be closeted gay men, known for giving oral sex in darkened cabins on cargo ships, sometimes to sleeping or groggy crewmates. The identity of the phantom was usually known but not made public and occasionally he would receive a black eye but in other cases his presence would be silently accepted. The ship was called a *lattie on water*. The following description is from an article from *Mister* magazine, published in 1982, which explains the term *trade curtain*: 'Sometimes eight people shared a cabin. If privacy was required, one strung a "trade curtain" around the bunk, and that was it!'[29]

Martin remembers how one word was invented:

One day we were sitting in the cabin and this thing transpired. Someone said, 'What are we having for a bevvy tonight, girl?' because we'd have a cocktail before we went to the bar ... We'd have various spirits left over. Passengers leave you a couple of bottles in the cabins when they'd left. And we had some vodka and some Martini, and someone said 'Oh I'll tell you what we'll do. Have some vodka and Martini, we'll call it a vodkatini.' And of course that drink came out. I wouldn't say I invented it, but that's the way things came about, you know.

There was a distinction between the camp men who identified as gay and more masculine men who did not claim a gay identity but would have taken a male partner. Prior to decriminalization and the subsequent Gay Liberation movement this kind of 'trade' identity was pretty common. Drag queen Betty Bourne described one of the sea queens she knew, Big May:

She'd been on the boats for years and years. They'd have a husband for the voyage . . . Seafood is the Polari word. They were all very married, they were in couples. There was the butch and the bitch, it was very aping the heterosexual thing. We called ourselves girls. It's to do with clinging to our youth, desperately and pathetically.[30]

The queens would occupy a long bench, known as a meat-rack, and flirt with the men they liked in order to acquire a husband. Martin describes what he'd do if he saw someone he liked:

I'd say, 'Oh vada girl, I'm going to have him for trade.' And you did. I used to have my blue eyes heavy with mascara and I'd sit there fluttering my eyelids like Bette Davis. Invariably I'd end up getting them in a matter of three months, I mean, in those days there weren't any stewardesses on the ships, it was just men.

In other cases, Martin describes how some men would dispense with the flirtation but lay claim to a particular man based on his occupation. 'You might walk on a ship and say "I always go with the chippie," which was the carpenter, and he might come round later and knock on your door. I mean he might be married, he might be straight, but it wasn't gay.'

While the sea queens spoke Polari, their husbands did not, with Mark giving an illuminating account of an interaction between himself, his sea queen friend Fishy Frances and his husband:

Say me and Frances are sitting and talking, my hus-band's there. I'd say, 'What are you doing tonight?'

She'd say, 'What I'm going to do girl,' she'd say, 'I'm going to go round and dohbie the riah.' Dohbie is wash. And she'll say, 'I'll dohbie the riah dear, I'm going to do the brows, and then I'm going to get the eke on.' Well my husband will understand that she's going to go round the cabin and get ready. He knows she's putting on make-up, because that's 'putting eke on', you see. But *he* wouldn't use it.

Similarly, officers would have been more circumspect about their Polari use, and in some cases would have only been able to let their hair down on shore leave.

Hospitality work on the cruise ships tended to be carried out mostly by younger men; by their early thirties, many had moved on to other jobs, with four to six years being considered a normal term of employment. And from the 1970s, there was a change in employment policies of many shipping companies, with staff from countries like India being hired (often working for less money) while many British staff were given 'golden hand-shakes' to leave in the 1980s. The 1975 Sex Discrimination Act and Equal Pay Act, along with other societal changes, resulted in increasing numbers of female staff being employed in cruise ship hospitality positions. This inevitably had an unfavourable impact on the sexual dynamics between the gay and nominally 'straight' seafarers, and in any case shoreside was starting to become less homophobic, so there were various pushes and pulls which saw an end to the party. The glamorous age of the cruise liners had had its heyday and many of the gay men who had worked on the ships came home, settling in port towns or cities like Liverpool, Aberdeen, Southampton or Portsmouth.

She's got it all on today, dear: a sailor in drag on SS *Caronia*, 1950s

Frank, one of my interviewees, has fond memories of his time on the ships: 'It was a very good grounding for me, I had a wonderful time. I loved every minute of it. People would deny it, but it actually happened. And God, it did happen!'

The drag scene

Back on shore, Polari flourished backstage in the theatres of London's West End as well as in the private drinking clubs popular with actors and office workers. Just as on the ships, Polari was a way of introducing younger gay men to the 'scene', and not just in the big cities. For some gay men, the introduction to a secret language was also an indication that some sort of established network existed beyond their immediate vicinity. John, quoted in an interview in the 1970s magazine *Lunch*, says:

> I used to have sex in the cottage . . . It wasn't until I was about sixteen and a half that I met this person and he was a taxi driver by the name of Ronnie and he proceeded to tell me what a golden little chicken I was and all the rest of it. Not in those precise words because I didn't know the parlare then. She wasn't an experienced queen.[31]

One of my interviewees, Sidney, who grew up and came out in Ipswich, describes a more limited gay scene but one where Polari was still in vogue:

> When I was in Ipswich up until the age of eighteen, I was sort of out from the age of about sixteen and

Ipswich at that time had a very limited gay thing going on and there was a bunch of geriatric old queens sitting around in a living room sized pub, and they actually gave lessons. So that was my sort of initiation into it. It was quite extensive.

Importantly, Polari was not just a set of words that you used if you were gay; it also offered an alternative way of looking at the world, a different set of values to the mainstream worldview which criminalized and ridiculed gay people. If you referred to something as *bona*, it didn't just mean that it was good; you were labelling it good through the shared values of the gay subculture of the time. Similarly, there was an outlook projected by Polari speakers which combined humour – often black humour – sarcasm, affection, irony and bawdiness, which functioned as a way of coping with the homophobia of the period. One of my interviewees described how he'd arranged to meet an older friend, known as Mother, in a bar. The friend was very late and my interviewee was just about to leave when he arrived with the words, 'Your Mother's been arrested, ducky!' The friend had been detained by the police for cottaging – a humiliating experience which he made light of by the humorous and matter-of-fact way he announced it. Subsequently, he received the maximum penalty during his appearance in court, for making a speech criticizing the police for picking on gay people as opposed to catching real criminals. Truly a bold queen.

The chatter of Polari-speaking queens, centring around who was sleeping with who or critiquing fashion choices, may have appeared silly and camp but it helped to turn values on their head. Appearing to worry about the state of your *maquiage* after being beaten up or raising a quizzical eyebrow at the arresting police officer's *naff riah* is one way of appearing above the threats of the Establishment. Polari enabled the performance of sangfroid, something akin to the quips of a variety of fictional heroes when in danger, from James Bond to Penelope Pitstop. Polari can help to turn power structures upside down – everything is viewed through irony-tinted spectacles. However, making a joke out of everything perhaps highlights a potential limitation of Polari – the extent to which it can be used to express authentic emotions like sorrow.

Instead Polari was much more likely to be used for comedy – to have a camp laugh with friends or to try to impress someone you fancied. With its ever-present bitchy edge, this could sometimes result in verbal mock-fights between established queens who would perform for a crowd, trying to outdo one another. One of my interviewees, Barry, describes how he needed to develop a sense of critical wit against them:

> The older ones were so quick and so cutting, you had to think of a retort that was funnier and cleverer than theirs and say it back at them straight away. Of course, eventually this just became a second nature.

Here's a snatch of one of Marc Fleming's drag acts.[32] He's just sung 'Nobody's Sweetheart', altering the lyrics to include a bit of Polari – 'As I mince down the street you'll see / Why they don't even know it's me!' – and then turns his attention to a hapless woman in the audience:

Hello dear, how are you? I see you've got a bad throat as well. You're wearing a cheap chiffon round it anyway. Is that your boyfriend with you? Your mother? Lovely fella. I knew him when he was one too. You're rather lovely – wet-look shoes, or have you been pissed on again? And I love that shirt dear, that chocolate brown, at least it won't show any stains does it?

To an extent, the sharp tongues of Polari speakers are a reflection of the way they were treated by others while growing up. Boys who didn't conform to the rigid and narrow set of gender norms imposed by society in the twentieth century were likely to encounter all manner of violence – both physical and verbal – and it is perhaps unsurprising that some of them would have developed the art of the withering putdown as a form of defence. Peter Burton notes:

> Polari has about it a particularly brittle, knife-edged feel. Nothing – in my chicken days – was more daunting than an encounter with some acid-tongued bitch whose tongue was so sharp that it was likely she would cut my throat with it. Those queans [sic], with the savage wit of the self-protective, could be truly alarming to those of us of a slower cast of mind.[33]

Unsurprisingly, drag queens or female impersonators, whose acts often featured sharp-witted critiques of members of the audience, were some of the most adept users of Polari, acting as its High Priestesses. While chorus boys and other assorted performers would have known and used Polari, it was normally reserved for backstage, rather than being used in front of a paying audience. However, in gay-friendly establishments drag acts could incorporate Polari into their patter, relying on the fact that audience members would understand what they were saying. Many of the drag queens who performed on the London gay scene and elsewhere in the 1950s and onwards never became household names, and there are few recordings of them, but their names were spoken with reverence by the men I interviewed, and they retain legendary status for those who knew them. The list includes Mark Fleming (Auntie Flo), Mrs Shufflewick, Lee Sutton, Phil Starr, Regina Fong, David Raven (Maisie Trollette) and James Court (Jimmy Trollette). David and James, of course, signalled their allegiance to Polari by including a Polari word in their drag names – their double act was called The Trollettes, combining *troll* with the *-ette* suffix, which, as seen in the previous chapter, was a commonly utilized linguistic feature. My partner, Tony, recalls seeing The Trollettes perform at the Two Brewers in Clapham in the 1980s, being 'absolutely terrified that they might pick on me'.

Another way that drag queens incorporated Polari into their acts was in parodies of songs – a sensible decision, as many audience members would have known the original lyrics so it would have been easy to understand the Polari versions.

One of Phil Starr's songs is a version of 'The Old Bazaar in Cairo' – originally written by Charlie Chester, Ken Morris and Clinton Ford. However, Starr reworks some of the lyrics to feature a number of Polari words. Early in the song he refers to *brandy* and *shandy*, the former being Polari for bum and the latter possibly referencing a hand shandy (male masturbation). In other lines he sings 'Old queens sold here 50p a lump' and 'Bet you look a smasher in an old loin cloth'. Here's the song's climax:

> You can purchase anything you wish.
> A clock, a dish, and something for your Aunty Nelly.
> Yasmacks, pontefracts, a little bit of fish.
> Stompers, poppers, anything you wish.
> You can get a blowjob or have it up the dish
> In the Old Bazaar in Cairo.[34]

The original lyrics of the song do refer to 'A clock, a dish, and something for your Aunty Nelly', although it is perhaps a coincidence that *dish* and *aunt nell* are also Polari terms. And in an earlier line of the song, Starr's pronunciation of *clock* sounds suspiciously like *cock*. After that the only other original bits of the song are the words 'yasmacks' and 'pontefracts' – with the final parts heavily referencing Polari (*fish*, *stompers*, *blowjob* and *have it up the dish*).

Similarly, Lee Sutton's act was sprinkled with Polari. This one is a parody of 'Sing a Song of Sixpence':

> Sing a song of sex pots, a pocket full of fun.
> Five and twenty chickens well and truly done.
> On the kitchen table they were most obscene.
> Now wasn't that a bona nosh for some old greedy
>   queen.[35]

However, the *pièce de résistance* (that's your actual French) of lyrical Polari is Lee Sutton's *fantabulosa* 'Bona Eke'. An increasingly cruel parody of the song 'Baby Face' (written by

The gentle art of understatement: Phil Starr (right) and his friend
Dockyard Doris, 2001

Harry Akst and Benny Davis in 1926), in Sutton's act he sings
the song twice, once straight through, and the second time with
explanations for the audience. In the transcript below, the parts
in parentheses are spoken to the audience.

(We're going to do a little number now. Er, this may be
a bit of a mystery to some of you because it is written

in a foreign language. But in the second half we do explain it. What it's all about. We do our best.)

Bona eke
You've got the campest little bona eke
And when you vada me it leaves me weak
Bona eke
My heart starts a racket every time I see your packet

Bona eke
Your bon polari almost makes me spring a leak
I'd grant your every wish
I'd even grease my dish
Just to see your bona eke

You've got a tatty gaff
And all your drag is naff
But I love your bona eke

What's more your riah's cod
And all your pots are odd
But I love your bona eke

Your lallies look like darts
And you've got nanti cartes
But I love your bona eke
(Explanation time . . .)

Bona eke
(nice f . . . wait for me)

You've got the campest little bona eke
(you've got a nice face for a woman, even though you
    are a fella)
And when you look at me it leaves me weak
(when you look at me I feel as though I've done seven
    days inside)
Bona eke
(nice face)
My heart starts a racket every time I see your
    packet
(I get so excited when I look at your wages)

Bona eke
(nice face)
Your bon polari almost makes me spring a leak
(whenever you speak your mind I almost lose control
    of myself)
I'd grant your every wish
I'd even grease my dish
(I'd even cook for you)
Just to see your bona eke
(nice face)

You've got a tatty gaff
([*Irish accent*] your flat is full of potatoes)
and all your drag is naff
(your wardrobe's worse than mine)
But I love your bona eke
(nice face)

What more your riah's odd
(patriotic hair – red and white with a navy-blue
    parting)
and all your pots are cod
(there's something fishy about your teeth – take 'em
    out – have a whale of a time)
But I love your bona eke
(nice face)

Your lallies look like darts
(your legs are so thin if they were bowed you could
    take up archery)
and you've got nanti cartes
(your old grey mare has nothing to pull)
But I love your bona eke![36]

What I find most interesting about this song is how many of Sutton's translations appear to be wrong or designed to lead the audience astray. For example, 'I'd even grease my dish' is translated as 'I'd even cook for you' (as opposed to 'I'd lubricate my bum for you'), and 'My heart starts a racket every time I see your packet' is translated to 'I get so excited when I look at your wages', as opposed to 'I get so excited when I see the bulge in your trousers'. Sutton was a master of Polari, so this is no mistake. Instead, he was deliberately toying with the audience – those who knew Polari would have understood the lines as they were intended, and then found it even funnier that Sutton was giving more innocent translations, while those who didn't know Polari might have been able to guess that they were being given the euphemistic versions of the lines, due

Housewives' Choice:
Lee Sutton

to Sutton's faux-naif delivery and the fact that other audience members were laughing louder than would be expected.

In a similar way, *nanti cartes* is translated as 'your old grey mare has nothing to pull', instead of 'no penis'. Here it appears that *cartes* is referring to a cart that is being pulled by a horse – although it is clear by the idiom 'your old grey mare has nothing to pull' that Sutton is giving the right translation after all – just in more subtle language. The song is a tour de force (that's also your actual French) of Polari, showcasing Sutton's extraordinary talent for punning and creative language, which was present throughout many of his routines. While the *Round the Horne* team are often most strongly associated with clever, comedic uses of Polari, it is the drag queens, and chiefly Lee Sutton, who truly had the most bona Polari of all, with 'Bona Eke' representing the layered jokes, the mixture of affection and criticism, the delight in wordplay, the performativity and the extremely rude humour that made Polari what it was.

Earlier in this chapter I noted how men who didn't identify as gay (despite having sex with men) would not have used Polari, although through contact with other gay men, they would have understood it. However, we shouldn't assume that a camp identity automatically meant you would use Polari. Drag queen Ron Storme, interviewed for *Summer's Out*, described his relationship with the language:

> I understand Polari. I know what they're talking about, but I've never had – I do use it on occasions. People think they can get one over on me by talking Polari but I know exactly what they're saying and talking about. I've never had a cause to use it. They've always referred to me as a posh queen but I'm just a working-class girl.[37]

Coming from a working-class family, Ron toured with drag review shows in the Second World War and then organized drag balls at Porchester Hall in the late 1960s, decorating the building with stock that had been loaned from Selfridges. The events attracted up to eight hundred men. Storme appears ambivalent about Polari. He also implies that his distancing from Polari marks him as posh, although he appears uncomfortable with that label too. From interviews with other gay men, it was clear that those with more middle-class backgrounds seemed less knowledgeable about Polari and were not as keen on using it. John, interviewed for an oral history project, confirms how Polari was a marker of social class as well as camp identity:

Ron Storme ... and observer, 1970

I learned 'palari' when I was in the theatre, but it was a common language . . . It was common only among a certain class in the gay world. It was usually people like myself who were in the chorus, the common end of the structure, who used it.[38]

From Ron's concerns about being seen as a posh queen for not using Polari, and John's description of Polari as a 'common language' used by people at the 'common end of the structure', we can see that, for some, Polari was associated with being working class. This is probably the result of several factors: the fact that working-class men – once out – may have felt they had less to lose, societally, if they wanted to camp it up; the earlier links through to marginal communities and identities like beggars, Dilly boys and travelling fairgrounds; and the fact that Polari was often used to converse in a matter-of-fact way about topics that were illegal and sexually taboo. Men from more well-to-do backgrounds were perhaps just as likely to go cottaging or want to pick up trade, but their upbringings might have made them a little more uptight about discussing their sex lives with gusto because it was 'simply not done'. Middle- and upper-class characters like Leonard in the novel *The Youngest Director* or the barrister Melville Farr (played by Dirk Bogarde) in the film *Victim* experienced conflicting identities – being part of the Establishment, which condoned oppression of LGBT people, while yearning for same-sex relationships. The rules of 'polite society' that they had grown up with might have made them uncomfortable with the explicitness of Polari phrases such as 'have it up the dish', 'bona nosh' and 'nanti cartes'.

Polari had a range of uses and meanings for LGBT people. For some it served as one of the first indications that they had made contact with an underground gay network, and learning Polari was a way of becoming initiated into that world and recognizing others. Once established as the language of the secret gay community, Polari enabled the expansion of a 'safe-ish space' beyond that of people's homes or private clubs to locations where gay and straight people mixed together and strangers might be able to overhear conversations. However, the strange-sounding words could also be used to confound and confuse people who had figured out that the speakers were different to them in some way.

As a means of providing a way of talking about topics considered important to gay men that did not have suitable coverage in English, Polari enabled communication and the creation of a sense of community and shared values. It allowed its users to show off their linguistic skills and make others laugh. However, it could also be used to wound or criticize – we should not assume that all members of a community exist in perfect harmony with one another or always bear each other goodwill. Members of the gay community had common goals but would have come from very different backgrounds and we should also bear in mind that a common goal – to hook up with an attractive man – might result in competition and conflict. In addition, Polari was a marker of a camp identity, a self-declared 'gay' identity (as opposed to 'trade') and a working-class identity, and individual gay people had to take into account these intersections of identity in deciding whether or not Polari was for them.

With its ability to enable a cautious or secret expression of gay identity, Polari was a handy tool that made life for LGBT people a little easier in the unforgiving and ignorant social climate of the 1950s. However, in the decade that followed, its status as an underground language was set to change – with a popular radio series revealing the secret to millions of listeners. It is time to go *Round the Horne*.

5

'I'm Julian and this is my friend Sandy'

In 1996, a few months before I'd settled on Polari as a PhD topic, a very arch friend called Julian had produced a cassette released by the BBC of an ancient radio series called *Round the Horne*. 'Listen to this, you!' he said, slipping the cassette in as we sat in his student bedroom, eating his famous tuna fish cheese bake. It was very silly and old-fashioned, a kind of Gang Show that made me recall my time in the Cub Scouts. There was no swearing but a lot of slyly rude jokes and punning. I only recognized one of the voices, that of Kenneth Williams, who seemed to be the star of the show and appeared to be having the time of his life. He'd been in dozens of Carry On films that were a staple of British Bank Holiday television in the 1970s and '80s, and I also knew him from his voicework on a children's animation show called *Willo the Wisp*. He often played snooty, camp, sexually repressed characters and had an unmistakable voice – a kind of strangulated Cockney with a very affected drawl laid over the top, like one of those knitted dolls you put over a toilet roll that my nanna had in her bathroom.

He'd died a few years earlier and his diaries had been published soon afterwards. I'd bought them because he was gay and in those days we were all so starved of anything culturally relevant to our sexuality that we'd lap up anything we could get. They were a long, sometimes miserable read. He came across as unfulfilled and increasingly bitter in his later years – a tremendously talented man who entertained so many people but never really found happiness.

In the *Round the Horne* sketches Julian and Sandy usually appeared at the end of each episode. Years later, when I was studying the language that tabloid newspapers used about gay people, I identified a set of stereotyping adverbs that journalists often employed: *screamingly*, *outrageously*, *shamelessly* and *flamboyantly*. They may as well have been describing Jules and Sand. A pair of out-of-work actors, in each sketch they had wound up in some new occupation and would shriek and exclaim, with Sandy encouraging Julian to 'unburden' himself of some secret shame while bits of Polari were seamlessly incorporated into the dialogue. Considering that the BBC was the subject of Mary Whitehouse's puritanical scrutiny at the time, it is amazing that Julian and Sandy got away with it. This chapter describes how they did.

Bona to vada your dolly old eek

Julian and Sandy find their way into this book because they are the most famous fictional characters to have ever used Polari, as well as standing in for representations of a type of person who spoke it (despite being a stereotypical, exaggerated comedy representation). They are also responsible for introducing Polari to a much wider audience than ever before, the consequences of which are discussed in the next chapter. For

Kenneth Williams (Sandy): 'People need to be peppered or even
outraged occasionally'

now, we'll look at how they came about, why they were scripted as using Polari and what their Polari was like. We should bear in mind that here we're dealing with a form of scripted Polari that was written to be spoken rather than being fully spontaneous, and it was also used on a largely non-gay audience. So it is a filtered version of the language and while it cursorily resembles the way it would have been used in private real-life situations, there are also some differences.

Considering its gay content, it is perhaps surprising to learn that *Round the Horne* was broadcast on Sunday afternoons and intended for a family audience. It was a staple of the mid-1960s, running from 1964 to 1968 and attracting around 9 million listeners each week. Along with its high ratings it won the Writers' Guild of Great Britain Award for the best comedy script in 1967. It consisted of a series of regular comedy sketches (often film and TV spoofs or musical numbers) fronted by the show's 'straight man' (in both senses of the word), Kenneth Horne, a balding, avuncular figure who introduced and interacted with the comedy characters. The other Kenneth – Kenneth Williams – played Sandy, while Hugh Paddick voiced Julian. Paddick was the less famous actor but also appeared as a (coded) gay soap opera director in the film *The Killing of Sister George* (1968) and played a Polari-speaking Robin Hood in the comedy film *Up the Chastity Belt* (1971). Of the two characters, Kenneth Williams's Sandy is a little more boisterous and dominant while Julian is implied to be more attractive and talented but sometimes appears to lack confidence.

Round the Horne was written by Marty Feldman and Barry Took. In 1997, the year before he died, Barry Took agreed to be interviewed by me and, consequently, insights I gained from him are woven throughout this chapter. That the Julian and Sandy sketches occurred at the end of each episode indicates they were the highlight of the show. Barry Took agreed, telling me that one week Marty had become tired of them and wanted to leave them out, although Took disagreed, so they compromised by writing their absence into a sketch ('No Julian and Sandy') and having them appear at the end, complaining that it was a disgrace and suggesting what they could have been written as doing.

As well as the interview with Took, I have relied on other interviews from a range of sources, including the Polari speakers

Hugh Paddick (Julian): love the seaweed drag

I spoke to, and my analyses of all the sketches, which I transcribed from cassettes released by the BBC. Looking through the transcripts, it was never explicitly stated that Julian and Sandy were gay. The word *homosexual* never occurs in them, while *gay* occurs four times, referring to a woman who keeps an 'understanding pub in the city' called the Gay Bargee, and a gents' boutique called the Gay Huzzar. However, the characters' sexuality is implied throughout, with their camp voices, frequent use of innuendo and references to male friends including Gordon (the leather-wearing, motorcycle-riding, rough-trade type mentioned earlier), Jock (a rugby-playing sailor – also implied to be trade), Reynard LaSpoon (a choreographer) and Pandro Wildebeeste (a film director, and a possible reference to Peter Wildebloode).

Despite not explicitly identifying themselves as gay, Julian and Sandy's popular and continued presence on *Round the Horne* goes somewhat against the grain of the view that gay characters were marginalized and problematized in the media, especially prior to the decriminalization of homosexuality. It is true that gay characters, especially in mainstream film, TV and radio, were few and far between across the entirety of the twentieth century. In the UK, they were often found as one-note comedy roles well into the 1980s, with characters played by Charles Hawtrey sometimes coded as eccentrically gay, while other comedians like Frankie Howerd and Danny La Rue incorporated camp or drag personas, followed by Larry Grayson and John Inman in the 1970s. Gay men were (just about) acceptable to the public, then, if they were funny, camp and cosy. Julian and Sandy formed part of a long line of this kind of character – they were amusing rather than sexually threatening, although

Hard at it: Barry Took and Kenneth Horne

compared to other comedy characters like John Inman's Mr
Humphries in the 1970s BBC sitcom *Are You Being Served?*
Julian and Sandy are a little more daring in their suggestions
of relationships with other men and offer hints regarding a
network of fictional gay establishments (including the steam
room at the Royal Borough of Tufnell Park Slipper Baths and
the Marine Commando Club in Paddington). Perhaps the fact
that they were disembodied characters – we could only hear
their voices – made them less threatening and allowed them to
be a little bolder than their contemporaries. The writing is also
more central to the humour than for characters whose home
was on TV or film, where visual performance and flamboyant
costumes were able to grab some of the laughs. And as we will
see, there was also an amount of ad libbing, which resulted
in Kenneth Williams in particular pushing the boundaries of
acceptability in a way which caused conflict behind the scenes.

Considering that they were the stars of *Round the Horne*, Julian and Sandy's conception was surprisingly accidental. They were not what Took and Feldman had originally envisaged for the series. Instead Took describes how they had started out as much older and were 'terribly booming old boys'.[1] As it was common for actors to do housework between engagements, the writers had thought it would have been funny to have 'these old theatrical chaps going to Kenneth Horne to do his washing up'. However, the producer found them sad rather than funny and instructed the writers to 'make them chorus boys'. And so Julian and Sandy were born. Both took their names from the writers of musicals. Julian was named after Julian Slade, who co-wrote *Salad Days* with Dorothy Reynolds, while Sandy was named after Sandy Wilson, who wrote *The Boy Friend* (in which Hugh Paddick had starred).[2] Ironically, we rarely get to hear much about Julian and Sandy's theatrical careers, with the sketches instead focusing each week on a different enterprise that they have started up (a running joke being that none of these schemes must have lasted longer than a week, implying their incompetence or inability to commit to anything). However, members of the Royal Ballet Company apparently loved Julian and Sandy, possibly recognizing themselves in many of the sketches – to them, it was a shared secret. As a pair of *wallopers* (dancers) or West End queens, Julian and Sandy were drawn from a long-standing tradition of gay chorus boys who probably would have danced and belted out songs in complicated ensemble musical numbers behind the leading actors.

Prior to the decriminalization of homosexuality in 1967, for many gay men Julian and Sandy would have been their only clue that people like them (albeit comedy caricatures) existed. Female impersonator Bette Bourne described how 'Even if you lived in a little village in the back of Hicksville – and you had to be listening to it on the crystal set with the bedroom door locked, and it on very softly – you still had Julian and Sandy giving you *courage mon ami*.'[3] Two of my interviewees, Sidney and Jim, talked about the importance of *Round the Horne* to their lives while they were growing up. Jim related that aged twelve or thirteen, 'living in the middle of nowhere in Yorkshire . . . I used to listen to *Round the Horne*. I didn't know anything about gay or anything in those days, just that I liked looking at men, you know. But I used to think that it was absolutely wonderful.' Whereas Sidney joked that in his home town of Ipswich in the 1960s, 'If you farted little old ladies would come up to you in the street and say, "Oh, I hear you farted dear."' He describes listening to *Round the Horne* every Sunday afternoon and 'it was part of the scene'. Julian and Sandy thus had an unexpected educational effect, introducing a newer, younger generation to Polari and, indeed, the existence of a gay scene. Up until that point you were unlikely to have heard Polari unless you had connections with other gay men – the sketches changed that. They also took Polari out of the dockland pubs, the cruise ships, the private drinking clubs and the cruising grounds of towns and cities, making it known across the whole of the UK.

Something about Mary

In order to understand the sketches a little better, we need to consider the social context of the 1960s in the UK. From today's perspective the 1960s are often reduced to a few colourful tropes – they were 'swinging', everyone was high on LSD and marijuana, and it was the age of 'free love', hippies and 'flower power'. Film footage of the time – of young people who were involved in the counter-culture – does give the impression of a revolutionary decade. Politically, there was growing aware-ness of the need for equality in terms of ethnicity, gender and sexuality. The 1960s saw the invention and distribution of birth control tablets for women as well as the legalization of abortion and the decriminalization of homosexuality in the UK. This, along with the explosion of creativity in fash-ion, music and film, means that we shouldn't underestimate the transformative effect of the 1960s on people's lives. The UK was a remarkably different place in 1970 compared to 1959. However, the changes were perhaps not as immediately widespread and far-reaching as documentary footage would have us think. Dominic Sandbrook describes Swinging London more as a 'small social network' which wasn't especially open or classless but instead was an elite phenomenon. He argues that it was a case of one form of snobbery replacing another.[4]

Social and cultural changes *were* underfoot but they more directly affected younger people living in cities. For other seg-ments of the population, particularly those living in smaller towns or villages, or who were older, change was more incre-mental, continuing into the 1970s and beyond. And despite the '60s being the 'swinging' decade, it began with Britain enshrin-ing into law some of the most oppressive forms of censorship relating to depictions of sex in the Western world, with the Obscene Publications Act (1959) making the sale of 'hardcore' pornography illegal through to the end of the century. While most Western countries had legalized pornography in the 1960s and '70s, British lawmakers refused to do so.

Culturally, Brits can come across as having an uptight attitude towards matters sexual, perhaps due to a hangover of the famously 'proper' Victorian era, and the legacy of a disapproving Church. The advice 'Wrap up well, it's cold outside' is not just taken literally but psychologically. Even now, British people are not thought of as especially passionate – words like reserved tend to be used about us – while anthropologist Kate Fox talks of a social awkwardness about the English which is far from sexy.[5]

The undisputed queen of censorship was Mary Whitehouse (CBE), founder and president of the National Viewers' and Listeners' Association (NVLA). Socially conservative and motivated through her strong Christian beliefs, Mary was the scourge of the 'permissive society', campaigning against moral degradation, wherever she thought she saw it. In horn-rimmed glasses, steel hairdo and high-necked twin-set, she cut a formidable figure which was often parodied (she is a Halloween drag queen dream). One of Mary's first public proclamations involved a long article in the *Sunday Times* in 1953, advising mothers on how they could avoid making their sons gay.[6] She also famously prosecuted the magazine *Gay News* for blasphemy in 1977 for publishing a poem by James Kirkup called 'The Love That Dares to Speak Its Name'. The poem involved a Roman centurion fantasizing about the body of Jesus Christ. Mary's prosecuting barrister, John Smyth, told the court, 'It may be said that this is a love poem – it is not, it is a poem about buggery.'[7] *Gay News* lost the case, although it raised £26,435 in donations to cover the £7,763 costs and one of

Oh Mary, get her!
Gay News badge
featuring Mary
Whitehouse

its journalists, Peter Burton, noted that Mary had done 'the publication a great kindness because she made us international news. Really, it was a big world-wide story, thereby raising our visibility, raising the readership, letting lots of lonely people, who didn't know we existed . . . We couldn't buy publicity like she gave *Gay News* and gays generally.'[8] Despite the good publicity, it is still illegal to publish the poem.

The repressive attitude towards sex in the UK resulted in some sex shops illegally selling under-the-counter hardcore pornography, risking police raids and fines, while legal depictions of sex were tame and, from a current perspective, rather strange. Through the 1960s and '70s a genre of film called the sex comedy demonstrated a peculiarly British take on sexuality – it was permissible if it was funny. The Confessions Of series and the Carry On films played at cinemas and were hugely popular. A deliciously awful sex comedy called *Come Play With Me* holds the distinction of being one of the UK's longest-running screenings (playing at Soho's Moulin Cinema for 201 weeks from 1977 to 1981), and reveals a great deal about how much bad acting the British public would put up with in order to see a few naked bodies.

Hugh Greene became Director-General of the licence-payer-funded British Broadcasting Corporation in 1960. He took on a failing institution which was losing viewers to the new commercially funded network ITV. Greene responded by taking the BBC in a new direction, giving representation to working-class people along with a range of more realistic characters and depictions of life.[9] Mary Whitehouse launched her Clean Up TV campaign in January 1964, the same month that Greene received a knighthood, asserting that under Greene the BBC was spreading 'the propaganda of disbelief, doubt and dirt . . . promiscuity, infidelity and drinking'.[10] Unsurprisingly, Greene was an ally of *Round the Horne*, and according to Barry Took he defended the programme because he officially saw nothing to object to in it. However, Took suggests that in reality Greene 'liked dirty shows'.[11] He probably also liked the idea of getting one over on Mrs Whitehouse whenever he could.

How to get away with dirty jokes

While radio programmes didn't need to worry about any form of visual content, there was a danger that their language could be scrutinized and censored. Any form of swearing was still seen as taboo – through the 1960s Mary Whitehouse's favourite target was the BBC sitcom *Till Death Us Do Part*, which featured a character called Alf Garnett who regularly used the word *bloody*. This word came in for a lot of attention from Mrs

Whitehouse (although Garnett's racist, sexist and homophobic language did not). If *bloody* set the bar regarding what was frowned upon, then the cutting-edge comedy of the time needed to be creative in terms of what it could get away with.

Whitehouse did complain about *Round the Horne*, although it was another character, J. Peasemold Gruntfuttock (also voiced by Kenneth Williams), who earned her ire, for using some quasi-religious phrases in a way that she felt was disrespectful. She, along with Conservative MP Sir Cyril Black, managed to have the script to one sketch changed, although Hugh Greene stood by the writers and refused to tell them to 'tone it down' overall.[12]

So how did Julian and Sandy escape Mary's fury? First, the writers went down the sex comedy route by employing an extremely high ratio of euphemism and innuendo. As a result, Jules and Sandy were able to insinuate sex without ever using a swear word. The scripts relied heavily on double meanings in order to reduce the amount of offence caused as well as to protect younger listeners who would only understand the literal meaning. This was something which was even reflexively joked about in one of the sketches:

> Sandy: . . . we could have been in a railway booking office and I could have said, Jule is checking his departures and looking up his *Bradshaw*.[13] Haaaa!
> Mr Horne: No, no, no, no, no, oh no. I don't think so. The audience may have seen a secondary meaning.
> Sandy: Them? Secondary meaning?

Julian: What?
Sandy: They don't even see the first meaning. Just
    laugh at anything that might be dirty don't they.
    Disgusting![14]

Sandy brings to mind the story of the Emperor's New
Clothes, whereby audiences understand that the sketches
are supposed to be rude and feel prompted to laugh, thereby
showing they are sophisticated enough to 'get' the joke, even
when they don't. The audience laughter is certainly a part of
the sketches, acting as a prompt to make listeners think more
carefully about some of the lines. Consider:

Sandy: Yes, or there's 'The party's over, it's all over
    my friend.' I mean, yes yes, it's lovely, no, it's
    lovely, that is poignant.[15]

Sandy's 'I mean, yes yes, it's lovely, no, it's lovely' is in
response to audience laughter which interprets the lyrics of the
song he quotes as containing a double (and very rude) meaning. The joke requires the listener to carry out a reparsing of
the phrase 'The party's over, it's all over my friend' as well as
making some sort of guess as to what exactly is all over Sandy's
'friend'. The word *it* was often the culprit of these kinds of
jokes, standing in as a general reference for sex ('we are the
Universal Party, so called because we're at it right, left and
centre'[16]) or a sexual body part ('I used to stand there with it
fizzing in me hand'[17]).

In another sketch, Julian says that the zoological society are
so pleased with him and Sandy that they 'made us fellows'.[18]

A potential triple meaning exists here. On the surface is the innocent proposition of the society inviting Julian and Sandy to join their 'fellowship'. However, 'made us fellows' could also imply that Julian and Sandy were turned into men (presumably because their homosexuality made them something other than men), while a third interpretation is that the zoological society, recognizing that Julian and Sandy were gay, decided to treat them by creating two fellows for them to take home and keep.

Euphemisms for homosexuality abound in the sketches. When Julian engages in a bit of catwalk modelling, Sandy remarks, 'Watch him Mr Horne, he's on the turn.' On 'Lazy Bona Ranch' Julian refers to 'a crying need in this country today for men like us to get out into the open' and a dog called Cyril is referred to as 'half and half' in 'Bona Pets'. These sketches could be seen as implicitly referencing someone as being gay or bisexual. The phrase 'I've got his/your number' occurs in three of the sketches and was also used to imply that the speaker has identified someone as gay.

Julian and Sandy also indexed their homosexuality by cheerfully referencing the fact that their sexual practices were illegal. In 'Bona Law', where Julian and Sandy have set themselves up as legal advisers, Mr Horne asks if they can help him. Julian responds with, 'Well it depends on what it is. We've got a criminal practice that takes up most of our time.' The 'criminal practice' in question refers to their paid profession but simultaneously functions as a dig at the pontificating legal jargon that viewed homosexuality as a 'criminal practice'. In another sketch, 'Bona Nature Clinic', Sandy welcomes Mr Horne by describing himself and Julian as being 'your actual homeopathic practioners'. This is not a double entrendre as such but a parody

Your actual artiste's impression: Julian and Sandy

of the phrase 'practising homosexuals'. Sandy follows on with an even bolder statement: 'Yes, yes, we're not recognized by doctors.' The double meaning here is that while homeopathic medicine is not taken seriously by most doctors, the medical profession also viewed homosexuality as an aberration that could be 'cured' through the sorts of humiliating and painful programmes described in the previous chapter.

Finally, taking on a drag identity was also presented, jokingly, as illegal. In 'Bona Bouffant', Julian advises Mr Horne to purchase a toupee, asking, 'Could I interest you in a flame-red shoulder-length wig?' Mr Horne replies, 'Well, not me, but you might interest the chief of police.'

Julian and Sandy are not usually viewed as political. If anything, it is easier to make a case that they are apolitical 'Uncle Tom' figures who conformed to the screaming sissy stereotype that was soon to be vilified by the Gay Liberationists to come. However, these remarks on the legal status of LGBT people and the way they were viewed by doctors indicate a more politically aware side of the sketches, albeit one that can be overlooked amid the general absurdity. But the fact that these mentions were few and far between enabled them to escape the ears of Mary Whitehouse and her supporters. Too many of them, and they would have been subject to inquiry.

Julian and Sandy could not be viewed as activists in the way that the Campaign for Homosexual Equality or the Gay Liberation Front advocated acceptance and legal change. They didn't represent themselves as 'normal' or as the same as heterosexuals, and they also didn't ask for equal rights. They recognized the oppressive society that they lived in, but only in a 'blink and you'll miss it' way. Instead, they concentrated on living their lives without shame or apology. By making a joke out of them they showed the world that attempts to subject them had utterly failed. If this was activism, it was by laughter and stealth – with Polari being one of their most effective weapons. In many ways, then, they have a lot in common with the Sisters of Perpetual Indulgence, described later.

A dish that's fit for a queen

When they conceived the chorus-boy characters of Julian and Sandy, Barry Took remembers that he and Marty used to hear Kenneth Williams and Hugh Paddick talking in Polari so they thought it would be a good idea to incorporate what they did in their private lives into the script.[19] As mentioned, Williams used small amounts of Polari in his diaries when he was stationed in Singapore. His entry for Friday 24 October 1947 (when he was aged 21) reads 'Met 2 marines – very charming. Bonar Shamshes.'[20] An editor's footnote to this entry says that Stanley Baxter (a friend of Williams) claims Williams did not speak Polari in Singapore but that he clearly knew it. *Bonar* is most certainly a variant of the more widely used *bona* although *shamshes* is not one of the more widely used words. It most probably is an alternative (bordering on Back Slang) spelling of *smashers*, probably being slang to refer to attractive men, although it could also refer to teeth in a similar way that *stampers* or *stompers* refers to shoes. However, considering the extensive set of diaries written by Williams, his use of Polari in them is pretty scant. Another instance is 'Went to Singapore with Stan [Baxter] very camp evening, was followed, but tatty types so didn't bother to make overtures.'[21] The word *tatty* suggests that Williams didn't approve of the available talent – a related Polari word, *tat*, is more commonly used to refer to cheap, unfashionable, poor quality or scruffy clothing or household goods.

Williams largely seems to have stopped using Polari in his diaries by the end of the 1940s. We need to be careful about assuming too much from this, especially as Took recalls Williams and Paddick speaking it in the mid-1960s, but we can definitely conclude that Polari was used in the army- and theatre-based gay circles in which Williams moved during the mid- to late 1940s. Perhaps Williams did not identify fully as a Polari speaker as he got older, or it could be the case that the language was on the wane for most of the period when he was writing his diaries. He refers to having a *Barclays* on other occasions in the diaries, which is probably Rhyming Slang for a *wank* (masturbation), although like *shamshes*, this is not a core Polari term.

However, Polari occurs in every Julian and Sandy sketch. Indeed, it is there from almost the start. Every sketch (with a couple of exceptions like 'No Julian and Sandy') begins with Mr Horne calmly introducing a new segment, as if on a magazine-style show. Here's the start of 'Bona Bijou Tourette'.

Well, now to most people travel means holidays. With the travel allowance of fifty pounds it's becoming more and more difficult to find a foreign holiday that one can afford and that's why when I was leafing through my monthly copy of *Breezy Pics* incorporating the *Leather News* and *Amateur Paediatrician* and I came across an advert for a travel agency offering cheap tours. I hurried over to their address in Chelsea right away. The sign on the door said Bona Bijou Tourette. Knock and troll in. So I knocked and trolled. Hello, anybody there?

While Mr Horne's introduction doesn't always include Polari, the next part of the sketch does, with Julian saying, 'Oh hello, I'm Julian and this is my friend Sandy,' and Sandy responding with, 'Oh hello Mr Horne, how bona to vada your dolly old eek again,' or words to that effect. These two statements quickly became catchphrases, and Sandy's contains a relatively high amount of Polari (four words), although it's likely that audience members would be able to translate it without too much difficulty. Apart from another of Sandy's phrases – 'Order lau your luppers on the strillers bona' (which occurs in three sketches) – many of the Polari words in the sketches were isolated instances, surrounded by English words and usually in familiar contexts so that listeners would be able to understand them. After all, there's no point in having jokes that are in a language that most of the audience doesn't know. Enough Polari was there to show that Julian and Sandy were authentic members of the gay subculture, to contribute towards their slightly exotic otherness, and occasionally to obscure gay content, but the original intention of Polari – to disguise one's sexuality or the content of one's speech – was minimal. There was a nod to that, but if it had been done seriously, the sketches wouldn't have worked.

Another issue was that the scriptwriters knew of Polari from their time working in theatre, but neither of them identified as gay, so their knowledge was not especially extensive.

Barry Took described his route into showbusiness to me as first having taken a job at a musical publisher, which led to work as a trumpet player, then with dance bands, and he eventually became a musical comic in the West End. His choreographer introduced him to Polari so he'd come to it through the theatrical route as opposed to learning it in gay bars and clubs. However, the actors behind Julian and Sandy, Hugh Paddick and Kenneth Williams, who were gay, knew more of the language. When interviewed, Barry Took recalled the long Polari phrase that Williams occasionally ad libbed into the script whenever Julian was called upon to play the piano:

> Sandy: Jule, get on the piano.
> Julian: Shall I?
> Sandy: Get on the piano, order lau your luppers on
> the strillers bona. Yes, sit down Mr Horne, we'll
> give you a sample Mr Horne . . .[22]

'Order lau your luppers on the strillers bona' means go and play something good on the piano. However, Took had difficulty remembering the phrase and when I prompted him, he was unable to translate it into English. At the time, he said that none of the other members of the show knew what it meant either, but they were all too embarrassed to admit it so the phrase was allowed to remain. That Williams held such power is fascinating. For all the writers may have known, he could have been inserting very sexually explicit pieces of Polari into the Sunday-afternoon listening experience of millions of viewers, and while most of the audience wouldn't have understood it, clearly some of them would.

There is evidence from Williams's diaries that the working relationship between him and the writers was not always a smooth one, as this entry from 1968 indicates:

Monday 8 April
'R.T.H.' Barry Took was in a v. funny mood and suddenly got quite snappy about the show becoming filthy. 'We might as well write a series called Get Your Cock Out,' he kept crying.[23]

Barry Took confirmed that he would have been uncomfortable with the type of swearing used in television sitcoms such as *Steptoe and Son* and *Till Death Us Do Part*, telling me that there were no swear words in *Round the Horne* as the writers were from a different generation. However, if we consider the sketch 'Rentachap' (where Julian and Sandy are employed to do housework for Mr Horne), there is evidence that Williams playfully used his status as an 'expert' Polari speaker in a way that borders on the obscene:

Mr Horne: Well, do the best you can – here's the
  dishcloth.
Julian: We couldn't wash up in here. All the dishes
  are dirty.
Sandy: Speak for yourself!
Mr Horne: Well, well, I'm sorry, I'd have washed up
  if I'd known.[24]

To a non-Polari speaker this excerpt seems pretty innocent, and most of the audience would have understood the

pun around the word *dish*, where Sandy's 'Speak for yourself!' comment seems to imply that he views himself as a
dish – with *dish* being slang (but not Polari) for an attractive man. However, for a well-versed Polari speaker, *dish*
would have an alternative meaning – referring to a man's
anus (see Lee Sutton's 'grease my dish' line, quoted in the
previous chapter). So Sandy's throwaway line in response
to 'All the dishes are dirty' takes on a different and much
ruder meaning.

During my interview with Barry Took, it became clear that
the Polari meaning of *dish* was unknown to him – he told me
that the line 'all the dishes are dirty' had been put in due to
its alliteration, and was surprised when I explained the other
meaning. And while the 'Speak for yourself!' line appears in
the BBC broadcasts, if we look at a book of the scripts released
by the BBC in 1974, it is missing:

> Kenneth Horne: Well, do the best you can – here's
> the dishcloths.
> Sandy: Ugh! Green and yellow – we can't be doing
> with that.
> Kenneth Horne: What's the matter with green and
> yellow dishcloths?
> Julian: Well see for yourself treash. We're wear-
> ing blue – doesn't match at all. No anyway,
> we couldn't wash up in here – all the dishes
> are dirty.
> Kenneth Horne: Well, I'm sorry, I'd have washed
> them if I'd known.[25]

The mismatch between the official script and the actual recorded dialogue is fairly substantial here, giving an idea of the extent to which Williams and Paddick were ad libbing.

Another potentially rude use of Polari is in 'Bona Rags', when Julian looks through Mr Horne's wardrobe and exclaims, 'Ooh! Look! He's got a baggy old aris!' *Aris*, sometimes pronounced *harris*, most likely refers to *arse*, coming from a chain of rhyming slang. One derivation gives *arse* as rhyming with *bottle and glass*, then *bottle* rhymes with *Aristotle*, resulting in the first part, *aris*, being used, and practically taking us back to the word *arse*.

In another sketch, 'Bona Dance', Julian refers to Mr Horne in the following way: 'Scotches may be a bit naff, but his plates are bona.' A simple translation of this would be that Mr Horne's legs are bad but his feet are nice. Two of the Polari words, *scotches* and *plates*, seem to be derived from rhyming slang – with *scotch* coming from *scotch egg* which rhymes with *leg*, and *plates* from *plates of meat* which rhymes with *feet*. However, *plate* can also refer to oral sex, either because it rhymes with *fellate* or because it comes from *plate of ham*,[26] which is rhyming slang for *gam* – a shortened form of *gamahuche* via French, which refers to oral sex. Again, when interviewed, Barry Took was unaware of the oral sex meaning associated with *plate* – he told me that the word came from army or navy slang – and while Mr Horne's 'feet are nice' translation is totally valid as a translation from Polari, we must also bear in mind that an equally valid meaning is that Mr Horne gives good blow-jobs.

Indeed, a long-standing joke throughout the sketches was that Mr Horne was actually a closeted gay man, which would perhaps help to explain the fact that he appears to seek out

Julian and Sandy in their various enterprises around fifty times. And in some of his introductions to the sketches he hints at diverse sexual interests (as in the reference to the magazine *Breezy Pics* incorporating the *Leather News* and *Amateur Paediatrician* in the sketch mentioned earlier). Horne's use of Polari is not as extensive as Julian and Sandy's, but as the sketches progress he does begin to use it too. For example, at two points in the sketch 'Bona Prods' (one of the more risqué title names), Mr Horne engages in a little Polari of his own:

Julian: We are the Cecil Bs of the 16 De Mille.
Sandy: Yes.
Julian: Small budget pictures really.
Mr Horne: Would I have vadaed any of them do you think?
Sandy: Ooo! He's got all the Polari in'ee.
Julian: I wonder where he picks it up.

Mr Horne: I take it you're engaged in something pretty exciting at the moment.
Julian: No, no not really, we're just standing here with our hands on our heads talking to you.
Mr Horne: Oh bold, very bold!
Sandy: I wonder where he spends his evenings.

In both cases, his Polari is recognized by the other two characters, who remark on it as potentially revealing a secret about Horne's sexuality. This use of an ostensibly masculine middle-class man dropping an odd Polari word into the conversation as a password nicely conveys one of the ways that

Polari was not necessarily the province of camp queens but had more covert functions.

Looking at the bigger picture though, Julian and Sandy's employment of Polari is relatively spartan in two ways: first, they used only a small amount of the potential Polari vocabulary that might have been available to them – 53 words out of over 400 word types. Second, the number of times they actually use Polari is low – I identified 815 uses of these 53 Polari words in total, and considering that the sketches contained about 33,000 words in total, only about 2.5 per cent of them are actually in Polari. None of the words for money or numbers, derived from the older Parlyaree, are used, nor are the extensive set of words relating to sex and sexual body parts (apart from the ambiguous uses of *plates*, *dish* and *aris* described above). Julian and Sandy's Polari differed, then, from more naturalistic non-scripted uses of the language in two distinct ways – first, it was simplified, and second, it was sanitized. As mentioned earlier, we need to take into account the fact that the show was broadcast to a large mainstream audience who wouldn't have been aware of Polari. Another scripted form of Polari – Lee Sutton's 'Bona Eke' – is denser and more complex and also has more sexual content. However, 'Bona Eke' was aimed at a smaller, mostly gay audience, some of whom would already have known Polari, and they would have been less likely to take offence at the rude jokes. Additionally, Sutton did provide translations of his Polari lyrics (despite some of his translations being purposefully incorrect). Julian and Sandy only explicitly translate on a couple of occasions. In 'Le Casserole de Bona Gourmet' (note the use of 'sophisticated' French), Julian offers to serve 'your jugged riah. That's Polari for hair.' However, this is in itself a pretty complicated case, where Julian is relying on the fact that *hair* and *hare* are homophones – the dish he's actually referring to is jugged hare (not hair). No wonder, then, that they felt the audience needed a little help with that one.

The jugged *riah* sketch continues with another demonstration of the way that Polari words were incorporated into the sketches, by taking advantage of the fact that some of them had innocent English meanings:

> Sandy: We got it from our special charcuterie.
> Mr Horne: Charcuterie.
> Sandy: Hm.
> Mr Horne: Your butcher?
> Julian: Oh you think so? It must be the way I've had me hair done.

Mr Horne's remark 'Your butcher?' is interpreted by Julian as 'You're butcher!', taking advantage of the matching pronunciation of *your* and *you're* in English as well as the fact that if the suffix *-er* is attached to the adjective *butch* (meaning more butch), it is identical to the English noun *butcher*. This demonstrates a somewhat Shakespearian use of punning, helping to explain why Took and Feldman were viewed as being among the top comedy writers in the late 1960s. For me, 'Your butcher' is just as clever as 'Now is the winter of our discontent made glorious summer by this sun [son] of York' (*Richard III*).

And perhaps unsurprisingly, Shakespearian references run through the sketches. In 'Bona Books' Julian and Sandy update Shakespeare's plays to include Polari: 'Much Ado About Nanti', 'All's Bona that Ends Bona', 'Two Homees of Verona' and 'As They Like It', with Julian performing his own take on the Seven Ages of Man (Omee) monologue. The line 'Then a soldier, full of strange oaths and bearded like the pard', becomes 'Then a soldier, all butch and full of strange Polari', while 'His youthful hose, well saved, a world too wide for his shrunk shank' is 'His youthful hose well saved, a world too wide for his shrunk lallies'. In 'Bona Law', Sandy argues that Julian 'loved not wisely, but not too well', reversing Othello's speech after he has killed Desdemona. And earlier in that sketch Sandy joyfully exclaims, 'Oh though, oh time has not withered nor custom staled *his* infinite variety', paraphrasing from Enobarbus in *Antony and Cleopatra*. It is true that Julian and Sandy were actors, although they were more likely to have been found in West End musicals than Stratford, so this detailed knowledge of the Bard's plays doesn't fully scan. Instead, these references are probably more indicative of the educational backgrounds of the *Round the Horne* team, although as noted, the punning of both Shakespeare and Julian and Sandy themselves ultimately makes their combination in the sketches a successful one.

Another aspect of the Shakespearian Polari in the 'Bona Books' sketch is that it gave the audience a better chance to understand the Polari words. As I mentioned in the previous chapter, it's interesting how drag queens incorporated quite a bit of Polari into well-known songs, which would have acted as a kind of framework to help audiences understand what was being said. So incorporating Polari into phrases that many people already knew well would be a successful strategy, ensuring that the language was not too mystifying to the point where it ceased to be funny.

In a few sketches, Polari is used when Julian and Sandy are enthusing about some man they fancy. In 'Bona Performers' Sandy describes the act of the Great Omee-Palone, a strong man, as follows: 'Well, he comes on wearing this leopard skin you see. He's a great butch omee, he's got these thewes like an oak, and bulging lallies. Ohh!' Using another Shakespearian word, *thewes* refers to muscles, possibly forearms or thigh muscles. Translated, Sandy is saying that the man has thighs like an oak and bulging legs and is very masculine. A British family radio audience would hardly have been ready for a woman to give such admiring praise over a man's body, let alone another man. But Polari helped people to say the unthinkable.

Another rather daring use of Polari is in the sketch 'Bona Books'. Sandy tells Mr Horne, 'We're just filling in as book publishers; normally, if you'll forgive the expression, we're actors by trade.' Julian follows up with, 'Trade's been a bit rough lately. Had to take whatever we can get.' Again, the double meaning of *trade* as both a Polari word and a mainstream English one helps to construct Julian and Sandy's sexuality in a way that gives them the perfect get-out clause. The reference to *trade* as being *rough* is especially bold, giving the well-versed Polari speaker full certainty regarding what they are referring to. The phrase 'take whatever we can get' further adds to the insinuation (take *what* exactly?), and even the throwaway line 'normally, if you'll forgive the expression' is suggestive that Julian and Sandy are glibly claiming a 'not normal' identity.

But for Mrs Whitehouse, on the other hand, such an exchange might have left her none the wiser. And even if she had been able to work out that this was a reference to *rough trade* or had had it explained to her, there was the danger of hearing Julian and Sandy's cackling insinuation, 'Ooh, she's got all the Polari, hasn't she. I wonder where she picks it up?'

Considering Mary Whitehouse's long-standing disapproval of homosexuality and the fact that she had already complained about another sketch in *Round the Horne*, the fact that she did not make any sort of formal complaint about Julian and Sandy is likely to be attributable to the obfuscating effect of their Polari, at least in part. Even if she had been able to crack the code (and let's face it, you didn't need to be Alan Turing to do so), any complaint she'd made would have been bogged down in the mechanics of what Polari meant and what the writers intended, complicating matters so much that she was simply better off sticking to straightforward cases like *bloody*. Ultimately, Julian and Sandy got away with far more 'subversive' material than Alf Garnett and many of Mary's other targets. They were just too clever for her.

It's over, it's all over my friend

Over fifty sketches and 9 million listeners indicate just how popular Julian and Sandy were in their day. After a successful fourth season of *Round the Horne*, a fifth one had been planned, but then tragedy struck. On Valentine's Day 1969, while onstage at an awards ball, Kenneth Horne suffered a heart attack and died. He was 61. The series was revamped as *Stop Messing About* (a Kenneth Williams catchphrase), but the cast had been devastated by Horne's death and Barry Took felt unable to continue. It was the end for Julian and Sandy.

A compilation LP was released in 1976 entitled *The Bona Album of Julian and Sandy*, featuring a kind of 'best of' of the sketches, with Barry Took taking Mr Horne's 'straight man' role. A book of the sketches, *The Bona Book of Julian and Sandy: Leaves from their Round the Horne Journal*, was published in the same year. From the 1990s onwards, compilations of the original sketches started to be released by the BBC, first on cassette, then CD, then on streaming devices, introducing Julian and Sandy to newer generations of listeners (myself included). As a repository of Polari, this is the largest in existence.

The last ever performance of Julian and Sandy in public occurred on television, not radio, on 28 December 1987 when Barry Took wrote a one-off sketch for Terry Wogan (who assumed the character usually taken by Mr Horne) in a programme called *Wogan's Radio Fun*. Julian and Sandy described how they had sunk half of Julian's pension into opening an (ill-fated) guest house or *bona lattie* ('an omee from omee') in the Algarve and were now planning on returning to the West End for a new show. The sketch ends with them singing a hit from the show, which comedically segues into 'The Lambeth Walk' (a popular East End song). Despite being twenty years on from their heyday, the sketch holds up well, with Williams and Paddick not appearing to need their scripts and displaying the same energy and chemistry as always. Williams, whose low opinion of many of his fellow actors was later revealed upon the publication of his diaries, had only praise for Paddick, referring to his kindness, subtlety and brilliance as a performer.[27] The sketch had to be cut short due to the amount of audience laughter and there was apparently talk of a revival. But Kenneth Williams died three months later, so it was not to be. Hugh Paddick died in 2000, and Mary Whitehouse a year later. She lived just long enough to see social attitudes changing, with graphic depictions of sex, including erections and gay sex, becoming legally available in the UK from the start of the twenty-first century.

From a contemporary perspective it is easy, too easy in fact, to dismiss Julian and Sandy as silly or even unhelpful gay stereotypes. Obviously not all gay men are like them (though I've met more than a few who are, and I've always thought there is a lot to admire in men who don't wear a mask so they can appear 'masc'). When Julian and Sandy appeared on the radio they had the job of representing all gay men everywhere, and in the absence of a wider range of characterizations, this is a big ask. However, considering the time, they were ground-breaking. Unlike some of the other mid-century depictions of gay characters in mainstream fictional contexts, they were neither victims nor villains. They did not die at the end of the episode. They did not go to prison. They did not end up alone, drunkenly crying into a pillow. They had one another and they were having fun. And importantly, I don't think they would have *cared* if you liked them or not. I get the impression that they would have made short shrift of any form of homophobia or gay liberationist critique with a barbed remark of their own – they could certainly give as good as they got, a trait common to many Polari speakers. In terms of providing a positive image of gay men at a time when almost every other message was negative and disapproving, Julian and Sandy were revolutionary, and the fact that they were loved by audiences, both gay and straight, indicated that society was getting ready to accept gay people, especially if it was someone they knew rather than an abstract demonized figure in the tabloids. As Barry Took said, 'The secret of Julian and Sandy is that they are cheerful outgoing people, and there is no hint of sadness or horror in the situation.'[28]

On the one hand, Julian and Sandy breathed life into Polari, introducing it to a new and in some cases much younger generation of speakers. But on the other, they may have helped to hurry along its demise, as the next chapter will show.

6

The Lost Language

In 2001, I finished my PhD thesis on Polari. A year later it came out in book form (*Polari: The Lost Language of Gay Men*) with an academic publisher, enabling my starry-eyed mother to go into Waterstones and order it very loudly, saying, 'and that's my son who wrote it!' The book contained the following phrases: *cultural economy, performativity theory, sociolinguistic coding orientation* and *vari-directional double-voicing* (yes, me neither). Around the same time I published a much shorter dictionary of Polari (*Fantabulosa*), with a longer, more general 'gay slang' supplement. Through these books I was deemed worthy of a lectureship at Lancaster University and then I decided that really, I'd had quite enough of Polari. It was difficult enough to find speakers in the 1990s and I didn't think there was much more to say on the subject. I moved on to look at other topics, but Polari wouldn't leave me alone. I started to be contacted regularly by students who wanted to interview me for their essays or journalists who wanted to publish a piece on Polari. I tried to help as much as I could, but sometimes felt a bit like Shirley Bassey – always being asked to sing 'Big Spender'. Then, in 2005, Sue Sanders, Elly Barnes and the group Schools Out initiated LGBT History Month, inspired by the American LGBT History Month which began in 1994. The British LGBT History Month is in February (which in the UK is a month that could usually benefit from a bit of rainbow magic) and involves local LGBT communities working with museums, galleries, libraries and universities in order to put on a programme of events and talks. I began to be asked to give public talks about Polari. This was no longer scary, although talking to 'the public' is a little different to lecturing to a room full of students. I had to admit that 'Big Spender' is a pretty good song, so I dusted off my sequinned dress and started singing.

For my first public outing, I am asked to speak at a museum which has an exhibition based on the *Hello Sailor* book I wrote with Jo Stanley, about gay life at sea. There is a nice mock-up of a gay sailor's cabin, complete with Dusty Springfield albums and 1960s beefcake posters on the walls. My talk occurs in the main bit of the museum, squashed in between some exhibits, with people randomly walking past. It is a bit noisy but there is a good crowd and the seats get filled. I start talking and then see a face from the past at the back of the room. It's an ex-boyfriend who I haven't spoken to in years. It throws me off kilter and I forget how to speak, causing the audience to laugh. I look up and he has moved away. I manage to regain composure and continue like nothing has happened. Then, half-way through the talk, there is a disturbance. A couple with two young children had settled in the chairs at the start, probably to rest their feet, not knowing what the talk was about, and once it had begun, being typically British and polite, the poor things had become trapped into listening. After about twenty minutes I realize that the youngest son has become bored and he suddenly stands up and runs down the aisle. I freeze and fortunately his dad jumps up and grabs him just before he reaches me, pulling him backwards. If they're reading, I'm sorry you all got stuck in my talk – I tell people now that if they need to leave, to use the loo or whatever, then they can just get up and go.

At another talk I get my facts wrong and announce to the audience that Maisie Trollette has died, when in fact she is very much alive (sorry Maisie). Everyone is too polite to correct me. And in another one I encounter a butch young man who tells me that he dislikes the whole idea of Polari and that he doesn't understand the desire of people to use labels like *gay* and *straight* as they are restrictive. While most of the people who come to my talks find Polari funny or fascinating, it's useful to get an insight into an alternative perspective and the young man's attitude echoes some of the voices that we'll hear in this chapter, which turns to the period of the 1970s and '80s, when Polari largely fell into disuse. I'll start by considering the extent to which we have evidence that Polari actually did decline before going on to the reasons why people no longer used it. But in order to make sense of these reasons, it's helpful to think about what it was like to be gay during this period and how new ideas about sexuality were starting to influence the younger generation.

Polari in danger

Within linguistics there is a sub-field around the notion of *language death*, a concept that evokes the idea of a language as a living being. This is an idea from the nineteenth century, with one scholar asserting that languages were organic bodies which 'develop as possessing an inner principle of life, and gradually die out because they do not understand themselves any longer, and therefore cast off or mutilate their members or forms'.[1] Studies around language death have looked at the ways languages tend to get replaced by other languages that are viewed as more prestigious, or involve cases where a country undergoes a huge natural disaster, environmental change (for example, through deforestation) or invasion, with its population becoming severely depleted or forced to disperse. The survival of a language is often linked to its potential to help its speakers earn a living, and at present hundreds of languages around the world are being eroded, often as parents make the pragmatic choice to encourage their children to learn and speak languages that are going to help them to find work. Many of these are languages or dialects in countries such as India and Australia or regions such as the Pacific Islands and North America. While the process behind language death is often understandable, something irreplaceable is lost from the world when it happens. Languages are not just different collections of words for the same things; they also reflect the speaker's way of thinking as well as encoding knowledge about a group's history, culture and environment. While we should not force people to learn and continue to use languages if they do not want to do so, I believe that it is important to document all languages and provide the means for people to learn and continue to use them without suffering penalties. There are also individual benefits to being multilingual in terms of improving cognitive function and the sense of social bonding with others, as well as a connection with the past that we can get from learning the language of our ancestors.

In 2010, Cambridge University labelled Polari an 'endangered language', with the term 'endangered' bringing to mind species of wildlife that are being hunted out of existence. However, it is a bit of a stretch to place Polari's decline along the same lines as the loss of a language like Domaaki, which is spoken by several hundred people in a few villages in the northern Gilgit-Baltistan region of Pakistan. Its speakers are viewed as having a low social status and are discriminated against, so they are choosing to speak other languages that are more highly regarded. However, I don't think that the majority of people who used Polari spoke it as a full language, and no people have been documented as having Polari as their native or only language. Polari speakers were fluent in (and often relied heavily on) English too. Additionally, people did not choose to stop speaking Polari for reasons of survival; as we shall see, there was a complex set of interacting reasons for its demise. Indeed, the combination of factors in Polari's decline are unique and for that reason are worthy of study in and of themselves, but it is also important not to view Polari as the same as the many other languages across the world that are disappearing.

A distinction is sometimes made between language death as sudden or gradual, where a sudden death is often linked to a dramatic disaster falling upon a population of speakers whereas a gradual one takes place over generations. While Polari's demise does appear to have been fairly sudden, and we may want to argue that some Polari speakers died due to HIV-AIDS in the 1980s, thus hastening the process, I think it is more likely that the decline had already been going on from

at least the start of the 1960s, so has more in common with
the idea of a gradual death, lasting several decades. As well as
its original set of speakers choosing to use it less and less over
time, there is also the fact that it was no longer as likely to
be 'passed down' from older, established members of the gay
scene to younger, newer members.

The men I interviewed in the 1990s all agreed that Polari
was no longer popular on the gay scene, although they did note
exceptions where it was used. David told me, 'There's lots of
people in Brighton who know of it, and there are still several
people who still use it at dinner parties when they get a bit
bevvied – you see *bevvied* is another one – getting drunk . . .
People do still use it, but only if you're in an age group over fifty.'
Freddy Bateman, interviewed for BBC Radio 4 in 1995, stated,
'I just use *vada*. And *bona* they use. But that's about all you
hear nowadays. You don't hear a lot now. I don't know anyone
who actually speaks the whole Polari.'[2] These two statements
suggest that Polari was confined to older men who would use it
in more private settings within long-established social networks
and that it was much reduced in terms of the set of words that
were used by its speakers. One aspect of the interviews I carried
out was that some of the men I spoke to were self-admittedly
a little rusty when it came to the technical aspects of Polari,
and attested that they no longer used it regularly. However,
actor Robbie Bonar, who goes by the stage name Champagne
Charlie, recalls hearing it regularly in the theatre in the 1980s
and '90s, suggesting that this is one context where it continued
to be used, albeit in a somewhat reduced way.

For the reasons discussed earlier in this book around the
lack of documentation, it is difficult to ascertain a specific date

or period when Polari started to fall into disuse. Statements from people who knew Polari or knew of it can perhaps help us to narrow the field down slightly. Tony Papard, for example, describes discovering the existence of the London gay scene in 1967 at the age of 22. He met his partner of 21 years, George, in the Biograph Cinema in Victoria, and learnt about Polari from him:

> George and his friends all used a strange language which I knew nothing about, except vaguely remembering it and not understanding it from Jules and Sandy on the radio. It was, of course, the polari gay slang, a mixture of Italian, backslang and theatrical slang. It was dying out in the 1960s, but George and his friends continued to use it, and some words like 'cod' and 'naff' have now come into general usage, while most others have fallen into disuse.[3]

After the decriminalization of homosexuality, the first legally produced periodicals aimed at a gay audience started to be published. Magazines and newspapers such as *Lunch*, *Jeffrey*, *Quorum* and *Gay News* were available in certain newsagents or via mail order in the early 1970s, and the fact that with rare exceptions these publications did not use Polari offers more evidence that by this point it was no longer in fashion. There are a couple of notable cases where Polari was mentioned in the gay press, discussed below, but they tend to provide reasons why it was *not* used rather than giving us evidence that it was.

There are cases of Polari being used in the mainstream British media around this time, although they were also rare.

One instance is Hugh Paddick in the 1971 comedy film *Up the Chastity Belt*, who leads a troupe of gay 'merry men'. In one scene, Lurkalot (Frankie Howerd) tells Robin that it's marvellous how he robs the rich and gives to the poor, and Robin replies, 'You must be joking [, we] keep it all ourselves, how do you think we get all this bona drag?' Then in February 1973, in an episode of the long-running science-fiction television series *Dr Who*, Polari is used as a kind of 'insider joke' when alien characters claim to be speaking something called Tellurian Carnival Lingo:

> Vorg: I bet he understands the Palare! Listen to this.
> Shirna: Eh?
> Vorg: The Tellurian Carnival Lingo, watch! [To the
>   Doctor] Palare the carny?
> Doctor: I beg your pardon?
> Vorg: Varda the bona palone?
> Doctor: I'm sorry? Erm.
> Vorg: Nanti dinarli round here yer gills. Ha ha ha!
> Doctor: I must apologize. I'm afraid I do not under-
>   stand your language.[4]

There were a few other references. In Les Dawson's comedy series for Yorkshire Television (also in the 1970s), Roy Barraclough was a cravat-wearing gay man called Mr Bona, while another actor, Peter Wyngarde, who had played an effete detective in the programmes *Department S* and *Jason King*, released an album in 1970 which contained a song called 'The Skinhead and the Hippy', whose lyrics include the Polari phrase 'troll the Dilly'. And in a 1976 episode of his television family quiz programme *Larry Grayson's Generation Game*, the titular host interviewed a family with the surname of 'Eke', and made a number of jokes along the lines of 'eke to eke'. These cases indicate a very small acknowledgement of Polari coming from people working in its 'home' environment of the entertainment industry (now increasingly focused on television), but they are one-offs and there was nothing like the regularly scheduled sojourns in Polari that had been undertaken by Julian and Sandy in the previous decade. Let us jump back a little to a point towards the end of the previous chapter, then, when Julian and Sandy were at their peak of popularity.

No longer a secret

The popularity of Julian and Sandy should not be underestimated. Nine million listeners a week was a substantial proportion of the British population and the programme was clearly critically acknowledged too. Perhaps it is only coincidence that *Round the Horne* won the Writers' Guild of Great Britain Award for the best comedy script in 1967, the same year homosexuality was decriminalized. Whatever the reason, it was certainly viewed as being part of the zeitgeist, further evidence that the public were ready to accept the change to the law rather than protesting en masse.

The simplified use of Polari in the Julian and Sandy sketches was partly due to the writers not knowing a lot of the words themselves, partly to the fact that they didn't wish to use any of the rude ones, and partly because they didn't want to over-complicate things for the audience, most of whom didn't know Polari. As I noted in the previous chapter, Polari in these sketches was used in two main ways: as part of longer catch-phrases which were repeated across multiple sketches and thus likely to be remembered (for example, *how bona to vada your dolly old eke*), and in shorter bursts where it was usually easy for audiences to deduce the meaning of words through context, including cases where they would already be likely to be familiar with a phrase. In the following dialogue from 'Bona Guesthouse', Julian and Sandy incorporate Polari words (*riah*, *lattie*, *troll* and *palone*) into song lyrics that they were relying on audience members to already know.

> Sandy: [singing] I dream of Jeannie with the light brown riah.
> Julian: Yes, then there was [sings] Bless this lattie, butch and stout.
> Sandy: Or what about our duet?
> Julian: Oh yes.
> Both: [singing] We'll troll beside you through the world today.
> Sandy: Lovely!
> Julian: Tears to the eyes.
> Sandy: And the –
> Julian: And the big finish –
> Sandy: The big finish.
> Julian: Yes.
> Both: [singing] Some day she'll troll along. The palone I love.

The trick here is that a Polari word is placed in such a familiar context that it does not confuse the audience but instead teaches them the word's meaning. Although this could get a little laboured:

> Julian: Oh dear, I wonder if he's with BBC2. What
>   cossy did they say?
> Kenneth Horne: Cossy?
> Julian: Costume. Polari for costume.
> Kenneth Horne: Oh yes, they said a dinner-suit . . .[5]

So gradually, over many episodes and repeated exposure to the forty or so Polari words that Julian and Sandy regularly used, the language would start to be understood by the audience. It is unlikely that the majority of these words were picked up in any sort of mass way, although it's possible that *naff* (which occurred fifteen times across the sketches) was helped into mainstream slang through Julian and Sandy. As most audience members did not identify as gay they would have not viewed it as appropriate to incorporate bits of Polari into their regular language use, but they would have recognized Polari, if they heard someone else speaking it, and they would have understood that the people speaking were likely to be the same as Julian and Sandy, ergo gay, even if they weren't able to translate the full content of the conversation.

None of my interviewees explicitly gave anecdotes of this happening, but John, interviewed by Kevin Porter and Jeffrey Weeks, states that a reason for Polari's demise was that 'it really became like everything else. Everyone does it. So there's no more mystery about it.'[6] It's likely, then, that Polari's growing popularity within the gay scene from the 1930s through to the 1950s and its subsequent mainstream exposure in the late

1960s comprised two 'waves' that both contributed towards its being dropped by speakers. Polari had been attractive when it was a secret, the equivalent of a handshake allowing access to a fraternity. But it is impossible for something to remain a secret when it starts to become popular. It becomes a victim of its own success, with the people who initially adopted it viewing it as no longer belonging to them but being a thing of the masses. And by the time Julian and Sandy had finished with Polari, what was the point of speaking it if it made your Great-Aunt Beryl smile in acknowledgement?

So although Julian and Sandy were seen as responsible for introducing Polari to a new, younger generation of gay men, especially those not living in cities, by the time the radio show was broadcast, it was already seen as somewhat passé within more up-to-date gay circles. And even for those who were new to the language and might have used it, the end of the broadcasts also represented a kind of cut-off. With no more Julian and Sandy, there were no other regular sources of Polari that they could turn to. One of my interviewees, John E, cited the decline of Polari as related to the fact that *Round the Horne stopped* making new episodes. I suspect that there were other factors at work, though, and let us turn now to that other key event of 1967 – decriminalization.

The age of gay liberation

The Sexual Offences Act was passed under Harold Wilson's Labour government on 4 July 1967 and received Royal Assent on 27 July 1967. The Act legalized homosexual acts, with a significant number of caveats attached. Fred Dyson, a miner, describes how he was on a bus with a friend when he heard the news: 'I got hold of him and I give him a great big kiss and everybody on the bus were looking but I weren't bothered. I just kissed him. I said: "You can all look, it's legal now."'[7]

Decriminalization had been a long time coming, and when it finally arrived it was both huge and something of a let-down. The Wolfenden Report, which had recommended decriminalization, had been published ten years earlier, and while the Act was a breakthrough, for some it was felt to be too little too late. The term *decriminalization* rather than *legalization* or *equalization* is used when talking about the Act because gay sex was legal only in certain circumstances – between two consenting men over the age of 21; neither of whom were serving in the armed forces or the Merchant Navy; and in the privacy of their own homes, behind a locked door and with no one else on the premises. Residents of Scotland, Northern Ireland, the Channel Islands and the Isle of Man were not included. Cases involving group sex, cruising or sex in semi-public spaces could still get you arrested, and in fact police persecution of gay men was not only to continue for decades to come but became more fervent in some quarters. In Manchester, for example, James Anderton – chief constable from 1975 until 1991 – carried out a campaign of harassment of gay people, resurrecting a Victorian law to charge one venue where men danced together with 'licentious dancing' and investing considerable amounts of the police budget into surveillance of cruising grounds.

Tony Papard describes how for his boyfriend and their friends, the openness about homosexuality resulted in the police taking more of an interest in it:

George and his friends who were part of this prior to
the 1967 Act said this legislation led not to liberation,
but to a massive police clampdown. When it was all
underground and secret, and only the initiated few
knew about it, apparently all sorts of things went on in
the gay clubs. Once it became partly legalized, however,
any sex on the premises would cause a police raid and
probably closure. Even cottages became the subject of
more police raids following the Act.[8]

Tireless gay activist Peter Tatchell's research indicates that

the liberalisation of 1967 was not as liberal as many
people believe. An estimated 15,000–20,000 gay and
bisexual men were convicted in the decades that followed. That's because homosexuality was only partly
decriminalised. The remaining anti-gay laws were
policed even more aggressively than before, by a
State that continued to oppose LGBT acceptance and
equality.[9]

And despite the change to the law, attitudes did not change
overnight. Many gay people still lived in fear of their friends and
families finding out about their sexuality, and they continued
to be victims of homophobic abuse and violence. Various religious organizations continued to view homosexuality as a sin,
and as Terry Sanderson's MediaWatch column in *Gay Times*
magazine carefully documented over the 1980s and '90s, some
newspapers were unremittingly vile. But from this point on the
rules had changed – decriminalization enabled organization,

demonstration and education by and of gay people. There was now an openness and a sense of engagement that ran counter to the environment of fear and secrecy which had enabled Polari to flourish. David attributes this sense of openness to Polari's demise: 'I think it [Polari] stopped when the gay scene became so open. It changed incredibly.'

This openness also brought with it the establishment of a legal gay scene where money could legitimately be made by catering to a gay clientele and providing premises for them to socialize. John describes the change as follows:

> The gay culture suddenly became more open. There were established gay pubs and bars. Some of the big brewers actually stuck by and kept them open because they brought in revenue, the violence level was low ... so it wasn't an encumbrance or embarrassment or a burden to them. There were plenty of straight landlords, particularly women, who were quite prepared to run them, because they loved all the gay guys ... The actual culture of staying in this in-built language suddenly died out because there was nobody actually living it.

Partly due to frustration at the half-measure effect of the Sexual Offences Act, but also because the Act enabled gay people to collectivize in a way that had been difficult before, the Gay Liberation Front was established in the UK. Taking the lead from the riots in protest at the raiding of the Stonewall Tavern in Greenwich Village, New York, Hugh David dates Britain's first gay rights movement march as taking place in November 1970.[10] The GLF established a new language around homosexuality. They adopted the word *gay* as an identity label; it was a word that had been used for decades already by people who had sex with same-sex partners – particularly having an association with the upper classes and upmarket drinking establishments, as well as being popular in the U.S. since the 1950s.[11] Derived from a more positive concept, *gay* was felt to be less derogatory than *queer* and not as clinically Establishment as *homosexual*. It also could be an acronym that worked well on placards: Good As You. Along with *gay*, concepts like *gay pride*, *gay liberation* and *coming out* were developed and popularized by the GLF. This more politicized terminology was of a very different sort to the language used by Polari speakers, whose words were more about hiding one's sexuality while simultaneously assessing your chances of sex with whoever's just walked through the door.

The Gay Liberationists were young, educated and determined. Their views about political change and the world they wanted to live in were connected to, influenced by, and in some ways paralleled the Civil Rights and students' movements of the 1960s and the Women's Liberation movement of the 1960s and '70s.[12] Sexism in particular was seen as very strongly linked to homophobia, with the view that binary labels like *gay/straight* and *masculine/feminine* created hierarchies whereby some identities were constructed as better than others and thus awarded more power and privilege. Heterosexual men were seen as maintaining power by subordinating other identities, while mainstream society forced everyone into restrictive identity boxes. Gay Liberation was going to help people to break free of such narrow roles and express their bisexual, androgynous nature in equal relationships and social bonds.

Out and proud: members of the Gay Liberation Front

These new ideas about gender were a breath of fresh air, and many Liberationists helped to perpetuate a sense of pride and honesty about sexuality that had never been seen before. But some liberationists had problems with the 'old ways' of being gay, and as a result poor, politically incorrect, sex-obsessed Polari was to come in for particular criticism.

Backlash

The Gay Liberationists of the 1970s changed political thinking about homosexuality in a remarkable way. Before them, the most well-established gay rights group in Britain was the Campaign for Homosexual Equality. Beginning in 1954 as the North-Western Committee for Homosexual Law Reform, the CHE had similar goals to the hat-and-tie-wearing members of the Mattachine

Society in America, founded in Los Angeles in 1950. The CHE were equally respectable, their objective being assimilation into mainstream society rather than changing or challenging the status quo, whereas the GLF was more concerned with building a community around the notion of gay identity. The differing ideologies of the two groups sometimes resulted in clashes. However, neither organization was particularly supportive of the kinds of camp gay men who spoke Polari.

At best, camp was viewed as apolitical. David, in describing to me why Polari fell out of fashion, stated, 'People . . . They think it's silly, *naff*.' In the struggle for equality, camp was not seen as having much to contribute. A famous essay by Susan Sontag called 'Notes on "Camp"' in 1964 argued that a camp sensibility was 'disengaged, depoliticized or at least apolitical'.[13] Andrew Britton's critique of Sontag goes further, describing camp as an anaesthetic 'allowing one to remain inside oppressive relations while enjoying the illusory confidence that one is flouting them'.[14] No matter that it was camp men and drag queens who had fought back during the Stonewall riots, forming a line to do high-kicks à la The Rockettes (the female dancers at Radio City Music Hall). Gay Liberation saw homophobia and sexism as linked because gay men were viewed as being 'like women' in various ways (including being penetrated during sex or having 'feminine' qualities such as being gentle or interested in domestic activities). So the Liberationist perspective tended towards challenging the view that gay men were like women, which at times could override the aim of celebrating gender diversity and fluidity. By the 1990s, these early steps in the movement were being retrospectively viewed as not necessarily helpful, with

DISSENTING ADULTS

Placards at dawn: the Gay Liberation Front
and Campaign for Homosexual Equality

commentator Andy Medhurst writing that the Queer Theory 'take' on camp is that 'Sontag got it wrong'.[15] Indeed, as the next chapter will show, camp can be deliciously political. It can be anything it wants to be, really.

But Liberationist thinking of the time did not see things this way. Some aspects of camp were seen as degrading both to gay men and women. There was a view that if gay men acted like women, then they insulted women and mocked themselves. They were buying into the heterosexual man's lie that women were silly and weak by aping those characteristics – a bit like when black actors played stereotyped 'lazy slave' or Uncle Tom roles in films. The Gay Liberation Front Manifesto was written in 1971 and revised eight years later. It argued that gay people should be outside the boundaries of the gender system, but in taking on butch or femme roles they were simply continuing the oppression: 'those gay men and women who are caught up in the femme role must realise, as straight women increasingly do, that any security this brings is more than offset by their loss of freedom.'[16]

Increasingly, voices started to be heard from gay people who viewed camp as problematic. Here's a letter written to *Gay News* in 1976, published the year after the film version of Quentin Crisp's autobiography, *The Naked Civil Servant*:

[Quentin Crisp] has set the 'gay' world back twenty years . . . As far as I am concerned, being 'gay' means that I am perfectly normal, with one slight difference – I prefer to see another man. I can . . . see no point in trying to ape a female. There are a great deal like me. Our local has a good number of 'affairs' and although in the 'Camp' life it would be boring, our lovers chat about food, clothes and the men about cars, television etc, just as normal couples do . . . There is no need to slap us and the hets in the face with 'high camp' . . . Quentin, keep it to yourself. No need to write books about it, have it on the box. Who wants to know?[17]

One of my interviewees, Sidney, recalls that around this period 'people were recoiling from effeminacy'. Camp entertainers who had broken into the mainstream came under criticism, with John Inman and Larry Grayson both coming in for particular flak. Had Julian and Sandy still been around in the 1970s, it's likely that they would have copped it too. As actress Maureen Lipman stated, '[They] were no threat – they weren't going to steal your husband or demand equality.'[18]

In the book of the television series *Are You Being Served?* David Walker, a campaigner for gay rights since 1969, remarks on John Inman's role:

When this flamboyant image screamed across the screen, it was like a nail in the coffin of what we were trying to achieve. The majority of people saw gay men as being very waspish, skipping around the place with limp wrists, and that's exactly what they saw on *Are You Being Served?* Of course there were protests, because if you want a large section of the community to be accepted, sending them up like that does no end of damage.[19]

Oh, the drama of it all! John Inman was picketed at a concert performance and there was a campaign to have his character taken off the air, as this article from the *Daily Express* describes:

Are you being unfair? Actor John Inman – 'I'm free' – has angered homosexuals with his portrayal of the limp-wristed shop assistant, Mr Humphries, in the B.B.C. TV series 'Are You Being Served?' Members of the Campaign for Homosexual Equality plan to picket his concert appearances in protest over the mincing high-pitched voiced Mr Humphries. They began their protest at Brighton by handing out leaflets before his show at the town's Dome Centre Hall. A campaign official said yesterday: 'He is contributing to the television distortion of the image of homosexuals.' They complained that he depicts homosexuals as . . . sexually obsessed, too extravagant in manner and too keen to dress up in drag.[20]

There were few gay characters in the mainstream media at the time, but those who did appear usually followed the Julian and Sandy model – funny or eccentric, not overtly political, archly feminine. It drove some of the Gay Liberationists mad – they hated what they saw as the silly behaviour, the 'effeminacy', the use of drag which made fun of women. Looking back on it, they wanted to educate the public that many gay men were not flamboyant or camp – and those stereotypes stung, with the men who perpetuated them being seen as complicit with the enemy. However, maybe there was a bit of internalized homophobia going on there, too. A fear that maybe a few of the stereotypes weren't always short of the mark. One thing is certain: the Liberationists brought a lot of baggage with them on their political journey – understandable considering what they had grown up with and what was still going on. Equality was still a very long way off. But where did that leave Polari?

> camp is a form of minstrellisation . . . parlare is a product of a culture that is deeply ambivalent and even while it celebrates effeminacy, 'obviousness' and casual promiscuous sexuality (precisely the elements that the straight world most abhors) [it] can never really accept that these are good . . . The terms of address that are distinctively gay are always used in a negative mocking way: 'Ooh, get you Duchess'.[21]

The feminist writer Mary McIntosh published the above analysis of Polari in the CHE-based *Lunch* magazine in 1972 (the word *lunch* was used by Polari speakers to refer to a man's crotch). I think McIntosh is right in that she identifies a kind of ambivalence in Polari – a mixture of attack and defence, demon-strating affection through insult, laughing at dark circumstances; Polari is nothing if not complicated. McIntosh's article reflects this, recognizing that 'in some groups there is a reluctance to abstain altogether from parlare; it represents after all, whatever warmth and solidarity the gay world was able to create'.

McIntosh was not herself against Polari although her article indicated an acknowledgement of a growing debate around the role of camp in the brave new world of Gay Liberation pol-itics. However, shortly afterwards *Lunch* published a follow-up article by another writer, Jonathan Raban, which, although not referring to Polari explicitly, gave the thumbs-down to gay slang:

> Gay slang is a means of group self-advertisement; like full drag or the one-piece leather suit, it is a succinct way of putting one's propensities on show. In large cities . . . we all have to do this to some extent; we have to communicate with others with brevity and speed, in an instant code of badges and symbols. But the obvious trap facing any member of a recognisable minority is that his symbols will consume him; that his identity will disappear into the narrow funnel of his clothes and slang. He will become no more than a shrill mouthpiece for a sectarian lobby, determined, in the case of the homosexual, by a language of body parts and fucking . . . Isn't it time for everybody to tidy their toys away, to put the old uniforms in the trunk in the attic, or donate them to Oxfam, and to take a few, at least, of the bricks out of the walls of the ghetto?[22]

There were also concerns that some of the words in Polari propagated racist and sexist values. The linguistic drag involving pronoun switching and appropriation of female names raised a question relating to what role gay men had for women in their worldview. Some camp men had viewed women as rivals for the masculine straight men they desired, particularly when they began to be employed on cruise ships, while a word used by some Polari speakers, *fish*, was used disparagingly and dismissively to refer to women. Additionally, there were words that categorized people according to their nationality, ethnicity or sexual preferences for such people, leaving the whiff of racism behind. *Schvartza* meant black man and *chinois* referred to a Chinese person. Additionally *dinge* meant black and a *dinge queen* was a man who liked black men. The author Michael Carson demonstrates the rather dismissive attitude that some Polari speakers had towards different races in his semiautobiographical 1988 novel *Sucking Sherbet Lemons*. The book's teenage protagonist, Benson, encounters an older gay man at the local library when he is looking at a book called *Tribes of the Southern Sudan*: 'When I saw you having a vada in the dinge section, I said to myself, Andrea – my name's Andy in real life actually, dear – Andrea, I said to myself, there's a gay one if ever I saw one.'[23]

I occasionally encountered attitudes that could be viewed as reductive, sexualizing and dismissive towards black and Asian men when I interviewed older (white) Polari speakers, which always put me in a bind, as the speakers were doing me a favour by agreeing to be interviewed. I was supposed to listen, rather than judge them. The goal was to give them a voice, but I worried that they might come under criticism if

I didn't filter out attitudes that were now widely seen as unacceptable. Such views were more commonly voiced in the past, as well as being more widespread across all sections of society. Julia Stanley in an article about gay slang written in 1974 notes that 'although gay slang is the vocabulary of people who are themselves outcasts from the straight culture, it is also sexist, classist and racist, and the existence of terms that reflect such attitudes binds us to the same value system that makes us outcasts'.[24] And in 1981, Gregg Blachford claimed that one of the reasons why homosexuals were rejected for not fitting into a prescribed pattern of masculine behaviour was their use of language:

> their slang ties them to the dominant order and offers no challenge to a society which labels all homosexuals as deviants and oppresses them as such, although effeminate homosexuals are more likely to be singled out for the brunt of any attack because of their visibility.[25]

The sense of sexual objectification afforded by Polari could also be seen as problematic. I previously noted how the pronoun *it* referred to an anonymous or casual sexual partner, and that words like *chicken* positioned younger gay men as food to be consumed. Within the context of gossip and cruising, the wide set of evaluative adjectives in Polari reduced people to whether they were hot or not. A term like *antique homie palone* might raise a laugh but there is also something dismissive about it, suggesting that older gay men were to be reviled or ignored. This is not specific to Polari speakers, nor did such attitudes go away because people stopped using Polari. A look at a website like Douchebags of Grindr indicates that, if anything, ageism and racism among gay people, especially in cruising contexts, is just as pervasive as it has ever been. And with some online dating apps enabling people to filter out other users according to their age and race, such people can become literally invisible in a way that was not the case when cruising happened face to face.

Some Gay Liberationists were aware of the ageist hierarchy within the established subculture and they wrote of it scathingly:

> gay men are very apt to fall victim to the cult of youth
> – those sexual parades in the 'glamorous' meat-rack
> bars of London and New York, those gay beaches of
> the South of France and Los Angeles haven't anything
> to do with liberation . . . these gay men dread the
> approach of age, because to be old is to be 'ugly' and
> with their youth they lose also the right to love and be
> loved, and are valued only if they can pay.[26]

Gay Liberationists problematized the older gay men who held such attitudes, although this could perhaps be interpreted as them rejecting such men too, and perpetuating the attitudes they criticized. The irony! It was certainly the case that as the 1960s and '70s progressed, the men who'd spoken Polari in the 1950s when they were younger were not young any more. Sidney characterizes Polari as an 'old person's language' by this point, while Jim E aptly describes the feeling among many younger gay men in the 1970s:

A lot of younger people didn't want to associate with older people, which to some extent I can understand, because I went to discos, when I was, 20, 22, 23, I didn't want someone who was 50 or 60 there. It was all right in a pub, but you wanted to let your hair down and go . . . But when you've got some old chap who's greatly overweight, with 15 double chins, he's got a naff haircut and is half bald, in green leather trousers and Hush Puppies and a white shirt, it doesn't work, and . . . it's like sitting next to a family in an airport when the children are screaming, you might be going first class but it ruins the whole flight. These things do make a difference.

The Gay Liberation movement was associated with young people, linked to the student protest movements of the 1960s. And as the 1970s progressed Polari was increasingly viewed as outdated and unnecessary, a camp hangover from a sad period in gay history where people had to hide in corners and men parodied women, objectified or judged one another and lusted after heterosexual-identifying men who might use them if there was nothing else around. Polari had become *naff* – a way of marking yourself as uncool, old-fashioned, and old, old, old. And a new way of being gay was now on offer – one that was about as far away from Polari as you could get.

The subcultural cringe

Gender fluidity did flourish in some quarters in the 1970s, especially among pop stars like David Bowie and Mick Jagger, who typified the androgynous, make-up-wearing, strutting, sexually ambiguous identities that were popular with both straight and gay audiences, and were eventually incorporated into the rebellious punk look of the mid- to late 1970s. As a result of counter-cultural and hippie fashions in the late 1960s, most men wore their hair longer than they would do after the 1980s. But while a few straight men felt freer to experiment with feminine fashions, many gay men were starting to move in the opposite direction. The following is a (hilarious) letter of complaint about the state of the nude male models who appeared in another one of those briefly existing gay magazines, *Quorum*:

> why so many with women's hairdos? A true homosexual prefers to look upon a virile physique with a clean-cut aspect of a real man in every respect – not a male body with a top-heavy head of feminine hair.[27]

Earlier, I quoted drag queen Lorri Lee who, in a 1981 documentary, gave a breakdown of the different types of queens. This lesson ended on a slightly sour note:

> You've got a new type of queen that seemed to hit the scene just lately, they're what we call the clone queens. Now the clone queens, they all look like each other, strange enough, every one, they're like an army of queens, they've got the short haircut, the little moustaches, the check shirt, and the faded blue jeans with the bovver boots and they're all going around spitting: 'Alright mate?' But they all do it, one spits, they all

A clone of your own: Tom of Finland drawings

spit, like a little crowd of sheep. And I suppose they find their security in numbers. There's no originality among those sort of people. If you're an individual you're definitely out.[28]

Clone queens, or clones, were the polar opposite of drag queens, although just like drag queens, they also engaged in a kind of theatre – aping a stylized, over-the-top type of masculinity as opposed to the hyper-realized and sometimes surreal femininity of the drag acts. Clones wanted to be Tom of Finland cartoons come to life – they were the precursors of the masc4masc profiles that were to become popular in twenty-first-century gay dating apps like Grindr. No wonder this put the noses of queens such as Lorri Lee, who suddenly had a lot of (younger) competition for the masculine men she desired, out of joint.

The term *cultural cringe* is sometimes used when one society begins to reject aspects of its own culture and instead appropriates elements of another culture which it looks up to, and something akin to this was starting to happen to British gay subculture from the 1970s onwards. The clone identity referred to so disparagingly by Lorri was imported from America. As James Gardiner writes, 'The American West Coast was Mecca for European queens in the 1970s; American-butch the dominant gay style.'[29] In the 1970s, British gay men started taking advantage of the fact that cheap flights to America were offered by the private no-frills airline Laker Airways, run by entrepreneur Freddie Laker. American gay subculture was more advanced, complete and self-promoting than the British one, and it provided a political and cultural template for British gay men.[30] With well-established gay scenes in cities like New York, San Francisco and Los Angeles, British men discovered a fashion for hyper-masculinity or 'butchness', as epitomized by the Marlboro Man in cigarette advertisements. Derek Ogg describes the effect that Laker's flights had on the British gay scene:

Clones, clones and more clones: the Castro, 1977

People were wearing hard construction helmets and cut-off jeans and work boots with rolled down socks and skimpy T-shirts in Scotland, in a climate which even in the summertime is pretty appalling . . . We felt international, we felt being gay was a passport to anywhere in the world . . . I don't think that he [Freddie Laker] knows how many young gay guys he flew virginally across the Atlantic to America to be absolutely stunned and astonished by the scene they saw over there. They brought back from the States a lot of the music and a lot of the attitudes, a lot of the politics and a lot of the social dynamics of the American gay scene.[31]

The fashion was for tight buttoned-up Levi's jeans, chaps, leather clothing, work boots, checked shirts or uniforms. Hairstyles were closely cropped (no more 'top-heavy heads of feminine hair'), accompanied by a sizeable moustache, while chest hair was on display through the top of an unbuttoned shirt or a tight, low-riding vest. And from the 1980s, chest hair was shaved off to allow gym-worked musculature to be displayed. Films like *Cruising* (1980) starring Al Pacino depict the clone 'look', while the pop group the Village People dressed as masculine stereotypes: cowboy, leather-man, construction worker, sailor and Native American, singing songs like 'Macho Man', 'Y.M.C.A.' and 'In the Navy' – offering a vision of a masculine, all-male, highly sexed environment. And as noted, going to the gym to build muscles became increasingly popular. Hugh David describes this change in definitions of gay masculinity as the result of 'burgeoning self-confidence' which 'ineradicably replaced the simpering Julian and Sandy stereotype',[32] and importantly, the expectations around gay relationships that gay men had were also to change. Like the earlier identity of 'trade', clones were also masculine, but while trade would have gay sex (when it suited them) and didn't identify as gay, clones *did* identify as gay. However, both clones and queens preferred masculine partners. The old queen–trade or butch–femme relationships were seen as problematic through Liberationist eyes, and so clones were a kind of merging of queen and trade into a 'new, improved' identity, both masculine and gay – desirable and desired. Gay pornography increasingly focused on butch men having sex with one another, and queens became desexualized.

In America, clones developed a rudimentary visual code for communicating sexual interests, based around displaying a coloured handkerchief from one of the pockets of their jeans. In the context of 1970s gay bars and discos, where loud music wouldn't always have facilitated conversation, the code supposedly provided men with a short cut to finding the perfect partner for the night. Worn on the left side, the hanky indicated that someone was active or a 'giver', while the right meant passive or 'receiver'. The colours corresponded to different preferences with slight variants in shade resulting in completely different meanings – robin's-egg blue, light blue, teal blue, navy blue and medium blue referred, respectively, to sixty-nining (mutual oral sex), regular oral sex, cock and ball torture, fucking and sex with policemen. God forbid that, like me, you suffered from colour-blindness, and despite the macho posturing of the clones, those references to specific colours like teal blue and robin's-egg blue make me think that the whole system must have been thought up by a gaggle of fussy interior designers clutching swatches. Equally, for Colin Spencer the 'butch imagery' was just as much an act as the make-up worn by Quentin Crisp or Peter Burton – the result of gay men caricaturing a society that still excluded them.[33]

Over the years, I've been contacted by a handful of Americans who were familiar with Polari, but on the whole it was not taken up in the u.s., although a case could be made for a few overlapping words between Polari and commonly used American gay slang, and we have seen how some words of American slang did penetrate Polari's lexicon during the Second World War. It has increasingly been American gay slang that has influenced the language used by gay people in the UK, though. Take, for example, the word *chicken*. The term had become unfashionable by the end of the 1990s and in the UK young gay men are now instead referred to as *twinks*, a u.s. slang word that comes from an American cream-filled

sponge cake called a Twinkie. The sexualizing food metaphor still holds, but now we refer to our young gay men as
American confectionary. The term *come out*, popularized by
Gay Liberationists, is derived from a longer phrase, *come out
of the closet* – originally U.S. slang which referred to revealing a secret. However, in Britain we normally do not use the
word *closet*, preferring *wardrobe* or *cupboard*. Polari speakers
had their own way of referring to men who kept their sexuality a secret – *black market queens*, a term that echoed the
secret, illegal economy that thrived during the Second World
War – although as time wore on this term fell into disuse and
was replaced by the Americanized *closet queen*. The switch
perhaps also reflects the tendency for slang to time-stamp its
users – and who was going to be turned on by someone still
using Second World War slang from decades ago?

Even the old Polari word *bold*, a favourite of Julian and
Sandy, gets little attention these days. Instead, there are different words, coming out of the Harlem drag queen scene and
popularized by the American television reality show *RuPaul's
Drag Race* – *fierce* and *sassy*. They are not direct translations
of *bold* but they're close enough, perhaps reflecting the change
from when to be obviously gay was an act of courage to a time
when it indicates a different kind of power.

~

It wasn't a single event or social change that resulted in gay
people largely abandoning Polari between the 1960s and
1970s, but rather an interacting set of factors, including the
decriminalization of homosexuality, the start of Gay Liberation,
mainstream exposure of Polari through Julian and Sandy,

influences from America, and the ageing and/or deaths of earlier generations of speakers. In the UK, the amount of social change between the end of the Second World War and the end of the 1970s was huge, with views around homosexuality and ways of being gay subject to considerable flux. Polari, useful in a more repressive time, was a casualty of this social change. However, the end of the 1970s could be seen as the beginning of a different, more oppressive period in LGBT history – so perhaps this would mean a further role for Polari.

At the outset of the 1980s, the promise of liberation was horrifically stalled when gay men started dying as a result of contracting a virus which was named as HIV (human immunodeficiency virus). Initially identified in American cities with large gay populations, the virus suppressed immune systems, leading people to die from opportunistic infections that in their late stages were referred to as AIDS (acquired immune deficiency syndrome). The virus was found in semen and blood, surviving in airtight conditions. Sharing needles, receiving blood transfusions and condomless anal or vaginal sex were the chief ways that HIV could be passed on. By 1994, in the UK there were 26,939 reported cases of people with HIV and 11,516 people diagnosed with AIDS, and 8,901 people had died as a result of AIDS-related complications.[34] Gay communities around the world showed a remarkable amount of cohesiveness, bravery and kindness in their response to the disease, although reactions from governments, the media and the public were sometimes motivated by ignorance and prejudice. In particular, some British tabloid journalists wrote appalling things about gay people in the 1980s[35] while the government passed a contentious law (Section 28) which forbade the 'promotion of

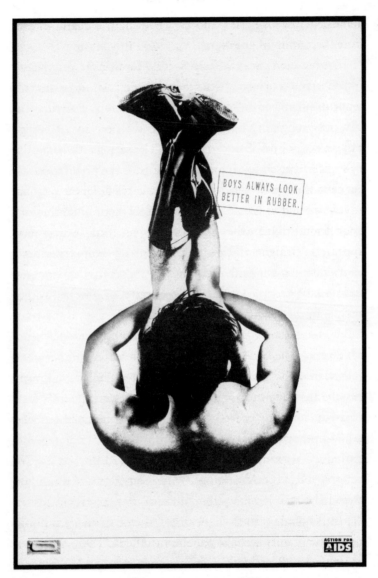

AIDS prevention poster, c. 1995

homosexuality' by local authorities, essentially banning schools from discussion of gay issues.

During the 1980s public attitudes towards homosexuality considerably worsened, with British Social Attitudes surveys reporting an increase in people saying that homosexuality was 'always wrong'. In 1983, 50 per cent of people answered this way; it was 54 per cent in 1984, then 59 per cent in 1985. By 1987, it had risen to almost two-thirds of the population: 64 per cent of people.[36] My own research carried out on personal adverts posted in *Gay Times* between the 1970s and the year 2000 found that in the 1980s there was an obsession with appearing 'straight-acting', 'non-camp' and 'non-scene', with many gay men stressing their butch bodies, jobs and hobbies, and seeming keen to put distance between themselves and other gay people.[37] HIV-AIDS and the wider response to it had contributed to a return to the intolerant views of the 1950s – but with a few differences. There was now much more discussion and awareness of homosexuality, so unless you went all the way into the closet, it was harder to keep your sexuality to yourself. Polari did not thrive during the 1980s, then – its camp qualities generally continued to make it superfluous to requirements during a period when the imperative was to be butch. And so not only did people's proficiency in Polari gradually erode, but knowledge that the language even existed began to be lost.

In November 2000, I got to set one of the daily polls on a gay community website called outintheuk. The majority of its users were British gay men in their thirties. I asked users of the site what their opinion of Polari was, giving five options. Eight hundred and sixteen people responded. The results of the poll are telling of the state of Polari at the start of the new millennium. Half of the site's users had never heard of it. Just under a quarter (23 per cent) thought it was an 'interesting piece of gay heritage'. Then there were three options that each received 10 per cent of the vote: it was 'harmless nonsense', 'due a revival' or 'old fashioned and encourages men to act camp so should never be brought back'.

Around the same time, a free gay newspaper called *Boyz* ran a debate about Polari that lasted for three issues.[38] Transcripts of phone calls to the paper's telephone service were published, and a *Boyz* editorial also gave an opinion. The debate began in June 1999 with a reader's view that 'camp words . . . such as lallies, bona and trade . . . [should be] consigned to the annals of gay history'. The reader called these words an embarrassment and a result of gay people carrying 'suppressed baggage' as the new millennium approached. In the following issue another reader agreed:

about that palare thing: too fucking right. Get rid of that bollocks and drag, and Kylie and little tight-arsed queens in T-shirts that don't reach down to their waist. I mean, some of them'd be half decent looking if they wiped all that shit off their faces and put away the feather boas. John Inman's bastard love children they are. It's 1999 for God's sake – are we really going into the millennium as overly-eager-to-please 70s sitcom characters, or as modern-thinking and behaving men?

However, another reader suggested that Polari detractors lighten up and noted, 'Why should we forget the days when gays were suppressed into using gay sign talk? It's part of our history . . . stop getting your lallies in a lather and find yourself some bona trade.' Another reader agreed, arguing, 'It's part of our heritage, and it was a language that was made up by gay men that were closeted so that they could communicate. Why should we turn our back on that? We should respect and remember them.' In the third week a reader rather bitchily remarked that it was notable that the two men who wanted to keep Polari 'live in the sticks', although three more readers phoned in to be supportive of Polari and camp men. Finally, *Boyz* magazine weighed in, siding with the men who disliked Polari, describing it as having no relevance for the year 2000 and calling it 'an attempt to play the benign, neutered, eager-to-please comedy "poof" for acceptance in the straight world'. The article viewed Polari as only spoken by elderly gentlemen and predicted that one day it would be regarded like the 1970s comedian Benny Hill, whose Chinaman impersonations are now seen as unforgivably racist. The article ends with the following:

> palare is evil. Lisping with a limp wrist and 'kicking up your lallies' to old hi-nrg isn't being 'zhoosy' or an act of agit-prop defiance, it just upsets your mother and makes you deeply unattractive to most other gay men. Spout your palare all you like, but live somewhere far, far away from us . . . like 1954.

I suspect that some elements of the *Boyz* debate may have been manufactured for controversy and that the editorial in particular was a bit tongue-in-cheek, especially considering the fact that it slipped in the Polari phrase 'your mother'. But the attitudes it expressed covered many of the views on Polari and the people who spoke it that had been coalescing since decriminalization in the late 1960s. The association of Polari with old men, camp men and, increasingly, men who lived in unfashionable parts of the UK ('the sticks') confirmed that it was seen as uncool and unattractive, while another set of speakers viewed it as historically relevant or still rather fun. These last two attitudes form the basis for the following chapter, which explains why Polari, or at least interest in it, still hasn't died completely but in fact started to undergo a revival in the 1990s. However, the form of this revival and the types of people who engaged in it are going to take us a very long way from the original set of speakers. Hang on to your handbag – things are about to get very strange.

7

She's Ready for Her Comeback

It is 2013 (I'm now 41), and my partner wants to go to Stoke-on-Trent for the weekend to see something called the Staffordshire Hoard – the largest collection of Anglo-Saxon gold ever found. We arrive at the Potteries Museum and Art Gallery but it is closed because Tony Robinson from *Time Team* is making a television programme about it, so we are told to come back tomorrow. It is our first time in Stoke so we decide to wander around the town centre a bit and eventually happen upon a slightly run-down area that has optimistically been called the Cultural Quarter. There are a few shops and cafes. Then I see it – the words 'Polari Lounge' above a shop front. In my head, an angelic chorus starts playing.

'What is this place?' I ask in genuine, non-ironic, childlike wonderment.

We go in. It is an LGBT-friendly cafe which has opened recently, with council funding and, if I've remembered correctly, a donation provided by pop star and local lad Robbie Williams. There are pamphlets on the tables describing what Polari is – and my dictionary is listed as a source of information. I am swooning with excitement. This is impact with a capital I, the equivalent

The Polari Lounge,
Stoke-on-Trent

of the Holy Grail for increasingly harried twenty-first-century academics who are now required to justify their existence.

I go up to the counter and order two coffees. The young man, barely twenty, who serves me, doesn't look at me. My default personality is shy but I want to talk to him. I'm so pleased. And I have so many questions.

'This place!' I say. 'I did a PhD on Polari! I wrote a book about it!'

No response.

'That's me!' I point at the leaflet.

'That's nice,' says the man serving. 'I'll bring the coffees over when they're ready.'

I go back to our table, deflated.

'But that's me!' I say again. 'This is my PhD come to life as a cafe!'

'He probably didn't think any of this up. It's just a job for him,' consoles my husband.

We drink our coffees and leave. I remember how in the 1990s, I never had trouble getting people to talk to me about Polari. I catch sight of my reflection on the way out and realize I am now middle-aged, and I announce this fact mournfully.

My husband says: 'Look love, we've given up a weekend to see some bits of metal that someone's dug up from a field. Of course you're middle-aged. And I hate to be the one to tell you but you've been middle-aged for quite some time. I make it at least since 1997.'

About a year later I check and the Polari Lounge appears to have closed down. Maybe it was something related to their customer service training. Still, it is Stoke's loss. And Polari's.

~

When we last left Polari, at the end of the previous chapter, it was pretty much over. It isn't going too far to say that Polari had virtually become a dead language. Perhaps that's no big deal. It's happened before and will happen again. People stop using languages and they die and are forgotten, or crop up in very restricted contexts. However, despite Polari reaching the end of its shelf life around the start of the 1970s, this wasn't the end of the story. In fact, things were going to take an interesting turn after that point, with Polari undergoing not exactly a full revival but a revival of interest, resulting in various groups of people using it, in very different ways and for very different reasons compared to the original set of speakers. Some of the activities around Polari that I'll relate in this chapter give me the distinct impression that that it's gone on a rather different journey to many languages that undergo the process of language death. I don't want to argue that Polari has been revived and is now flouncing around as a kind of camp zombie language, but rather that there's become a kind of death cult around it. It is worshipped, there are myths that are told about it, there are rituals, and it even feels as if it is imbued with the magical power to grant fame and fortune to a select few.

But let's rewind a bit to the start of the 1990s when there were still pockets of people speaking Polari around the UK, many who are now of retirement age. Gradually, over the 1990s, life was starting to improve for gay people. The age of consent for gay male sexual intercourse was lowered from twenty-one to eighteen in 1994 (still not equal with heterosexual people – that wouldn't come for another six years – but it is a step in the right direction). The discovery of combination therapies meant that the life expectancies of people who had HIV were greatly lengthened in many cases. Gay people slowly started to crop up more often in mainstream television and film, coming in a wider set of flavours. There were also a number of television programmes aimed at gay audiences. In the late 1980s, Channel 4 launched *Out on Tuesday*, a weekly rather highbrow documentary programme (later called *Summer's Out* or *Out*), while BBC2 followed a few years later with the more populist *GayTime TV*. In 1999, Channel 4 broadcast a gay drama serial, *Queer as Folk*. The press started to be occasionally nice about gay people, or at least were not consistently horrible. Part of this change is the response to HIV-AIDS from within the gay community itself and the fact that the homophobic backlash of the previous decade prompted mobilization among those communities on a grand scale. Organizations like Stonewall, Outrage, the Terrence Higgins Trust and the Sisters of Perpetual Indulgence were responsible for lobbying for changes to the law, taking the media to task for its homophobia and distributing information about HIV and safe sex. And this last group in particular were also at the vanguard of Polari's rehabilitation, using it in a completely new way, challenging established thinking that camp was not political.

High Polari

The Sisters of Perpetual Indulgence, who we met earlier in the book, are another American import, being founded in the U.S. in the 1970s. Put simply, they are a loose-knit organization of men across several cities who dress as nuns. In the U.S. they were one of the first groups to mobilize in the fight against HIV-AIDS, handing out leaflets about safe sex in areas like the Castro in San Francisco. Their members can be viewed on several levels – as drag queens, as ministering to the spiritual needs of LGBT communities, or as political activists who wish to parody, question or reclaim traditional notions of 'virtue'. During the last decades of the twentieth century some mainstream religious organizations had slightly softened their harsh views about LGBT people, preaching a message of loving the sinner but hating the sin – effectively disallowing gay relationships while trying to come across as inclusive and loving, a strategy also known as 'having your (hateful) cake and eating it'. Notable exceptions to this rule included more accepting groups like the

Metropolitan Community Church and the Quakers. Whether we believe in some form of higher power or not, religious organizations have, at times, provided people with a sense of social cohesion and a way of marking important life events with rituals around births, marriages and deaths. Gay people have often been excluded from such rituals or have had to hide their sexuality in order to participate in mainstream religion. On the other hand, with its emphasis on the physical, it's possible to criticize some aspects of the gay subcultures of the twentieth century (and indeed the present) for downplaying spirituality. The Sisters therefore help to redress this imbalance for gay men by placing an overtly gay twist on religion – mocking and questioning the intolerance of mainstream religions while simultaneously creating a religious arena for gay men which is both tolerant of male-male desire and camp, and able to meet the different spiritual needs of individual gay men. By the 1990s, there were Orders in Canterbury, London, Manchester, Nottingham, Newcastle, Oxford and Scotland.

Same-sex relationships were not legally recognized in the UK in the 1990s, meaning that partners of loved ones would have no automatic inheritance rights, no visiting rights in hospitals and no say in how funerals should be conducted. The ceremonies carried out by the Sisters both pointed out this institutional homophobia and provided a framework by which LGBT people could celebrate or console one another at times of great joy or sadness. Their ceremonies included marriages and house blessings, and they also named notable LGBT figures as saints, including Harvey Milk, Peter Tatchell and Armistead Maupin. One such canonization was carried out on the film-maker Derek Jarman (unlike in Christianity, the

Sisters sometimes canonized living people), with the ceremony conducted by the London House at his home in Dungeness in 1991. An aspect of some of these ceremonies involves the use of what the sisters refer to as 'High Polari'. One of the Sisters I interviewed had the following to say about the motivation behind Polari's use:

Dolly [one of the Sisters] was concerned that because camp is unfashionable with the younger gays and radical queers, Polari would just be lost. The other motivation was that the Sisters of Perpetual Indulgence were thinking of conducting their ceremonies in Polari, mirroring mass being conducted in Latin. Ultimately, we decided that having ceremonies that no one but the celebrants understood wasn't helpful (just as the Church had done!). We do use a little Polari in ceremonies, for the exotic feel, but we're careful to make sure people can get the meaning from context.

As a 'dead language', Polari is to gay men what Latin is to Catholics. Here's an excerpt from the canonization of Derek Jarman:

Sissies and Omies and palonies of the Gathered Faithful, we're now getting to the kernel, the nub, the very thrust of why we're gathered here today at Derek's bona bijou lattie. The reason being that Dezzie, bless his heart-face, is very dear to our heart. Look at him, his little lallies trembling with anticipation, heart of gold, feet of lead, and a knob of butter. So, perhaps we could take a little time to reach out and touch, to handle for a moment Dezzie's collective parts.[1]

And the following is an excerpt of a blessing or prayer taken from a website (now closed) run by Sister Muriel of London:

May all our dolly Sisters & Brothers in the order receive multee orgasmic visitations from the spirit of Queer Power in 1998,

May you have multee guilt free charvering from now until 'The Victory To Come',

May our fight against homophobia and in-bred stigmatization bring forth a new millenium of love & freedom,

May our blessed Order Of Perpetual Indulgence continue to breed new and delicious acolytes across the world,

May we never forget our nearest & dearest who have been lost to us by HIV/AIDS,

May we not forget those who are living with it day by day,

May we as Sisters encourage all those with the fear of opening the closet door to have the courage to get their hands on that door-knob,

May we all continue to bring joy to the gathered faithful when we manifest together on the streets,

May Perpetual Indulgence always be our aim, and may the blessings of this beloved Celtic house be upon you and your happy parts now and forever.

Ahhhhh-men!

High Polari differs from the more informal versions of Polari spoken in private conversations or the scripted version spoken by Julian and Sandy, in that it occurs in a mock-ceremonial, sermonizing and ritualistic context. Despite this, it retains the same sense of camp and innuendo, although alongside this is a sense of celebration and pride, which suggests a more political stance. The sense of subversion of mainstream values and humour remains the same as in the old uses though. Ian Lucas writes that the Sisters' use of Polari was

> one of the structuring elements of the ceremony; it helped formalize responses between the Sister Celebrant and the Gathered Faithful. In this sense, it helped define the event itself. Responses were conditioned and directed through the formal use of Polari . . . For those members who were unsure about the sincerity of the canonization, the use of Polari offered a refuge, a semi-comprehensible sanctioning and mystifying of the Event.[2]

As mentioned earlier, the Polari dictionary sent to me by one of the Sisters contained lots of words that were taken from Cant, one of the earliest linguistic relatives of Polari, but it had little direct acknowledgement of the Polari words that were used by many of the speakers in the 1950s. Thus, although High Polari is a later instantiation of Polari, it actually contains words taken from much older sources.

The use of High Polari by the Sisters indicates there had been something of a turnaround in terms of the relationship that gay men had with camp in the post-liberation era. Andy

Medhurst has described how rumours of the death of camp have been somewhat exaggerated:

> Camp . . . was weaned on surviving disdain – she's a tenacious old tigress of a discourse well versed in defending her corner. If decades of homophobic pressure had failed to defeat camp, what chance did a mere reorganization of subcultural priorities stand?[3]

And far from being apolitical, some campaigners for gay rights, reacting to inadequacies in political responses to the HIV-AIDS crisis, recognized and redeployed camp strategies in a political stance that was difficult to ignore by using equal amounts of humour and outrage to disseminate its message. A good example of this is the way in which camp was sometimes deployed at funerals of gay men who had died of HIV-AIDS, mixing outrage with celebration.

Perhaps we have to acknowledge the timing in Polari's journey from being seen as silly, apolitical and even politically incorrect in the 1970s to its deployment in a serious political campaign in the 1990s. A lot had happened in the twenty years between these points, and there was now enough distance from Polari's heyday for it no longer to arouse such a virulent sense of disapproval among this new crop of political activists. The Liberationists of the 1970s can come across as a little bit earnest – well-intentioned but keen to be taken seriously – and some wanted to distance themselves from aspects of gay culture that marked people as stereotypically gay. Part of this, I think, was due to growing up in a homophobic climate themselves, when camp, pathetic or villainous gay characters were the only

On the throne: the London House of the Sisters of Perpetual Indulgence
canonize Derek Jarman, Dungeness, 1991

representations available to them. But in rejecting Polari and
camp, they were rejecting aspects of their culture, and it feels
like a shame that they only saw the negatives. The next generation of gay activists viewed things a little differently. By now
there was more of a sense of an established gay culture with
its own history that was beginning to be properly documented.
The testimonies of older people were starting to be taken seriously as opposed to the feeling that they had little to tell us
and we needed to move on from them as quickly as possible.

And homophobia had not gone away after Gay Liberation.
If anything, the lesson of the 1980s was that things were going
to get worse for gay people, and the tragedy of HIV-AIDS, rather
than giving those in power the chance to embrace and console,
had simply unleashed knee-jerk moralizing, tabloid scorn and
Section 28.

Camp enabled gay activists to rehabilitate aspects of their culture and history that had been sidelined – and, importantly, it injected a bit of much-needed fun and light-heartedness back into political activism. Just as the gay men of the 1950s had used Polari to laugh in the face of arrest, blackmail and bashing, the campaigners of the early 1990s incorporated Polari as a way of defying closed-minded politicians and showing that even in the shadow of HIV-AIDS it was possible to squeeze in a camp innuendo. Derek Jarman died of an AIDS-related illness in 1994, aged 52. During a time when there was considerable stigma around HIV-AIDS, Jarman's canonization by the Sisters, including the touching of his 'collective parts', is indicative of a kindness and a desire to destigmatize that was sorely lacking in other quarters. And as always when Polari is used, there is that sense of the mocking of earnestness, the back-handed compliment, the toppling of the idol. Ian Lucas notes that

> at the same time as Derek Jarman, as a person living with AIDS, was having his own body revered he was also the object of ridicule. He had become through the use of Polari in an irreligious manner, the site of the sacred and the profane. This was furthered by the Crowning of the Saint with a 'bona helmet on his riah' and a necklace made of cock-rings and pornographic pictures.[4]

Jarman took these aspects of the ceremony in his stride, though, and viewed his canonization as an important event in his life.

A slightly different view of Polari's rehabilitation links to the notion of fashion cycles. In 1937, fashion historian James

Laver devised a law which charted how attitudes towards a particular fashion change over time. For example, when something is ahead of fashion and yet to be adopted by the masses, it is often viewed as indecent, shameless or outré. Once it becomes fashionable it is seen as smart, but after that, attitudes start to become more negative. After one year it is dowdy, after ten years hideous, and after twenty years it is ridiculous. But then something interesting happens, and gradually the fashion is rediscovered and reappraised. At thirty years it is amusing, at fifty it is quaint, then it is charming at seventy, romantic at a hundred and beautiful at 150.⁵ We can't fully apply Laver's Law to Polari as I'm not sure that the exact numbers would work perfectly, but it has certainly gone through some of its earlier stages – smart in the 1950s, dowdy in the '60s, hideous to ridiculous in the '70s and '80s. And by the 1990s it was on the way to being amusing.

Putting aside the reasons for the Sisters' rehabilitation of Polari, they threw it a lifeline that was to have unexpected repercussions and ensure that it would never be truly forgotten. Later I'll discuss how the Sisters' use of Polari inspired projects by artists and members of more established churches (the latter resulting in your actual controversy), but for now I'll pick up a different thread – one which sees Derek Jarman's canonization being taken note of by academics and queer theorists.

An academic pursuit

Around the start of the 1990s, the concept of queer theory became popular within academic and activist circles. It was part of a new 'postmodern' way of thinking which was often

unfortunately expressed by academics who favoured an in-
accessible, jargon-heavy writing style (much more difficult to
decipher than Polari). This was a shame and also a bit of an own
goal because one of the points of queer theory was to question
the existence of fixed social hierarchies and shed light on the
ways that certain types of people are kept down or excluded
from power. But if you throw around a lot of big words and
write in such a highfalutin way that most people can't make
sense of you, then you're definitely going to be excluding a lot
of people yourself.

That aside, a central aspect of queer theory was that gender
is a kind of performance – and we get our lines and stage
directions from the society and time period that we grow up
in. So we learn how to behave as a man or a woman based
upon copying other people around us and we also learn how
to organize our sexuality into little boxes or categories based
upon what society at a given point tells us are the acceptable
boxes that exist. But over time and across cultures, these boxes
and ways of being a man or woman can change. To an extent
this seems to make good sense. We've seen in previous chapters
how there were different categories or 'boxes' linked to men
who had relations with other men. If we think about, say, the
Mollies of the seventeenth century, or the queens and trade
of the early twentieth century, and then go on to consider the
clones of the 1970s or more recent categories like twink, bear
or pansexual, we can see that there are different ways of cat-
egorizing men who have sex with other men, but they are not
permanent identities and they are subject to what a society
will condone at a given time. The point of queer theory, then,
was to show (or 'deconstruct' in queer theory parlance) how

these different boxes or identity categories came into being, sometimes through an analysis of a society's history, laws and media. Queer theorists tended to have different goals to, say, the Gay Liberationists, because the latter were more about saying, 'We are an identity, we exist and we want equality,' while queer theorists were more likely to say, 'These kinds of identities aren't as fixed as we think, so nobody is "anything" really.'

It was within this academic climate that research into sexuality began to get seriously under way, which included the creation of a sub-field that concentrated on the relationship between language and sexuality. Although largely represented by American researchers who organized themselves around the term 'Lavender Linguistics', there were a few British studies during this period, some which discussed Polari. Ian Hancock was one of those who wrote about Polari early on from an academic perspective, although the chapter he published in 1984 focuses on it in relation to other British languages used by travellers, and not from a gay perspective.[6] This was followed by Jonathon Green, who gave a brief overview in 1987, although it was not until 1994 that Leslie Cox and Richard Fay considered Polari as part of a broader examination of different ways that gay people used language.[7] A few years later Ian Lucas looked more at Polari's uses in the theatre, including its incorporation by the Sisters of Perpetual Indulgence.[8] In addition, there was a growing body of research on gay and lesbian history, which also referenced Polari, usually considering less the words themselves and more how Polari enabled secrecy during oppressive times. While some histories featured gay men and lesbians who had lived extraordinary or high-profile lives, others were more concerned with the lives of 'ordinary' people and included testimonies of gay men and lesbians.[9] These histories usually briefly referenced Polari alongside mention of the Julian and Sandy sketches. A television programme called 'A Storm in a Teacup', shown in 1993 as part of the *Summer's Out* series, featured interviews with Polari speakers as well as three scripted conversations containing Polari, performed by actors and set on a London bus. The first one appears to take place in the Second World War and is between two sailors on shore leave, the second is between two women in the 1960s, while the third features two gay men in the 1970s, one who speaks Polari, the other who is critical of it, using the phrase 'phallocentric discourse' and bringing to mind the Gay Liberationists of the previous chapter.

In some quarters Polari still appeared to be thriving. In a *Gay Times* article from 1995, journalist Peter Burton made note of the language he heard while watching the parade at Manchester Mardi Gras: 'almost everyone within hearing range is using Polari, the lost language of queens'. One drag queen is described as saying: 'Varda the bona cartes on the homis on the leather float. I've left my homi at home. He's not very social.'[10]

It was around this time that I came into the story. I doubt that I would seriously have considered basing a PhD thesis around Polari if it hadn't been for this small amount of existing research on the topic. The 1990s were a kind of sweet spot for Polari, when research on sexuality was finally starting to be seen as a respectable subject within academia and there were still enough Polari speakers available for someone to be able to locate them. The books I published on Polari in the early 2000s helped to cement its respectability as an academic topic, and along with other academics, I gave various interviews in the media and wrote articles on Polari for newspapers, gay periodicals and websites. Particularly with the growth of the Internet during this period, it became easier to find information about Polari and for people who were interested in it to form networks or get in touch with others if they were writing an article and wanted to interview someone. As a marker of how acceptable gay topics had become to the mainstream media, in 2010 I was interviewed about Polari for a piece that went in *The One Show*, an early-evening magazine programme aimed at a family audience, broadcast on BBC1. The piece was filmed in a very glamorous and atmospheric cabaret bar called Madam Jojo's in Soho. I'd already come into contact with the bar a few years earlier though, as you'll discover.

Brand Polari

After 1967, the decriminalization of homosexuality enabled people to establish a legitimate business or living from being gay for the first time in the UK. Prior to this, as described earlier, private drinking clubs and informal gay bars had been risky to attend as patrons could be arrested en masse. After 1967, gay bars and clubs became reasonably popular in most UK towns, with larger cities having numerous outlets. Establishments that catered to gay and lesbian clientele were often in peripheral parts of town centres and could sometimes be clustered together, with the same street having a gay pub, nightclub, cafe or restaurant, shop or sauna. Terms like 'gay village' were sometimes used to refer to these larger configurations of commercial outlets, and communities grew up around them, playing host to charities, medical and counselling services and meeting places for hobby and sports groups. There were increasing numbers of magazines and newspapers aimed at gay men and lesbians, which usually contained adverts for their target audiences. These included holiday packages, life insurance, greeting cards, clothing, films, books and music. For much of the 1990s, the Internet was mainly the province of academics and the highly computer literate; gay people still mostly made contact with one another face to face in actual physical locations. They talked to one another. They didn't use fake photographs to hide their identities, and they didn't 'block' anyone they didn't like the look of. It was indeed an amazing time.

To an extent, the legal establishment of a physical gay scene from the 1970s to the 1990s resulted in a commercialization of gay identity, perfectly in line with wider economic, social and political trends in Britain, which saw a move towards rewarding private enterprise, along with the notion of people exercising power through their spending choices. The lifestyle products marketed to gay and lesbian consumers not only helped to foster a sense of gay community and pride, but enabled the people involved in selling those products to make a living. However, advertising was often used in ways that 'sold' a some-what narrow view of gay identity – with young, bare-chested, muscular, white, handsome, butch-looking men appearing in a wide range of adverts targeted at gay men for all manner of products. It was in this climate that Polari started cropping up in various commercial concerns. One way was simply as a kind of brand – a word from Polari would be used to name a product or venue. This would typically involve a gay bar or shop. In Brighton's Kemptown (where I conducted a lot of my Polari research all those years ago), there was a gay-friendly cafe called Bona Foodie. In the Isle of Wight, a clothes shop was called Bona Togs, and don't forget the short-lived Polari Lounge in Stoke. In Dublin, a gay pub called The George offers 'Bona Polari' on a sign above the windows. It wasn't just pubs though. A dentist in Australia wrote to tell me that he had named his practice Polari:

I have two friends from Sydney, one of whom was 'raised' by drag queens when he first came out and they were the ones who first told me about the language. In fact, I liked the idea of a gay language so much that I decided to name my medical practice, catering largely to gay men and lesbians, Polari. You should see the looks I get when I actually explain to someone what it means.

Not all brands that used words from Polari were purely commercial ventures. There was a community theatre group in Manchester that went by the name of Vada, and a group aimed at providing support for older people in London called Polari. Here's an excerpt from a leaflet by the latter:

The love that dared not speak its name. Polari . . . The organisation was set up in 1993, choosing the name Polari for its associations with older gay people. (Polari was used as a covert gay language before the decriminalisation of homosexuality in 1967) . . . Firstly: Polari is actively seeking the views of older lesbians and gay people on how they want to be represented. Secondly: Polari is noting these diverse views and identifying the gaps through which people 'disappear'. Thirdly: Polari is producing leaflets about a range of social care and housing issues to different types of inquirers. Fourthly: Polari aims to encourage older lesbian and gay people to speak directly to housing and social care providers through a programme of education and training.

However, other appropriations of Polari – especially more recent ones – placed less emphasis on the gay community aspects that the language evoked and instead tried to position it as something that can enable you to be cool or chic, for a price. Indeed, there is now an online fashion brand called Polari, which sells a 'Polari is Burning' T-shirt containing a small ® (registered trademark) sign above the word Polari. The phrase is a riff on the title of the 1990 film *Paris Is Burning*, which documents drag queens living in New York City. It harks back to an older form of gay culture, but it is the U.S., not the UK, that is being referenced here, so there is a kind of transatlantic blending going on, a bit like the 1970s British clone who took his look from the streets of the Castro or West Hollywood.

At the time of writing the Polari fashion website contains slogans like *dish the dirt, and no flies* and *varda that bona omi*, and most of the clothes it sells are boldly emblazoned with the word *Polari* and are modelled by young, hip-looking twenty-somethings.[11] Who knew that Polari could be so cool?

And in 2013, in the trend-setting area of Shoreditch, London, a restaurant called Hoi Polloi created a cocktail menu with Polari-named drinks, including the Bijou Basket (consisting of gin, ginger wine and rhubarb bitters), the Riah Shusher (rhubarb and vanilla Tapatio Blanco tequila mule), the Bona

Hoofer (gin, spiced syrup and espresso) and Naff Clobber (Buffalo Trace, Benedictine and maple syrup). The cocktails were priced at around £9 each and were described in *Metro* newspaper in a column called 'Trend Watch', where the managing director of Hoi Polloi was quoted as saying that the concept came about because 'the theatre of the dining room is a perfect foil for the extravagance and camp of Polari.'[12]

Madam Jojo's in London's Soho also incorporated Polari as part of its brand. The burlesque bar opened in the 1950s and was popular with both gay and straight patrons. In 2004, I was contacted by a public relations firm who had been appointed by the bar. They had the idea of reviving Polari by getting their waiters to use it on customers when they were serving. They had a problem, though: they didn't have enough examples of Polari to revive it in this context, and they wanted me to provide some form of training in the language. So I dutifully created a kind of crash course in Polari, which was distributed among the waiters, enabling them to incorporate a set of words and phrases into their interactions with customers. The PR plan worked and as a result the Polari-speaking waiters of Madam Jojo's found their way into the news, with the BBC News website covering the story. The club's owner was described as saying that 'by offering staff at Madam Jo Jo's the option of learning and using Polari to refer to familiar aspects and objects of their works we are offering a fun, yet practical way of bridging any language gaps.'[13] I'm not fully sure that any language gaps were being bridged because Polari wasn't really getting that much use in 2004, but it was a nice idea to recreate a sense of a 1950s Soho experience and to keep Polari's memory alive.

However, with the examples discussed in this section there is something a little different happening, in that Polari is being used as a way not just of providing gay people with a sense of cultural identity, history and pride, but of ensuring the survival of a commercial establishment, product or brand and, implicitly, the livelihoods of those who are associated with that brand. The Polari words used in these forms of branding help to mark the products as gay, but I also think that, considering Polari's current standing in the fashion cycle, they give it a sense of cool credibility. It is amusing that in 1999 the London-based *Boyz* magazine was describing Polari as deeply uncool and something that was only credibly spoken in 'farmland or the kind of town where a trip to Woolworths is seen as going posh',[14] but just a few years later it was more likely to be associated with London's 'in-set' getting cocktail umbrellas caught in their facial hair. The wheels on Polari's fashion cycle were spinning pretty quickly, especially once it was seen as having the potential to sell things. I ought to note that I'm not disapproving of anyone's desire to make a living through selling some T-shirts or colourful drinks – we all have to do what we can to get by, after all. But it does show how what happened to Polari after its 'death' is in some ways just as interesting as how it was used when it was alive.

So Polari was first rediscovered by activists, then academics, and then artisans. But this isn't the end of the story. Another group – artists – were also poised to take it up from the late 2000s onwards. And you'd better hold on to your sheitel, because this is where Polari finds itself in even odder territory.

Highbrow Polari

Even as early as the late 1980s, Polari had been used by writers and film-makers as a way of adding a sprinkle of authenticity to stories that were set in mid-century Britain and featured gay characters or themes. We have already encountered Michael Carson's semi-autobiographical *Sucking Sherbet Lemons*, which features a Polari-speaking character called Andy who identifies as Andrea and uses words like *vada* and *dinge*.[15] Another novel, *Man's World*, written by Rupert Smith in 2010, combines timelines from the 1950s and 2000s in order to tell an interwoven story of gay Londoners, and includes bits of Polari speech. The 1998 Todd Haynes film *Velvet Goldmine* is set in the mid-1970s and contains a scene with two characters speaking in Polari, with subtitles appearing in the screen in English: 'Ooo varda Mistress Bona! . . . Varda the omie-palone . . . A tart my dears, a tart in gildy clobber! . . . She won't be home tonight.' Another 1998 film, *Love Is the Devil* – a biopic of the artist Francis Bacon – also contains a small amount of Polari: 'Oh do stop staring at Mr Knife and Mrs Fork George, the expression on your eke you'd think they'd been covered in poison. Oh try to relax. Give her another drink!'

As part of Polari's burgeoning association with culture, history and literature, it was perhaps unsurprising to see it starting to appear in increasingly highbrow circles. A literary salon created by the author Paul Burston was named simply Polari. Starting in the upstairs room of a pub in Soho, it is currently based in the UK's cultural heart – the South Bank Centre – and has been described by the *Independent on Sunday* as 'London's peerless gay literary salon'. The salon has hosted numerous popular contemporary authors who have written on gay themes, including Jake Arnott, Neil Bartlett, Stella Duffy, Patrick Gale, Philip Hensher, Will Self and Sarah Waters. There is an annual Polari book prize, which is awarded to the best debut books that explore the LGBT experience, and the salon itself has won awards. I am not sure that very much actual Polari gets spoken at the salon but as a word which means 'language' the moniker is fitting.

Polari is also the name of a slightly less well-known periodical of creative writing, based in Australia.[16] Describing itself as a journal which 'celebrates writing that addresses sexuality, sex and gender', it works 'contrary to the mainstream and revels in the margins'. Its website features pictures of literary figures such as Oscar Wilde, Gertrude Stein and Allen Ginsberg. As with the London-based literary salon, I don't think Polari itself is used very much (if at all) in the *Polari* journal, but instead it is the association with a historic, secret, marginalized form of language that is evoked by the title. Finally, *Polari* was the name given to an online magazine which ran in the 2000s, created by Chris Bryant and Bryon Fear.[17] I was involved in this and occasionally wrote columns for it – I recall how Chris told me at the launch that he wanted to provide a different kind of publishing outlet for gay people, something distinct from the many gay magazines and websites that were currently available, one that wasn't commercialized and didn't use sexy images as a quick way of getting people's attention. He vowed that it would never feature a picture of a bare-chested man. Over the course of the magazine's history it provided political commentary and articles on a wide range of cultural topics.

Uptown girl: Clementine the Living Fashion Doll

I attended the same launch event, which featured a short film that had been made by puppeteer and female impersonator Mark Mander. Mark has his own, original take on drag, having created a persona called Clementine the Living Fashion Doll. While Mark is British, Clementine has a heavily enunciated transatlantic accent, parodying the look and sound of glamorous movie stars like Joan Crawford. She consists of Mark's head super-imposed on a tiny doll's body – in his stage act, Clementine appears inside a booth, a bit like one used in a Punch and Judy show, with careful use of blacked-out clothing on a black background to hide Mark's body and create the illusion of Clementine. However, Mark also creates animations with Clementine, and it was one of these films which was used at the *Polari* magazine launch, with Clementine finding out about Polari (the language), through the discovery of the Polari dictionary I had published, *Fantabulosa*. Clementine was thus the latest in a long line of performing drag queens to use Polari, but she did it in a more didactic way, teaching her audience about its history (while gently poking fun at me). Unlike some of the earlier Polari-speaking drag artistes who tended to be modelled on working-class housewives and performed in rough-and-ready pubs, Clementine is a much more upmarket queen, playing at venues like Crazy Coq's, a beautiful Art Deco theatre space near Piccadilly Circus. Since the launch I've attended several of Clementine's stage performances there and am occasionally called to the stage as a member of the audience to be ridiculed. I'd view Clementine as a postmodern drag artiste, providing not only a parody of femininity but a parody of drag queens themselves.

So, we have come rather a long way in a short space of time. From Polari being the province of 'common' queens who gave each other female names and chattered endlessly about the latest trade, to Polari being seen as a politically incorrect horror-show a couple of decades later, it is now moving in some of the most highbrow literary circles. I wonder what the Polari-speaking hairdressers, chorus boys and cruise-ship waiters of the 1950s would have made of its appearance in such rarefied company, or for that matter what the placard-holding Gay Liberationists of the 1970s would have thought of the rehabilitation of all this camp nonsense if they'd been transported to the present day in a time machine. I should stress that it's not the language of Polari as such that has been rehabilitated and reclaimed, but more the idea of it. Still, I sometimes feel that Polari has whizzed from one social extreme to the other and now it's just as marginalized as it ever was.

One of the most interesting illustrations of the recent cultural and artistic rehabilitation of Polari is from a loosely knit group of Manchester-based artists, including Elaine Brown, Joe Richardson and Jez Dolan. In 2010, I was contacted by Elaine and Joe, who were part of an arts organization called the Ultimate Holding Group. They had created a project called EXAM which had been commissioned as part of the Queer Up North Festival and involved a one-day public immersive art event. They explained that it was a kind of GCSE exam in LGBT studies. The exam paper was mocked up to look just like one from an official examining board, and the people who volunteered to sit the exam did so in a large hall under proper 'exam conditions' in complete silence with the examiner telling people to 'turn their papers over' and that they 'may now begin'. The paper was marked and there was a results day when the volunteers found out how they had performed. The point of the

'You may now turn over your papers and begin': the EXAM project

EXAM project was to highlight how LGBT issues and people are usually absent from most aspects of the National Curriculum. Despite the repeal of Section 28 (in 2000 in Scotland and in 2003 in the rest of the UK), school textbooks still often feature 'normative' heterosexual families and tend not to give much space to topics like LGBT history, the persecution of LGBT people or the role they have played in furthering civilization. So the EXAM project aimed to address this by bringing LGBT people and issues to the forefront of education. The language portion of the exam was on Polari, which I thought was a nice touch, and Joe and I became friends, staying in contact in the ensuing years.

Later, Joe teamed up with Jez Dolan, who also happened to be one of the Sisters of Perpetual Indulgence (Manchester branch), where he is called Sister Gypsy TV Filmstar. They received council funding to continue incorporating Polari into art projects, which resulted in a flourish of creativity in the following years. I played the role of linguistic adviser to these projects, although in fact I usually felt more like an art groupie, following them around their launches and being frequently amazed at their fresh perspective on what by now was for me the linguistic equivalent of a very comfortable pair of slippers.

One project involved hijacking Bury's Festival of Light in 2012. Festivals of light are normally events that take place in winter evenings and are a kind of modern update on street parties or carnivals, designed to cheer people up on a miserable British November night. Bury is a small mill town in Greater Manchester which is known for black pudding and the Lancashire Fusiliers. During the Festival of Light, Joe and Jez used a projector to beam gigantic Polari phrases onto the outside walls of the Art Museum. As darkness fell over Bury, the words 'He's nada to vada in the larder' loomed high above the heads of the meandering crowds of locals, and I saw a handsome dad mouth the phrase quietly to himself, shaking his head in mild consternation. Polari was certainly confounding the *naffs* on a grand scale all over again, although I wasn't sure if I'd somehow missed the point (if this was another immersive art project, then who was it for?). The Art Museum also hosted a number of Polari-inspired pieces that Joe and Jez had made, including a ceramic dish onto which Joe had painted a pie chart. The chart displayed the percentages of words in Polari that were derived from different sources such as Cant, Back Slang and Cockney Rhyming Slang, taken from the Polari dictionary I'd published in 2002. The Polari definition of *dish* afforded the piece an additional pun.

Jez came up with a different take on Polari's etymologies by reworking a piece of existing artwork by Alfred H. Barr Jr called *Cubism and Abstract Art*, which aimed to map out the influences within different strands of art. Barr's work is a complicated-looking diagram which shows links between different art schools like Neo-Impressionism and Cubism, and also has a timeline, so as you look from top to bottom you see how different fields in art come in and go out of fashion. Jez took the basic structure of Barr's artwork, leaving in the boxes and lines, but changing all the labels so that they referred to the different influences on Polari over time (including many of the groups discussed earlier). Due to the fact that Jez couldn't fiddle about with the existing diagram's structure, this visual Polari etymology shouldn't be taken as a perfect account of the language's development, but I think he did a pretty good job of getting it as close as possible. But perhaps the group's most ambitious project was the creation of the Polari Bible.

The Polari Bible was originally published online.[18] It had been created by Tim Greening-Jackson (aka Sister Matic de Bachery), who used the Polari dictionary created by some of the other Sisters of Perpetual Indulgence as the basis of a computer program. This program converted an English version of the Bible into Polari. Jez had the text of the Polari Bible put into a huge, beautiful leatherbound book, and it was displayed in a glass case at the John Rylands Library in Manchester, alongside a range of important historic Bibles. The point of this was to highlight how religions are not very accepting of LGBT people but that they should be. Also, there was another level to it – about how powerful religious people get to decide what objects are sacred and which ones aren't. So the Polari Bible was treated by the artists and the John Rylands Library as a sacred object; you aren't even allowed to touch the thing without putting on a pair of very white gloves as the oils from

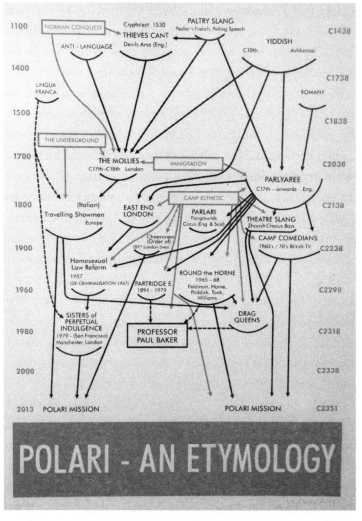

Polari – An Etymology

your skin will damage the delicate paper – a nice touch of High Camp. Jez organized a number of public readings of the Polari Bible, described in more detail later.

As well as the art exhibits and the Bible, the Manchester artists also put on a play about Polari's history, drawing on my books as source material. In fact, two plays about Polari took place in 2013, one written by Jez and his team, another by Chris of *Polari* magazine called *In the Life: A History of Polari*, starring Steve Nallon (who was famous for voicing Margaret Thatcher in the 1980s TV comedy series *Spitting Image*). The plays featured a mixture of music, dancing and acting, referencing the *Round the Horne* sketches, sailors, drag queens and trade. *In the Life* featured a scene where Melvyn Bragg interviewed Professor Peri Odical about Polari's status as a language, resulting in a lot of pontificating about anti-languages and lexicons. As parodies go, I got off lightly, while the performer Champagne Charlie (Robbie Bonar, not the nineteenth-century Champagne Charlie) performed a number of songs, including a cover of 'Bona Eke'. And around the same time, Polari went fully online, as Joe Richardson used the dictionary I'd published to create a phone app. One of the features of the app was that you could shake your phone and it would present you with a random word or phrase.

In 2015, two other artists, Brian and Karl, created a short film set on Hampstead Heath, called *Putting on the Dish*. The film involved a conversation on a park bench between two men, credited as Maureen and Roberta, and involved the most dense (and tense) use of Polari I've ever heard. Unlike the much earlier scripted version of Polari used by Julian and Sandy, the characters in *Putting on the Dish* don't give the viewing audience an easy ride or provide translations as they go along. Their Polari comes thick and fast – kudos to the two actors (Steve Wickenden and Neil Chinneck), who speak it as if they'd known it their whole lives.

In the Life, featuring Champagne Charlie (Robbie Bonar), 2013

One aspect of this short film which I found interesting was how the speakers seamlessly incorporated the different etymological influences or layers of Polari into their conversation. There are words like *bencove* and *chovey* from Cant, as well as Parlyaree words like *nanti* and *charver*, backslang words like *riah*, Cockney Rhyming Slang words like *kyber*, Yiddish words like *shyckle*, basic French like *mais oui* and 1960s/1970s slang terms like *remould*. This is recognizably Polari, but there's no way of knowing if the 'everything but the kitchen sink' version used by Maureen and Roberta would have been fully understood by twentieth-century speakers. From my interviews with Polari speakers, most of them tended to know a few core words and then used just as many terms that tended to be more limited to their immediate social circles. I also get the impression that as the decades passed, Polari gradually changed so that different words fell in and out of fashion at different points. The version of Polari used by Brian and Karl is similar to that found in the Polari Bible, in that it feels as though it has been influenced by the existence of dictionaries (including my own), which contain a good many of the known words of Polari taken from different points in time. As a result, these more scripted versions perhaps shouldn't be seen as completely authentic re-creations of the language, but that's not surprising – the ways that we represent the past are very much filtered through the lens of the present. I suspect that as time goes on, future attempts to re-create Polari may struggle to capture exactly how it was used.

Another nice example of a more contemporary repurposing of Polari was in a short book called *Cruising for Lavs*, written by George Reiner and Penny Burke (proceeds of the book were donated to the charity Lesbians and Gays Support the Migrants). The book follows a dialogue between the two authors, with George describing his life to Penny, as a young man growing up in Cornwall, then moving to London as a student. As with the Brian and Karl film, the authors of the book use Polari from a mix of earlier sources, as well as throwing in a few new terms:

> I hear you ducky, strano is our way to do the rights. Girl, she's bold, we may zhoosh our riah, flutter our ogle riahs, and ask for a deek from those glenn hoddles, you know at the same tick we'd be saying nish thank you, kiss my aris![19]

It would miss the point to question the 'authenticity' of such modern texts – they are to be understood as coming from the voices of twenty-first-century speakers and are perfectly in keeping with the magpie-like way that Polari speakers mixed and matched words from different sources.

An unintended consequence of my research and publishing the dictionary is that I enabled Polari to be raised from the dead for brief moments, but sometimes I feel it is more like a kind of anachronistic Frankenstein's monster version of the language. As linguists are trained to be dispassionate creatures, being more concerned with charting the ups and downs of a language as opposed to getting into debates about which way of using language is the 'right' one, I'm liable to simply see this new development in Polari's story as an interesting turn of events rather than anything else. But others may think differently.

This chapter reveals that Polari managed to stay dead for only a few years before someone spilt a few drops of enchanted blood on it and it came back – not in its original form but in a different, ghostly way. It appeared in strange rituals spoken by men dressed in robes, it graced the cocktail menus of the hippest places in London, it is on the lips of authors and play-wrights, and it found itself projected onto the side of a museum so it could confuse the British public en masse. As dead languages go, Polari is having a pretty fabulous afterlife and is now mixing with a much swankier set of posh queens. Who would have thought it?

Seriously, though, I'm glad that Polari is no longer seen as apolitical. In the pictures of Derek Jarman taken during his canonization, the look of pride and amusement on his face says it all. It's perhaps the moment in Polari's long, complicated history that I'm most proud of.

We're pretty much caught up now, and there are only a few parts of Polari's story left for me to tell. I'm afraid that the last chapter is going to get a bit preachy and weepy, so you might want to have a lace hanky at the ready for the big finish.

8

In Conclusion

You may have gathered by now that I am often shy and awkward around new people. Compared to the other children, at school I was quiet and studious, and this has continued into adult life. Academia is generally a godsend for people like me – we can potter away at our little obsessions without having to come into contact with the 'real' world too much. We would not thrive in the real world. The university world protects us from them (and them from us, for that matter).

In some ways Polari was a challenging subject for me to study because I'm not one of the people who would have embraced it, even if I'd been around in the 1950s. I get embarrassed talking about my sexuality and private life, even among close friends. Phrases like 'ooh, vada the lallies on the bona omi, dear!' don't sit too well with me. So it would be lovely if there was an overarching narrative in this book about how a stuffy academic was tasked to interview fabulous older men who embraced their sexuality and were confident enough to be themselves, and through the magic of studying Polari the stuffy academic learnt how to embrace his sexuality and loosen up and be fabulous too. As this is real life, it didn't happen that

Are you wearing white gloves? The Polari Bible

way. But still, the stuffy academic has had a few glimpses of what might have been.

It is a dark wintry night in 2012 and I am looking for an art exhibition in a converted mill building in a part of Manchester I don't recognize. After a lot of getting lost I finally find it – it's up a creepy staircase which looks like a set from a horror film. Inside, it is a different matter completely: lots of bright light and wide open space with white walls and a few exhibits dotted around, browsed by fashionable people sporting interesting eyewear and monochrome polo neck jumpers. I am here to participate in a public reading from the Polari Bible. There are seven of us, and we are going to take turns and try to break the record for the longest reading of the Bible in Polari at any one sitting. As nobody has ever attempted this before, to my knowledge, we will have already made it into the record books once the first word has been uttered, but that's not really the point. It's more of a performance-as-art thing. Or an experience thing.

The Bible itself looks rather fancy and is on a lectern that has been set up in the corner of the room, with a dramatic spotlight shining on it. Jez, the first reader, takes the podium and starts relating how 'Gloria' created Adam and Eve:

> In the beginning Gloria created the heaven and the earth. And the earth was nanti form, and void; and munge was upon the eke of the deep. And the fairy of Gloria trolled upon the eke of the aquas. And Gloria cackled, Let there be sparkle: and there was sparkle. And Gloria vardad the sparkle, that it was bona: and Gloria medzered the sparkle from the munge.

The other speakers each take their turn. Everyone does it differently. One chap, Daniel, does it as a kindly Anglican bishop, as if giving a reassuring Christmas message. Another, who is an actor in real life, projects his voice to the back of the room and performs dramatically as if reciting a well-rehearsed piece of Shakespeare. It is then my turn. I get up and put on the white gloves. The page is open at the story of Sodom and Gomorrah – one of the best and silliest bits of the Bible, involving two presumably gorgeous male angels who beam down to Earth on an exploratory mission to check if Sodom's terrible reputation for 'grievous sin' is justified. They lodge with Lot, but the men of the city come sniffing round wanting some celestial trade, so Lot instead offers up his two virgin daughters. That's not good enough for the locals, who are fixing to break the door down to get to the angels inside. At this point the angels have had enough and make everyone go blind, and then decide to destroy the whole city as an afterthought. Lot and his family are allowed to escape, but for some unexplained reason are told not to look back at the brimstone and fire. Lot's wife can't help herself and is punished by being turned into a pillar of salt. It is like a nightmarish 1950s public information film, both deliciously ridiculous and horribly unfair. Lot's family are made homeless, even though they did nothing wrong, and Lot's wife gets a salty ending because she can't help a bit of rubber-necking. And what about the two poor daughters – who lose their mother and have a father who is actively complicit in their proposed abuse! It's such a shady tale that it should be an exemplar of why the Bible is neither true nor just. It has always annoyed me. So perhaps this is why something odd comes over me when I start reading. I am immediately possessed by the ghost of Kenneth Williams and begin to read the story in an exaggeratedly camp voice with lots of strangulated nasal 'oohs' and theatrical gestures – my wrists are so limp that I can't hold my hands up. The audience looks shocked, then bursts out laughing.

> And they screeched unto Lot, and cackled unto her – Where are the homies which trolled in to thee this nochy? Parker them out unto us, that we may know them. And Lot trolled out at the door unto them, and shut the door after her. And cackled, I pray you, sisters, nix so wickedly. Varda now, I have dewey palone chavvies which have not known homie; let me, I pray you, parker them out unto you, and do ye to them as is bona in your ogles: only unto these homies do nishter; for therefore trolled they under the shadow of my roof.

Afterwards, I realize that it felt rather liberating. It was nice making people laugh and being the centre of attention for a few minutes. It was also fun not caring what people thought. Perhaps Polari has helped me to accept myself after all. But the next day the feeling has worn off and I'm back to my old uptight self again. Still, the experience has given me an insight into what it might have been like to have been one of those bold queens who spoke Polari. And I have a new respect for them.

Still quite the scandal

Sometimes, from our perch of gay marriage, PrEP and Tom Daley calendars, it can feel as if the whole world is soaked in a rainbow of tolerance and celebration and that gay people finally have nothing to worry about. The year 2017 was the fiftieth anniversary of the partial decriminalization of homosexuality in the UK, and there was an explosion of cultural queenliness to celebrate just how far we have come. There were art exhibitions at Tate Britain and the Walker Art Gallery in Liverpool (where Jez's *Etymology of Polari* was displayed), and the mumsy old BBC ran a series of television programmes about gay lives and histories, including a monologue by a very camp hairdresser who knew plenty of Polari and wasn't afraid to use it. I was especially touched by an advert for the series which showed an elderly heterosexual couple embracing on a bus-stop bench and then being arrested by a police patrol team, with the tagline 'Imagine if being in love was a crime'. Even the National Trust got in on the act, laying on LGBT tours which gave a potted history of the queer history of Soho, complete with a little lesson on Polari for the uninitiated, and an 'immersive' recreation of the infamous Caravan Club and its raid in 1934. I dutifully put on my interwar drag, parted my hair and went to both, paying London prices for cocktails and dancing with the actors who had been employed as colourful 1930s inhabitants of the club. At the end of the evening a recording of sirens was played, signifying the raid, and we all filed out into the night, not to be locked up by sneering Lily Law, but just to go home.

Despite this celebration of LGBT identity, it's perhaps overstating the situation to say that all the battles have been won. The British Social Attitudes survey has a question on homosexuality which they ask every few years, and it is never far from my regard. From the peak of hostility in the 1980s (74 per cent of respondents believed that homosexuality is always or mostly wrong in 1987), attitudes have become more tolerant since then, falling to 28 per cent in 2012 (although that's 28 per cent too high).[1] As an indication of how far the journey to full acceptance is yet to go, I note that at the time of writing, apart from Liam Davis (currently at Torquay United), there is a dearth of openly gay male professional footballers in the UK – and considering it's our national sport, that's telling. Intolerance is still pretty deep in some quarters. Being born into a deeply religious family generally isn't good for gay people's well-being – we are, incredibly, just getting round to banning 'conversion therapies'. And attitudes across many parts of the world are much less tolerant than in the UK, and are worsening in some cases. Try being gay in Saudi Arabia or Russia or Nigeria – it ain't much fun.

Weirdly, even after all this time, Polari still has the power to provoke outrage. In the U.S., Erich Erving took the translated version of the Polari Bible in order to create something called the Polari Evensong, which was used by the Yale Divinity School, described as an experiment of employing a transgressive language to express worship and prayer. Just as Jesus had welcomed people who were outcasts and on the fringes of society (such as widows and sex workers, who were often overlooked by organized religions during his time), a Polari Evensong would be a bold move in terms of welcoming queer people in a way that had never before been attempted. Part of the text reads:

O Duchess, open thou our lips.
And our screech shall show forth thy praise.
O Gloria, make speed to save us.
O Duchess, make haste to help us.
Fabeness be to the Auntie and to the Homie Chavvie,
     and to the Fantabulosa Fairy.
As it was in the beginning, is now, and ever shall be,
     world nanti end. Larlou.
Praise ye the Duchess.
The Duchess's name be praised.

I was sent a recording of the evensong and it sounds beautiful – heavenly even. The words are sung in such a highly stylized way that it takes a while to realize that any Polari is being used – the effect is one of peace and reverence.

On 31 January 2017, to mark LGBT history month, student priests at Westcott House in Cambridge used the Polari version of the evensong in the college chapel.

It did not go down well.

On 3 February 2017, *The Guardian* reported that, 'The service had caused some members of the college "considerable upset and disquiet".'[2] As a result, the college principal, Reverend Canon Chris Chivers, was described as making a public apology, saying that this 'was not an authorised act of worship in line with the college's procedures'. He went on to say that 'the contents of the service are at variance with the doctrine and teaching of the Church of England, and that is hugely regrettable'. The incident was widely reported in the media, and commented on in social media, resulting in a variety of responses – some people finding it hilarious, others not able to see what the fuss was about, and others genuinely feeling that the use of Polari in the ceremony was inappropriate. Lest we assume that the detractors were all heterosexual, I noted at least one queer person on my Twitter feed who disapproved of the Polari Evensong.

For me, what's most interesting about the story is that it shows that, even in 2017, Polari is still able to cause controversy; it can still make people laugh, and it can still make people upset. And that's what it always did. It also indicates that while there have been huge advances since 1967 in terms of equal rights for gay people, there are still cases where Polari can reveal tensions in society. I also suspect that Polari's story is not yet over.

When I finished my PhD thesis I couldn't have predicted many of the ways that Polari has been reappraised in the following couple of decades, so I'm a little reluctant to make guesses about what the future has in store. At the talks I give I am often asked if it will make a full comeback, if LGBT people will start using it all over again. I am not sure if that will ever happen – it flourished in extremely oppressive conditions and hopefully Britain has seen the last of those days. As part of an expression of a camp gay identity I still think Polari has mileage, though, whether for further political purposes or just as a way of helping people get through a bad day. I recall how I imagined a heavenly chorus of Polari speakers making fun of my anxious bumbling during the first conference talk I gave, and I think everyone ought to have an imaginary bold drag queen or sour-faced *omee-palone* avatar to provide acid commentary during our moments of high drama. A shared sense of language and history also helps to strengthen the bonds of community – and with the closure of many gay pubs and bars across the country as a result of the gentrification of areas such as Soho, and the fact that people increasingly spend large parts of their social lives online, I feel that the sense of a gay community is a little looser than it once was. Perhaps this is also the effect of equalization – now we can get married, we can assimilate into the mainstream. We are no longer an anti-society, so we don't need an anti-language. But we should be careful of throwing out the baby with the bath water. Yes, it is good to remember our history, but there can be benefits to examining aspects of history and repurposing the best bits for contemporary times – taking them out of their glass cabinets and giving them a new lease of life.

So there are two things that suggest to me that Polari may not be over yet. First, one of its main features was its ability to adapt, to borrow shamelessly from other language varieties, to change and grow, and to embrace different social groups. The drag queens, the Dilly boys, the dancers and the sea queens – they all made Polari their own and they cut it to fit their own purposes. But nobody ever really 'owned' Polari. And it's still up for grabs. I suspect that this flexibility means that it will continue to be used, although probably in such a way that it continues to change. Second, Polari's capacity to surprise should not be underestimated. Once my PhD was finished and I decided to cut ties with Polari, I was continually thrown off-centre by the creative energy of people who wanted to do things with it that I would never have considered. I look forward to seeing what a new generation can do with it.

A few lessons learned

It is Easter 2017 and I am at the University of Nottingham for the Lavender Linguistics conference. It is the first time that the conference has been held in the UK, and in the academic circles in which I move this is a Big Deal. I have been invited to hold one of my Polari workshops and also to give the final plenary speech, which I have decided to call 'What Polari Did Next' and is based to a good extent on Chapter Seven of this book. It is a long time since my first Lavender Linguistics conference in 2000, when I locked myself in a toilet cubicle during the coffee breaks because I didn't know anyone and was too shy to socialize. Sixteen years later I am now a professor (famous in a small, dusty corner of academia), but I still hate conferences.

I give my talk about Polari at the end of the conference and briefly mention how one of the reasons for it dying out was that the speakers were increasingly seen as dated by the generation who came after them. As I am saying it, I realize that the same thing has begun to happen to me. Earlier in the conference I accidentally used the wrong pronoun on one of the conference attendees who identifies as trans, saying *she* when I ought to have used *they*. I recall all the times that I have winced at an older person for using the wrong word. Now it's my turn. I wonder if everyone will take their turn. At the end of my talk someone asks a question about the politically incorrect Polari speakers – how I dealt with the ethical dilemma of representing them honestly and respectfully in my research but also not being critical of them, as they constitute a vulnerable group and were doing me a favour by taking the time to talk to me. I remember how some of the language used and attitudes held by my interviewees had occasionally been shocking to me. I hadn't challenged them over it. Nor had I quoted those bits directly in my research, although I had referred more generally to politically incorrect Polari speakers.

They weren't saints. But they weren't sinners either – despite what the Church and the law and the doctors and the newspaper editors claimed at the time. They didn't choose who to fancy and I'm sure if they had been given a choice, under those circumstances, I wouldn't have blamed them for pushing some hypothetical 'Be Straight Now' button. But they made the best of it, which I'd like to think is a Very British Thing – but it's probably just a Very Human Thing. They broke the law every time they had sex and put themselves at risk just by going out to make contact with other people like them. And, really, the message here is that love, desire, romance, sex, connection, they all win. They win over hate, oppression, isolation, shaming and erasure. Had these people listened to the messages and warnings that society was telling them, had they stayed at home with a jigsaw of Henry VIII and his six wives, had they repressed their sexualities, then, well, there'd probably have been no need for decriminalization and the Gay Liberation Front and Outrage and Stonewall and Pride Marches and Tom Daley calendars. They created and maintained informal structures and networks which eventually became too difficult for the government to ignore, and that gives me a sense of certainty that in less tolerant parts of the world love will eventually win out there too.

So, we, I, owe a debt to them. The fact that I can live with my husband – that in 2017 we signed a bit of paper so that he magically turned into my husband after more than two decades – is down, in part, to the good-natured resilience of those bold queens on the scene and their outrageous Polari. They weren't political – not in that 'let's have a meeting brothers' sort of way. If anything, they were politically incorrect. But their very existence was a political act.

Paul O'Grady, interviewed in 2017, has spoken with characteristic frankness regarding the work that he and other drag performers carried out in earlier decades:

> The younger generation don't know, and I hate to sound like a pioneer, but it's because of our work that they're able to minnie up and down Old Compton Street and have a good time and get married and it's because of us lot that they can do that and I'm not looking for recognition, I'm just saying and stating a fact.[3]

He's right. So thanks Paul and all your mates. I don't know if I would have been as bold as you.

I took on the study of Polari because I thought it was funny and it would be enjoyable to solve the mystery of why it went away. I also wanted to give a voice to a group of people who

THE
POLARI
BIBLE

Seventh Edition

Containing the Authorized Version

*Diligently Translated out of the Originall
tongue in to High Polari by the Sisters of
Perpetual Indulgence & a Gentleman*

Appointed to be read in
discotheques & Turkish baths

*Publifhed in Manchester a notorious hotbed of
the sin of Sodom by the Larlou Press*

Copyright ©2003-2014 Tim Greening-Jackson
All rights reserved

Hopefully the Turkish bath won't crinkle the pages: the Polari Bible had been despised by society and so were at risk of having their voices lost to history forever. For a long time nobody had cared to hear their voices, and as they had to speak in code anyway, their voices couldn't be understood, even when they did speak.

Since then there have been many voices speaking about Polari and about those original speakers. However, when you try to speak 'on behalf' of another group, you don't speak with their voice. You still speak with your own voice, and you can end up saying more about yourself than you do about the people you wish to represent. As Christine Ashby writes, 'While the aim of giving voice is emancipatory, the researcher often benefits more from the telling than the researched.'[4] This is certainly true in my case. My study of Polari resulted in me getting a lectureship and the comfortable life that goes with that. I also got to meet some very interesting and inspiring people over the years, as well as forge some lasting friendships, so there were much greater social benefits. And I've had recognition benefits too – my university awarded me with a staff prize for 'research impact' relating to Polari in 2018 – an indication of how respectable LGBT research is now seen as. I hope it will inspire others in similar endeavours.

Less expectedly, studying Polari forced me to confront my shyness and to overcome it, at least to the point where it is manageable and I can stand up in a room full of people and talk, and even slightly enjoy the experience. A lesson I've learnt from all the time I've spent on Polari is not to take yourself too seriously, to laugh at your perceived flaws and to make fun of the various adversities that life inevitably throws your way every now and then. It's not so much that laughing at something bad will stop it from hurting you, but the laughter gives you a way of coping with that hurt. That's the message that the Polari speakers of the 1950s knew all about, that Julian and Sandy exemplified in the 1960s, and that the drag activists of the 1990s took on board. It's one of those messages that continues to be relevant.

Over the course of the last twenty years, I've tried to give a voice to the Polari speakers. What I didn't realize when I started out is that they'd help me to find my own voice. I leave them with a sense of gratitude.

Bona lavs and larlou!

Glossary

It is unlikely that twentieth-century Polari speakers would have used or even known all of the terms listed in this section. And as is discussed earlier in the book, a Polari word will possess multiple spellings, meanings, origins and in some cases pronunciations, owing to the secretive, unstandardized, constantly changing nature of the lexicon.

Numbers

½ **medza**
1 **una, oney**
2 **dooey**
3 **tray**
4 **quarter**
5 **chinker**
6 **say**
7 **say oney, setter**
8 **say dooey, otter**
9 **say tray, nobber**
10 **daiture, dacha**
11 **long dedger, lepta**
12 **kenza**
100 **chenter**

A

ac/dc 1. a couple. 2. bisexual
acting dickey temporary work
active butch or bull in trade
affair, affaire someone with whom you have had a relationship
ajax preposition: nearby, next to
alamo I'm hot for you!
almond rocks socks
and no flies honestly!
antique HP an old gay man
aqua, acqua water
aris arse
(the) arva, harva sex. Also 'the full harva' (anal sex)
aspro, aspra a prostitute

aunt nell 1. to listen. 2. ear.
   3. be quiet!
aunt nelly fakes earrings
auntie an older gay man

B

badge cove an old person
bagaga, bagadga a penis
balony, balonie rubbish
barkey, barkie, barky a sailor
barnet hair
barney a fight
bat, batts, bates 1. a shoe. 2. to
   shuffle or dance on-stage
batter prostitution. To go *on
   the batter* was to walk the
   streets as a prostitute
battery to knock down
battyfang to hide and bite
beak a judge
bean young
beancove a young person
bedroom a place where men
   can have sex, such as a toilet
   cubicle in a cottage
beef curtains 'flaps' on a
   woman's vagina
ben, bene good
benar better
bencove a friend
Beryl with a brooch the police
Betty Bracelets the police
bevvy, beverada, bevie, bevois
   1. a drink (especially beer).
   2. a public house. Also
   bevvied (to be drunk)
bevvy omee a drunkard
bianc, beyonek, beone, beyong
   a shilling

bibi bisexual
bijou small (can be used
   ironically on large things)
billingsgate bad language
bimbo a dupe
binco a kerosene flare
bins spectacles
bitaine a prostitute
bitch 1. a feminine or gay man,
   especially one who is the
   passive partner in sex.
   2. to complain
black market queen, BMQ
   a closeted gay man
blag to make a sexual pick-up
blazé queen an 'upmarket'
   gay man
blob queen a queen of no
   account who tends to
   follow a drag queen around,
   hoping that some of the
   glitter will fall off on her
blocked to be high on drugs
blow to give oral sex
bod body
bodega a shop
bodega homie male shopkeeper
bold 1. audaciously gay.
   2. unpleasant
bolus a chemist
bona good
bona house male brothel or
   pub/club used by rent boys
bona lavs best wishes!
bona nochy good night!
bona rack a gay establishment
   with a good reputation
bona vardering attractive
(the) bones one's boyfriend

boobs breasts
booth a room, especially
a bedroom
bowl brandy faeces
box bum
boyno hello!
brainless good
brandy bum
brandy latch a toilet cubicle
bugle a nose
bulge a man's crotch
bull a masculine woman
butch masculine

C

cabouche a car
cackle talk
cackle fart an egg
camisa, commision, mish
a shirt
camp funny, exaggerated,
flamboyant and heavily
stylized
**camp name, christening, other
name** an opposite-sex name
given to a Polari speaker,
usually to reflect a key
aspect of their identity,
appearance or personality
**capella, capolla, capelli,
kapella** a hat or cap
cark it to die
carnish food, often meat
carnish ken an eating house
caroon a crown (old money)
carsey, karsey 1. a house.
2. a toilet. 3. a brothel
cartes, cartzo genitals,
especially penis

catever, kerterver bad
cats trousers
Cavaliers and Roundheads
uncircumcised and
circumcised penises
chant to sing
charper to seek
charpering carsey a police
station
charpering omee a police
man
charver to fuck
charvering donna a prostitute
chaud a penis
chaud's mudge a foreskin
chavvy, chavy a child
chemmie a shirt or blouse
chenter a hundred
cherry virginity
chicken 1. an attractive man
(usually aged under 25).
2. a young boy
chinker, chickwa five
chivvy to persecute
cleaning the cage out
cunnilingus
cleaning the kitchen
anilingus
clevie a vagina
clobber clothing
cod bad
cod rack a gay establishment
with a poor reputation
coddy, cody bad, amateurish
cods testicles
cold calling to walk into a
pub looking for company
colin 1. an erect penis.
2. a horn

Coliseum curtains foreskin

(the) colour of his eyes penis size

corybungus posterior

cossy costume

cottage a public lavatory or urinal

cottaging spending time in public lavatories in order to have gay sex

crimper a hair dresser

cruise to look for sex

cull 1. mate. 2 fool

culls testicles

D

dacha, daiture, deger ten

daffy drunken

dally sweet, kind

dander anger

dash to leave quickly

deaner, deener, dener, diener a shilling

dear, dearie friendly and/or patronizing personal term of address

delph teeth

dewey, dooe, dooey, duey two

dhobie, dohbie 1. to wash. 2. washing

diddle gin

diddle cove keeper of a gin or spirit shop. Can be extended to refer to a person serving behind a bar or working in an off-licence

(the) Dilly Piccadilly Circus

Dilly boy a male prostitute who worked around Piccadilly Circus

dinarly, dinarla, dinaly money

dinge black

dinge queen someone (usually a gay man) who seeks black partners

dish 1. bum or anus. To have it up the dish is to get fucked, while to grease the dish is to apply lubricant for sex. 2. an attractive man

dish the dirt to talk things over, gossip

dizzy scatter-brained

do a turn to have sex

do the rights to seek revenge

dog and bone a telephone

dolly smart or attractive. Can also be used as a term of address

dona, donner, donah, doner a woman

don't be strange don't hold back!

dowry a lot. Can be used to 'upgrade' any noun

dowry efink a sword

dowry lattie a palace

dowry omee a king

drag, drage 1. clothing typical of one sex or gender worn by someone who identifies as a different sex or gender. However, drag can

often be much more than
clothing, and reflects a
mental, emotional or sexual
state of being. Some trans
people have pointed out
that the real 'drag' is to
have to wear the clothing
that is socially expected
of them. 2. any clothing
not usually worn by the
speaker in their everyday
life. 3. *dressedas a girl*
(most likely a backronym)
drag up to wear clothes
associated with a different
sex or gender
dress up a bad (as in
unconvincing) drag queen
drogle a dress
dubes, doobs, doobies 1. pills.
2. marijuana cigarettes
duchess a rich or grand gay
man
ducky, duckie term of address,
used in a similar way
to **dear**
dyke, dike a lesbian

E

ear fakes earrings
ecaf, eek, eke a face
efink a knife
Eine London
esong a nose

F

fab, fabe, fabel good, great
fabularity 1. wonderfully
funny. 2. majesty

fabulosa wonderful
fag a gay man, usually
derogatory
fag hag a female friend of
gay man
fairy a feminine gay man
fake 1 noun: an erection.
2. to make. 3. used as
a premodifier to imply
that something is false
or artificially constructed
in some way
fake riah a wig.
fakement 1 a thing. 2 personal
adornments
fantabulosa wonderful
farting crackers trousers
fashioned used as a premodifier
to imply that something
is false or artificially
constructed in some way
fashioned riah a wig
fatcha to shave or apply
make-up
feely, feele, feelier, fellia a
young person or a child
femme 1. female. 2 a feminine
lesbian
ferricadooza a knock-down
blow
filiome 1. a young man. 2. an
underaged sexual partner
filly pretty
fish a woman (derogatory)
flange 1. a vagina. 2. to walk
along
flatties noun: 1. men (especially
those who make up an
audience). 2. dupes

flowery lodgings, accommodation, prison cell

fogle a handkerchief or neckerchief (usually silk)

fogle-hunter a pickpocket

foofs breasts

fortuni gorgeous

frock female attire

frock billong lallies trousers

fruit a gay man

full drag completely decked out in women's attire

full eke wearing make-up

fungus an old man

funt a pound (money)

G

gajo outsider

gam 1. oral sex. 2. leg

gamming oral sex

gamp umbrella

gardy loo beware!

gay homosexual

gelt, gent money (coinage)

gildy fancy

gillies women (especially those in an audience)

girl general term of address

Gloria God

glory hole a hole between two stalls in a public toilet – usually big enough to poke things through

glossies magazines

goolie black

goolie ogle fakes sunglasses

got your number 1. to know what someone is up to. 2. to identify someone as gay

groin, groyne a ring

groinage jewellery

gutless either very good or very bad

H

hambag, handbag money

hampsteads teeth

harris arse

head toilet

hearing cheat an ear

heartface term of address

hettie heterosexual

Hilda Handcuffs the police

HP a gay man (homee-palone)

HP **Arly** a version of Polari where *arly* is inserted after the first letter of a Polari word

husband a male lover, usually more than just a one-night stand, but can ironically refer to a short-term sexual partner

I

importuning cruising for sex

in the life gay

Irish a wig

it a short-term sexual partner

J

jarry 1. to eat. 2. to fellate

Jennifer Justice the police

Jew's eye something valuable

Jim and Jack a back

jogger, jogar 1. to play. 2. to sing. 3. to entertain

joggering omee an entertainer

joshed up looking your best
journo day
jubes, joobs 1. breasts (female).
   2. pectorals (male)

K

kaffies trousers
kapello a cloak
ken 1. a house 2. to know
kenza twelve
kerterver cartzo a venereal
   disease
kik to look
kik pipe television
kosher homie a Jewish man

L

lady a gay man
lag a slave
lallie, lally, lall, lyle, lally-peg
   1. a leg. 2. *lall* can also
   mean to receive
lally-covers, lally-drags trousers
lamor a kiss
lappers hands
large superlative
larlou amen!
lattie a house or flat
lattie on water a ship
lattie on wheels a carriage,
   car or taxi
lau to place, put or send
lav a word
lell to take
lepta eleven
lett to dwell, live or sit
letties lodgings
letty 1. a bed. 2. to sleep
lills hands

Lily (Law), lilly the police
lily pad police station
lingo a foreign language
lippy lipstick
long dedger eleven
lop to run
lopen running
lucoddy body
lunch a man's crotch
luppers fingers

M

mais oui of course
manky bad, poor, tasteless
   or dirty
manly Alice a masculine gay
   man
maquiage make-up or to put
   make up on one's face
Maria sperm
mart covers gloves
martini a ring
marts, martinis hands
Mary, Mary-Ann 1. a generic
   term for a gay man.
   2. a Catholic gay man.
   3. An exclamation
matlock mender a dentist
matlocks teeth
mauve gay
mazarine a platform below
   a stage
measures, medzers, metzers,
   metzes, mezsh money
meat and two veg a man's
   penis and testicles
meat rack 1. a male brothel.
   2. any place where large
   numbers of men are sexually

available 2. specifically, the iron railings outside Piccadilly Circus. Sometimes capitalized as Meat Rack

medzer, mazder half

medzer caroon half a crown (money)

mental the best! (or the worst!)

meshigener crazy

metties, metzies wealth

mince to walk with short steps in an affected or feminine manner

minces eyes

minge a vagina (derogatory)

minnie 1. a homosexual man. 2. to walk

moey, mooe 1. a mouth. 2. a face

mogue to tell a lie

molly a gay man

mother an older gay man

muck (stage) make-up

multy, multi, mutlee very, much, many, a lot

mungaree, mangare, munjarry, manjarie, manjaree, monjaree, munja, numgare 1. food. 2. verb: to eat

munge darkness

N

nada none

nada to vada in the larder a small penis

naff, naph 1. tasteless, bad. 2. heterosexual

namyarie, nanyarie 1. to eat. 2. food

nanna awful

nanti dinarly no money

nanti polari, nanty panarly don't speak

nanti pots in the cupboard no teeth

nanti that leave it alone, forget about it

nanti, nantee, nanty, nunty, nuntee a general negator that can mean *no, none, don't* or *nothing*

nantoise, nantoisale 1. no, none. 2. inadequate

nawks bosom

nelly a feminine gay man

nellyarda to listen

nishta, nish, nishtoise, nishtoisale, nix nothing, no

nix mungarlee nothing to eat

nix my dolly never mind

nobber 1. nine. 2. someone who collects money for a street performer

nochy night

nosh to perform oral sex

NTBH not available, or ugly (not to be had)

number a person, usually attractive

O

ogale fakes spectacles

ogle 1. to look longingly. 2. an eye

ogle filters, ogle shades sunglasses

ogle riah fakes false eyelashes

ogle riahs eyelashes

ogle riders eyebrows or eyelashes

omee-palone, homee-palone a gay man

omee, omi, omy, omme, omer, homee, homey, homi a man

on the team gay

on your tod alone

oney one

onk a nose

opals, ocals eyes

orbs eyes

order, orderly 1. to leave or go. 2. to orgasm (i.e., to come)

orderly daughters the police

otter eight

outrageous extrovert, loud, camp

oyster a mouth

P

packet a man's crotch

palaver 1. to talk. 2. an argument

palliass a back

palone-omee a lesbian

palone, polone, polony, pollone, paloney, polonee palogne a woman or girl

pannam, pannum bread

parker 1. to pay. 2. to give

parker the measures to pay the money

parkering ninty wages

parnie, parnee, parney 1. rainwater. 2. tears

passive a gay man who takes the insertee role in anal intercourse and may also be quiet and feminine

pastry cutter a man whose oral sex technique involves digging into the skin of the penis with his teeth

pearls teeth

phantom (gobbler) a closeted gay man in the Merchant Navy who would go round the cabins at night, lifting the sheets of the other sailors to administer oral sex while they slept (or pretended to sleep)

pig an elephant

pig's lattie a sty on the eye

plate to perform oral sex

plate the dish anilingus

plates feet

pogy pogey a little

polari, polare, palare, parlaree 1. the gay language. 2. to talk

polari lobes ears

polari pipe a telephone

poll a wig

pont, ponce a pimp

ponte, poona a pound (money)

pouf a gay man

pretty face an attractive man

punk a gay man

purple hearts the drug Drynamil

put on the dish, put on the brandy to lubricate the anus, in preparation for anal sex

Q

quarter, quater four
quartereen a farthing
quean's dolly a female friend of a gay man
queen, quean a gay man
queeny majestically feminine
queer ken a prison
quongs testicles

R

randy comedown a desire to have sex after the effect of taking drugs starts to wear off
rattling cove a taxi
real girl a biological female as opposed to a drag queen
reef to feel, especially to feel the genitals of a person
remould sex reassignment surgery
rent, renter, rent boy a male prostitute
riah hair
riahy hairy
riah shusher a hair dresser
rim anilingus
rosie rubbish bin
rough a masculine, working-class, often aggressive man
rough trade a masculine, working-class sexual partner who may not identify as gay and might become violent or demand money after sex
royal, royalty majestically gay or queenly

S

sa, say six
salter, saltee, salty, saulty a penny
savvy 1. to know or understand. *Savvy?* means *do you understand?* 2. knowledge, practical sense, intelligence
say dooe eight
say oney seven
say tray nine
scarper, scaper, scarpy, scapali to go, run or escape
scat faeces
scharda what a pity!
schinwhars, chinois a Chinese man or woman
schmutter clothing
schonk to hit
schooner a bottle
schumph to drink
schvartza a black man
scotches legs
screaming loud and camp
screech 1. mouth. 2. face
screeve 1. to write. 2. written material
sea food, seaweed a (homo) sexually available sailor
sea queen 1. a gay sailor, particularly a steward or waiter in the Merchant Navy. 2. a gay man who seeks sex with sailors
send up to make fun of
setter seven

shamshes 1. attractive men.
2. teeth (uncertain)
sharper, sharp 1. to steal.
2. a policeman
sharping-omee, sharpering-omee a policeman
she third person pronoun applicable to anyone
sheesh showy, fussy, elaborately ornamented or affected
shush to steal
shush bag a swag bag
shyckle, shyker, sheitel a wig
sister a friend who may have also been also been a sexual partner at one point
size queen someone who likes well-endowed men
slang to perform on stage
slap make-up
sling-backs high heels
smellies perfume
snuff it to die
so gay
soldi a penny
solicit to cruise for sex while wearing drag
sparkle a light
stampers, stompers shoes
starters lubricant used to faciliate anal sex
steamer 1. a prostitute's client.
2 a gay man who seeks passive partners
stimp covers nylon stockings
stimps legs
stretcher-case exhausted
strides trousers

striller(s), strill(s) 1. a musical instrument. 2. piano keys.
3. a musician
strillers omee noun: a pianist or musician
sweet good
sweet and dry left and right
swishing flamboyantly grand or camp

T

tat rubbish, worthless
TBH 1. sexually available (to be had). 2. gay
that's your actual French phrase used to draw attention to the fact that the speaker has used a word of two of French, as a way of appearing sophisticated
thews muscles, likely thighs but possibly forearms
thumping cheat a heart
timepiece a watch
tip to give oral sex
tip the brandy, tongue the brandy, tip the ivy anilingus
tip the velvet to give oral sex
tober omee 1. a rent collector.
2. a landlord
tober showmen travelling musicians
todge omee-palone the passive partner in gay sex
too much excessive, over the top (can be either good or bad, depending on the context)

tootsie trade sex between two feminine men

tosheroon half a crown

town hall drapes an uncircumcised penis

trade a casual sexual partner

trade curtain a curtain hung

tray three

treash term of endearment

tres sheeshwahz very chic

troll to walk around, perhaps with sexual intent

trollies trousers

trummus a bum

trundling cheat a car

turn my oyster up to make me smile

tush bum

two and eight a state

U

una one

uppers and downers drugs

V

vacaya a device that emits sound, such as a jukebox or record player

vada, varda, vardo, vardy, varder to look

vadavision, vardavision a television

vaf look at that wonderful thing (vada, absolutely fantabulosa!)

vaggerie, vagary, vagarie to go, travel, leave

vera gin

versatile bisexual

voche 1. a voice. 2. a singer

vodkatini a vodka martini

vogue 1. a cigarette. 2. to light (a cigarette)

vonka a nose

W

wallop to dance

walloper a dancer

wedding night the first time two men have sex together

willets breasts

winkle a small penis

wonga money, earned from questionable sources

Y

yews eyes

your actual intensifying phrase, for example, 'we are your actual homeopathic practioners'

Z

zelda 1. a woman. 2. a witch

zhoosh, jhoosh 1. clothing. 2. trim or ornamentation. 3. to drink. 4. to style (hair) 5. to primp or apply make-up

zhooshy showy

References

I What Is Polari?

1 Ian Hancock, 'Shelta and Polari', in *The Language of the British Isles*, ed. Peter Trudgill (Cambridge, 1984), pp. 384–403.
2 Richard Hudson, *Sociolinguistics* (Cambridge, 1980), p. 24.
3 Michael Halliday, *Language as a Social Semiotic: The Social Interpretation of Language and Meaning* (London, 1978).
4 Russell Davies, ed., *The Kenneth Williams Diaries* (London, 1994), p. 35 (diary entry from 8 December 1949).
5 Ibid., p. 38 (diary entry from 25 January 1949).
6 Ibid., p. 24 (diary entry from 5 March 1948); p. 25 (diary entry from 16 March 1948).
7 There are many variants of LGBT in existence which affix additional letters and symbols to the abbreviation. As it was difficult to pick one everyone agrees on, I have used LGBT as it is the most well-known abbreviation, although I acknowledge that there are many other letters that could be added to represent other sexual and gender identities.

2 Something Borrowed, Something Blue

1 William Wilde, 'Some Words of Thief Talk', *Journal of American Folklore*, XI/7 (1889), p. 306.
2 Thomas Harman, *A Caveat or Warening for Commen Cursetores Vulgarely Called Vagabones* (London, 1567).
3 Lee Beier, 'Anti-language or Jargon? Canting in the English Underworld in the Sixteenth and Seventeenth Centuries',

in *Languages and Jargons*, ed. P. Burke and R. Porter (Cambridge, 1996), p. 79.

4 Ian Hancock, 'Shelta and Polari', in *The Language of the British Isles*, ed. Peter Trudgill (Cambridge, 1984) p. 399.

5 Randolph Trumbach, 'The Birth of the Queen: Sodomy and the Emergence of Gender Equality in Modern Culture, 1660–1750', in *Hidden From History*, ed. M. B. Duberman, M. Vicinus and G. Chauncey (London, 1991), p. 112; Rictor Norton, *Mother Clap's Molly House: The Gay Subculture in England, 1700–1830* (London, 1992), p. 104.

6 Anonymous, *Hell Upon Earth: Or the Town in an Uproar. Occasion'd by the Late Horrible Scenes of Forgery, Perjury, Street-Robbery, Murder, Sodomy, and Other Shocking Impieties* (London, 1729).

7 Curzio Malaparte, *La Pelle* [1949] (Milan, 1981).

8 Tony McEnery, *Swearing in English* (London, 2005).

9 Norton, *Mother Clap's Molly House*, pp. 54–9.

10 Eric Partridge, *Slang Today and Yesterday* (London, 1970), p. 223.

11 Eric Partridge, *A Dictionary of the Underworld* (London, 1964), p. 497.

12 Partridge, *Slang Today and Yesterday*, p. 1391.

13 Eric Partridge, *A Dictionary of Slang and Unconventional English*, 8th edn, vol. II (London, 1974), p. 1318.

14 Eric Partridge, *Here, There, and Everywhere: Essays upon Language* (London, 1950).

15 Sydney Lester, *Vardi the Palary* [1937], cited in Partridge, *A Dictionary of Slang and Unconventional English*, vol. II, p. 1318.

16 'Bona Rags', *The Bona World of Julian and Sandy: Starring Kenneth Williams, Hugh Paddick and Kenneth Williams*, BBC Radio Collection (BBC Physical Audio, London, 2002, CD).

17 Partridge, *Slang Today and Yesterday*, p. 1391.

18 Thomas Frost, *Circus Life and Circus Celebrities* (London, 1876), pp. 305–11.

19 Philip Allingham, *Cheapjack* (London, 1934), p. 189.

20 Hancock, 'Shelta and Polari'.

21 Henry Mayhew, *London Labour and the London Poor*, vol. III (New York, 1851), p. 47.

22 Ibid., p. 47.
23 Lily Savage, *Lily Savage: A Sort of A–Z Thing*
    (London, 1998), p. 103.
24 Peter Burton, 'The Gentle Art of Confounding Naffs: Some
    Notes on Polari', *Gay News*, 120 (1979), p. 23.
25 Hancock, 'Shelta and Polari', p. 395.
26 Donald Kenrick, 'Romani English', in *International Journal
    of the Sociology of Language: Romani Sociolinguistics*,
    ed. Ian Hancock (The Hague, 1979), pp. 111–20.
27 George Henry Borrow, *Romano Lavo-Lil: A Book of the
    Gypsy* [London, 1874] (Gloucester, 1982).
28 Partridge, *Slang Today and Yesterday*, p. 249.
29 Matt Cook et al., *A Gay History of Britain: Love and Sex
    between Men since the Middle Ages* (Santa Barbara, CA,
    2007), p. 109.
30 Glyn Jones and Christopher Beeching, 'Bona Slang', letter
    to *The Guardian* (22 January 2005).
31 Sandy Wilson on *The Bona History of Julian and Sandy*,
    BBC Radio 4 (12 December 1998).
32 Peter Gordeno, 'The Walloper's Polari', *TV Times*
    (18–25 October 1969), p. 44.
33 Quentin Crisp, *The Naked Civil Servant* [1968] (London,
    1997), p. 26.
34 Daniel Farson, *The Gilded Gutter Life of Francis Bacon:
    The Authorised Biography* (London, 1993).
35 W. Somerset Maugham, *The Narrow Corner* [1932]
    (London, 2001), p. 40.
36 Crisp, *The Naked Civil Servant*, p. 20.
37 BBC1, *It's Not Unusual*, broadcast April 1997.
38 Hancock, 'Shelta and Polari', p. 391.
39 Henry Kahane, Renee Kahane and Andreas Tietze, *The
    Lingua Franca in the Levant: Turkish Nautical Terms
    of Italian and Greek Origin* (Urbana, IL, 1958).
40 Hancock, 'Shelta and Polari', p. 393.
41 Charles James Ribton-Turner, *History of Vagrants and
    Vagrancy, and Beggars and Begging* (London, 1887); Gamini
    Salgado, *The Elizabethan Underworld* (London, 1977), p. 138.
42 Jonathon Green, 'Polari', *Critical Quarterly*, XXXIX/1 (1987),
    p. 128.

43 Stephen Donaldson, 'Seafaring', in *Encyclopaedia of Homosexuality*, ed. Wayne R. Dynes et al. (New York, 1990), p. 1174.
44 Russell Davies, ed., *The Kenneth Williams Diaries* (London, 1994), p. 15 (diary entry from 11 September 1947).
45 Kellow Chesney, *The Victorian Underworld* (New York, 1972), pp. 328–9.
46 George Modelski, *World Cities: 3000 to 2000* (Washington, DC, 2000).
47 Julian Franklyn, *A Dictionary of Rhyming Slang* (London, 1960), p. 5.
48 Jonathon Green and Kipper Williams, *The Big Book of Filth* (London, 1999).
49 David Mazower, *Yiddish Theatre in London* (London, 1987), p. 9.
50 Emmanuel S. Goldsmith, *Modern Yiddish Culture: The Story of the Yiddish Language Movement* (New York, 1997), p. 15.
51 Only the spelling of this word suggests an influence from Yiddish, as the pronunciation and meaning are French.
52 Dudley Cave interviewed by Peter Tatchell, ww2 *People's War*, BBC Archives (15 October 2014), www.bbc.co.uk/history.
53 Ibid.
54 Crisp, *Naked Civil Servant*, p. 149.
55 Angus Calder, *The People's War: Britain, 1939–45* (London, 1969), p. 308.
56 Crisp, *Naked Civil Servant*, p. 152.
57 Burton, 'The Gentle Art of Confounding Naffs', p. 23.
58 Partridge, *Slang Today and Yesterday*, p. 1391; Hugh David, *On Queer Street* (London, 1997), p. 199.
59 I make a distinction between the way *fish* was used in an extremely derogatory way by Polari speakers to refer to women and way that *fishy* is used by U.S. drag queens as a compliment to refer to a convincing female appearance.
60 Dot Wordsworth, 'Polari a "Secret Language"? Nonsense', *The Spectator* (15 October 2016).

3 How to Polari Bona

1 Lee Sutton, *Presenting Lee Sutton, A Near 'Miss'?*
(EMI Records, London, 1968, LP); Lee Sutton, *Drag for Camp Followers* (EMI Records, London, 1971, LP).

2 Lily Savage, *Lily Savage: A Sort of A–Z Thing*
(London, 1998), p. 103.

3 Pamela Fishman, 'Interactional Shitwork', *Heresies*, II (1977),
pp. 99–101.

4 Paul Baker, *Using Corpora to Analyse Gender* (London,
2014).

5 BBC2, 'Lol: A Bona Queen of Fabularity', *40 Minutes* (1981).

6 BBC Radio Collection, *The Bona World of Julian and Sandy:
Starring Kenneth Williams, Hugh Paddick and Kenneth
Williams* (BBC Physical Audio, London, 2002, CD).

7 Russell Davies, ed., *The Kenneth Williams Diaries*
(London, 1994), p. 331 (diary entry from 28 August 1968).

8 James Gardiner, *Who's a Pretty Boy Then? One Hundred
and Fifty Years of Gay Life in Pictures* (London, 1997),
p. 123.

9 ITV, *The Naked Civil Servant*, broadcast 17 December 1975.

10 Sutton, *Presenting Lee Sutton*.

11 BBC2, 'Lol: A Bona Queen of Fabularity'.

12 Michael Davidson, *The World, the Flesh and Myself*
(London, 1962).

13 Sutton, *Presenting Lee Sutton*.

14 'Bona Beat Songs Ltd', *The Bona World of Julian and Sandy:
Starring Kenneth Williams, Hugh Paddick and Kenneth
Williams*, BBC Radio Collection (BBC Physical Audio,
London, 2002, CD).

15 Cited by Terry Gardner in Alkarim Jivani, *It's Not Unusual:
A History of Lesbian and Gay Britain in the Twentieth
Century* (London, 1997), p. 15.

16 Savage, *A Sort of A–Z Thing*, p. 103.

17 Ben Hunte on 'Gay Britannia', BBC Radio 4 Extra
(27 July 2017), www.bbc.co.uk/programmes.

18 'A Storm in a Teacup', *Summer's Out*, Channel 4 (1993).

4 A Bad Time to Be Gay

1 Dudley Cave interviewed by Peter Tatchell, ww2 *People's War*, BBC Archives (15 October 2014), www.bbc.co.uk/history.

2 Quentin Crisp, *The Naked Civil Servant* [1968] (London, 1997), p. 167.

3 Leonard England, 'A British Sex Survey', *International Journal of Sexology*, III/3 (February 1950), p. 153.

4 'A Storm in a Teacup', *Summer's Out*, Channel 4 (1993).

5 David Butler and Anne Sloman, *British Political Facts, 1900–1979* (London, 1980) p. 291.

6 Andrew Hodges, *Alan Turing: The Enigma* (London, 1983), pp. 149, 489; David Leavitt, *The Man Who Knew Too Much: Alan Turing and the Invention of the Computer* (London, 2007), p. 140.

7 Netta Weinstein et al., 'Parental Autonomy Support and Discrepancies between Implicit and Explicit Sexual Identities: Dynamics of Self-acceptance and Defense', *Journal of Personality and Social Psychology*, CII/4 (2012), pp. 815–32.

8 Glenn Smith, Annie Bartlett and Michael King, 'Treatments of Homosexuality in Britain since the 1950s – An Oral History: The Experience of Patients', *British Medical Journal*, 328 (2004), pp. 427–9.

9 Douglas Warth, 'Evil Men', *Sunday Pictorial*, 25 May 1952.

10 Alkarim Jivani, *It's Not Unusual: A History of Lesbian and Gay Britain in the Twentieth Century* (London, 1997), pp. 114–15.

11 John Vincent, *LGBT People and the UK Cultural Sector* (London, 2014), p. 10.

12 Peter Wildeblood, *Against the Law* (London, 1955).

13 Rodney Garland, *The Heart in Exile* (London, 1953).

14 Martyn Goff, *The Youngest Director* (London, 1961).

15 'A Storm in a Teacup'.

16 Hall-Carpenter Archives, *Walking After Midnight: Gay Men's Life Stories* (London, 1989), p. 52.

17 Crisp, *Naked Civil Servant*, p. 96.

18 'Stuart Feather and Bette Bourne talk about Polari', www.youtube.com, 28 May 2014.

19 Dudley Cave on 'A Storm in a Teacup'.

20 Joe Heaney, 'Desperately Seeking . . .', *Gay Times* (July 2002), p. 49.

21 Unnamed interviewee in Kevin Porter and Jeffery Weeks, *Between the Acts: Lives of Homosexual Men, 1885–1967* (London, 1991), pp. 75–6.

22 Crisp, *Naked Civil Servant*, p. 44.

23 Peter Burton, 'The Gentle Art of Confounding Naffs: Some Notes on Polari', *Gay News*, 120 (1979), p. 23.

24 Kris Kirk and Ed Heath, *Men in Frocks* (London, 1984).

25 Paul Baker and Jo Stanley, *Hello Sailor: The Hidden History of Gay Life at Sea* (Abingdon, 2003), p. 150.

26 William Brougham, 'Polari Remembered by Stan Monroe', www.youtube.com, 3 February 2017.

27 Julian, 'Julian's Column', *Gay News*, 11 (14 November, 1972), p. 10.

28 BBC2, 'Lol: A Bona Queen of Fabularity', *40 Minutes* (1981).

29 Michael Gavin, 'Gays All at Sea', *Mister*, 35 (1982), p. 27.

30 Bette Bourne on *The Bona History of Julian and Sandy*, BBC Radio 4 (12 December 1998).

31 D. Seligman, 'Coming Out', *Lunch*, 45 (1973), p. 11. Although the last sentence of the quote is ambiguous, I'm guessing that John is talking about himself in the third person, as opposed to the taxi driver, a feature of Polari discussed in the previous chapter.

32 Marc Fleming filmed at the Cabal Club, Soho, 1970s, 'Marc Fleming 1', www.youtube.com, 25 December 2013.

33 Burton, 'The Gentle Art of Confounding Naffs', p. 23.

34 Phil Starr, performing at Fudges, Brighton, 'Phil Starr', www.youtube.com, 27 January 2011.

35 Lee Sutton, *Drag for Camp Followers* (EMI Records, London, 1971, LP).

36 Ibid.

37 'A Storm in a Teacup'.

38 Porter and Weeks, *Between the Acts*, p. 138.

5 'I'm Julian and this is my friend Sandy'

1 Barry Took on *The Bona History of Julian and Sandy*, BBC Radio 4, December 1998.

2 *Salad Days* (commissioned in 1954) is a musical about a young couple who discover a piano that has the power to make all who hear it dance. *The Boy Friend* is a musical spoof set in the 1920s.

3 Bette Bourne on *The Bona History of Julian and Sandy*, BBC Radio 4, December 1998.

4 Dominic Sandbrook, *White Heat: A History of Britain in the Swinging Sixties* (London, 2006).

5 Kate Fox, *Watching the English* (London, 2004).

6 Ben Thompson, *Ban This Filth* (London, 2012), pp. 31–3.

7 Sandra Laville, 'John Smythe: The Go-to Barrister for Mary Whitehouse', *The Guardian*, 2 February 2017.

8 Alkarim Jivani, *It's Not Unusual: A History of Lesbian and Gay Britain in the Twentieth Century* (London, 1997), pp. 171–2.

9 Tony McEnery, *Swearing in English* (London, 2005), p. 107.

10 Thompson, *Ban This Filth*, p. 35.

11 *The Bona History of Julian and Sandy*, BBC Radio 4, December 1998.

12 BBC Home, *Round the Horne*, www.bbc.co.uk/bbc7/comedy/ progpages/horne.shtml.

13 *Bradshaw's Guide* was a popular series of railway guides and timetables, developed by George Bradshaw.

14 BBC Radio Collection, *The Bona World of Julian and Sandy: Starring Kenneth Williams, Hugh Paddick and Kenneth Williams* (BBC Physical Audio, London, 2002, CD).

15 'Bona Beat Songs Ltd', *The Bona World of Julian and Sandy*.

16 'Keep Britain Bona', *The Bona World of Julian and Sandy*.

17 'Bona Ads', *The Bona World of Julian and Sandy*.

18 'Time and Motion', *The Bona World of Julian and Sandy*.

19 Barry Took on *The Bona History of Julian and Sandy*, BBC Radio 4, December 1998.

20 Russell Davies, ed., *The Kenneth Williams Diaries* (London, 1994), p. 15 (diary entry from 24 October 1947).

21 Ibid., p. 8 (diary entry from 1 January 1947).

22 'Bona Guesthouse', *The Bona World of Julian and Sandy*.
23 Davies, ed., *The Kenneth Williams Diaries*, p. 324
    (diary entry from 8 April 1968).
24 'Rentachap', *The Bona World of Julian and Sandy*.
25 Barry Took and Marty Feldman, *The Bona Book of Julian
    and Sandy* (London, 1974), p. 37.
26 Julian Franklyn, *A Dictionary of Rhyming Slang*
    (London 1960), p. 108.
27 Davies, ed., *The Kenneth Williams Diaries:* 'Paddick did
    some v. subtle & brilliant things! In comparison, my stuff
    was very crude,' p. 605 (diary entry from 7 March 1980),
    'H.P. is a v. kind man', p. 694 (diary entry from 4 April
    1984).
28 Barry Took on *The Bona History of Julian and Sandy*,
    BBC Radio 4, December 1998.

6 The Lost Language

1 Otto Jespersen, *Language, its Nature, Development and
   Origin* (London, 1922), p. 65, citing Franz Bopp (1827).
2 *Word of Mouth*, BBC Radio 4, 19 September 1995.
3 Tony Papard, *The Gay Scene in the Past 40 Years
   or So* (2010), www.kemglen.talktalk.net/stradivarius/
   OurHistorypepard.html.
4 'Carnival of Monsters', episode 4, *Dr Who*, BBC1 (1973).
5 'Bona Studios', *The Bona World of Julian and Sandy:
   Starring Kenneth Williams, Hugh Paddick and Kenneth
   Williams*, BBC Radio Collection (BBC Physical Audio,
   London, 2002, CD).
6 Kevin Porter and Jeffery Weeks, *Between the Acts: Lives
   of Homosexual Men, 1885–1967* (London, 1991), p. 138.
7 Alkarim Jivani, *It's Not Unusual: A History of Lesbian
   and Gay Britain in the Twentieth Century* (London, 1997),
   p. 149.
8 Papard, *The Gay Scene in the Past 40 Years or So*.
9 Peter Tatchell, 'Arrests Didn't End when Gay Sex was
   Decriminalised in 1967 – They Rocketed', *iNews*
   (19 July 2017), https://inews.co.uk.
10 Hugh David, *On Queer Street* (London, 1997), p. 225.

11 Jeffrey Weeks, *Coming Out* (London, 1977), p. 190.
12 Mary McIntosh, 'Class', in *Lesbian and Gay Studies: A Critical Introduction*, ed. Andy Medhurst and Sally Munt (London, 1997), p. 234.
13 Susan Sontag, 'Notes on "Camp"', in *Susan Sontag Against Interpretation and Other Essays* (New York, 1966), p. 277.
14 Andrew Britton, 'For Interpretation – Notes Against "Camp"', *Gay Left*, 7 (1979), p. 12.
15 Andy Medhurst, 'Camp', in *Lesbian and Gay Studies*, ed. Medhurst and Munt, p. 280.
16 Gay Liberation Front, *Manifesto* (London, 1979), p. 9.
17 Patrick Higgins, *A Queer Reader* (London, 1993), p. 208.
18 *The Bona History of Julian and Sandy*, BBC Radio 4, December 1998.
19 Adrian Rigelsford, Geoff Tibballs and Anthony Brown, *Are You Being Served?* (San Francisco, CA, 1995), p. 29.
20 David Wigg, 'Are You Being Unfair?', *Daily Express* (12 October 1977), p. 5.
21 Mary McIntosh, 'GaySpeak', *Lunch*, 16 (1972), p. 8.
22 Jonathan Raban, 'Giggling in Code', *Lunch*, 20 (1973), p. 17.
23 Michael Carson, *Sucking Sherbet Lemons* (London, 1988), p. 203.
24 Julia Stanley, 'When We Say "Out of the Closets!"', *College English*, 36 (1974), p. 386.
25 Gregg Blachford, 'Male Dominance and the Gay World', in *The Making of the Modern Homosexual*, ed. Kenneth Plummer (London, 1981), p. 189.
26 Gay Liberation Front, *Manifesto*, p. 9.
27 S.H. quoted in *Quorum*, 3 (Harrow, 1972), p. 38.
28 BBC2, 'Lol: A Bona Queen of Fabularity', *40 Minutes* (1981).
29 James Gardiner, *Who's a Pretty Boy Then? One Hundred and Fifty Years of Gay Life in Pictures* (London, 1997), p. 148.
30 Jivani, *It's Not Unusual*, p. 174.
31 Ibid., pp. 173–4.
32 David, *On Queer Street*, p. 253.
33 Colin Spencer, *Homosexuality: A History* (London, 1995), p. 375.
34 Rachael Harker, *HIV and AIDS Statistics*, House of Commons Library (London, 2010), p. 3.

35 See Terry Sanderson, *Mediawatch: Treatment of Male and Female Homosexuality in the British Media* (London, 1995).

36 Alison Park et al., *British Social Attitudes: The 30th Report* (London, 2013), p. 16.

37 Paul Baker, *Public Discourses of Gay Men* (London, 2005).

38 *Boyz*, issues 408–10 (London, 1999).

7 She's Ready for Her Comeback

1 Ian Lucas, 'The Color of His Eyes: Polari and the Sisters of Perpetual Indulgence', in *Queerly Phrased*, ed. Anna Livia and Kira Hall (Oxford, 1997), p. 91.

2 Ibid., p. 90.

3 Andy Medhurst, 'Camp', in *Lesbian and Gay Studies: A Critical Introduction*, ed. Andy Medhurst and Sally Munt (London, 1997), p. 281.

4 Lucas, 'The Color of His Eyes', p. 91.

5 James Laver, *Taste and Fashion* (London, 1937).

6 Ian Hancock, 'Shelta and Polari', in *The Language of the British Isles*, ed. Peter Trudgill (Cambridge, 1984), pp. 384–403.

7 Jonathon Green, 'Polari', *Critical Quarterly*, XXXIX/1 (1987) pp. 127–31; Leslie Cox and Richard Fay, 'Gayspeak, the Linguistic Fringe: Bona Polari, Camp, Queerspeak and Beyond', in *The Margins of the City: Gay Men's Urban Lives*, ed. Stephen Whittle (Aldershot, 1994), pp. 103–27.

8 Lucas, 'The Color of His Eyes'.

9 Kevin Porter and Jeffrey Weeks, eds, *Between the Acts: Lives of Homosexual Men, 1885–1967* (London, 1991); James Gardiner, *Who's a Pretty Boy Then? One Hundred and Fifty Years of Gay Life in Pictures* (London, 1997); Hall-Carpenter Archives, *Walking After Midnight: Gay Men's Life Stories* (London, 1989); Hugh David, *On Queer Street* (London, 1997); Alkarim Jivani, *It's Not Unusual: A History of Lesbian and Gay Britain in the Twentieth Century* (London, 1997).

10 Peter Burton, 'Tony Warren Remembers: "A Life Lived in Whispers"', *Gay Times*, 206 (November 1995), p. 62.

11 See www.polaripolari.com.

12 'Trend Watch', *Metro*, 12 November 2013.

13 '"Fabulosa" Lingo Revived at Club', http://news.bbc.co.uk, 6 December 2004.
14 *Boyz*, 410 (1999), p. 3.
15 Michael Carson, *Sucking Sherbet Lemons* (London, 1988), p. 203.
16 See www.polarijournal.com.
17 See www.polarimagazine.com.
18 See www.polaribible.org.
19 George Reiner and Penny Burke, *Cruising for Lavs* (London, 2018).

8 In Conclusion

1 See www.bsa-data.natcen.ac.uk.
2 'C of E College Apologises for Students' Attempt to "Queer Evening Prayer"', *The Guardian*, 3 February 2017.
3 'Gay Britannia', BBC Radio 4 Extra (27 July 2017), www.bbc.co.uk/programmes.
4 Christine Ashby, 'Whose "Voice" Is it Anyway? Giving Voice and Qualitative Research Involving Individuals that Type to Communicate', *Disability Studies Quarterly*, XXXI/4 (2011).

Further Reading

Baker, Paul, and Jo Stanley, *Hello Sailor: The Hidden History of Gay Life at Sea* (Abingdon, 2003)

Cox, Leslie, and Richard Fay, 'Gayspeak, the Linguistic Fringe: Bona Polari, Camp, Queerspeak and Beyond', in *The Margins of the City: Gay Men's Urban Lives*, ed. Stephen Whittle (Aldershot, 1994), pp. 103–27

David, Hugh, *On Queer Street* (London, 1997)

Davies, Russell, ed., *The Kenneth Williams Diaries* (London, 1994)

Gardiner, James, *Who's a Pretty Boy Then? One Hundred and Fifty Years of Gay Life in Pictures* (London, 1997)

Green, Jonathon, 'Polari', *Critical Quarterly*, XXXIX/1 (1987) pp. 127–31

Hancock, Ian, 'Shelta and Polari', in *The Language of the British Isles*, ed. Peter Trudgill (Cambridge, 1984), pp. 384–403

Jivani, Alkarim, *It's Not Unusual: A History of Lesbian and Gay Britain in the Twentieth Century* (London, 1997)

Lucas, Ian, 'The Color of His Eyes: Polari and the Sisters of Perpetual Indulgence', in *Queerly Phrased*, ed. Anna Livia and Kira Hall (Oxford, 1997), pp. 85–94

Porter, Kevin, and Jeffrey Weeks, eds, *Between the Acts: Lives of Homosexual Men, 1885–1967* (London, 1991)

Acknowledgements

I'd like to thank the following people who contributed advice, information, time or assistance in various ways:

Nigel G. Backhurst, Sue Blackwell, Chris Bryant, Stefan Dickers, Martin Edwardes, Erich Erving, Jez Dolan, Bryon Fear, Tim Greening-Jackson, Craig Hutchinson, Martha Jay, Sally Johnson, Ian Lucas, Richard Maggs, Kevan Mai, Mark Mander, Andy Medhurst, Liz Morrish, Lynne Murphy, Joe Richardson, Mark Sebba, Aimee Selby, Alan Sinfield, Mark Spencer, Mark Spencer, Jane Sunderland, Joan Swann, Barry Took, David Watkins, the Sisters of Perpetual Indulgence and the Polari speakers whose interviews I quote from in this book.

Photo Acknowledgements

The author and publishers wish to express their thanks to the below sources of illustrative material and/or permission to reproduce it. Every effort has been made to contact copyright holders; should there be any we have been unable to reach or to whom inaccurate acknowledgements have been made, please contact the publishers, and full adjustments will be made to subsequent printings.

Courtesy AF Archive/Alamy Stock Photo: p. 165; courtesy the Bishopsgate Institute: pp. 62, 73, 113, 131, 174, 213, 247 (photograph © Gordon Rainsford); photograph © Christopher Bryant: p. 269; photo-graph © Les Chatfield: p. 154; engraving by Nathanial Dance, frontis-piece to Francis Grose, *Supplement to the Antiquities of England and Wales* (1787) © Trustees of the British Museum: p. 30; courtesy and © Jez Dolan: pp. 267, 274; photograph © Richard Dworkin: p. 227; courtesy and © Bryon Fear: p. 261; courtesy and © Tim Greening Jackson: p. 285; courtesy History and Art Collection/Alamy Stock Photo: p. 39; courtesy Imperial War Museum (Ministry of Information Photo Division photographer): p. 76; photograph © Jack de Nijs, Anefo: p. 70; photograph by John Pratt/Keystone Features/ Getty Images: p. 167; photograph © Julie Sorrell: p. 238; photograph by Graham Stark/Hulton Archive/Getty Images: p. 169; photograph © David Striker: p. 135; from John Thomson and Adolphe Smith, *Street Life in London* (1877), courtesy London School of Economics Library: p. 44; courtesy Trinity Mirror/Mirrorpix/Alamy Stock Photo: p. 160; courtesy the Wellcome Institute, James Gardiner Collection: pp. 65, 147; courtesy the Wellcome Library: p. 232.

Index